AN OUTLINE OF

French History

AN OUTLINE OF
French History

BY *René Sédillot*

Translated from the French by
GERARD HOPKINS

NEW YORK   ALFRED A. KNOPF   1953

L. C. CATALOG CARD NUMBER: 52–11755

THIS IS A BORZOI BOOK,
PUBLISHED BY ALFRED A. KNOPF, INC.

FIRST AMERICAN EDITION

PREFACE

NOT, SURELY, another history of France? Few subjects in the world can have been more thoroughly explored, alike by scholars rummaging through dusty archives and by more popular writers with the sweeping glance and the inclusive method. But there is always something fresh to be discovered, some obscurity to be explained. The historians of the day before yesterday were ignorant of too much. Many facts of which they knew nothing are only now coming to light. Their immediate successors, on the other hand, more eager to prove a theory than to tell a story, were to a very considerable extent swayed by their passions. Is there no way in which to write a history book that shall be at once truthful and complete?

In order to satisfy that dual demand a man must hover high above the centuries. To descend into the crowded field of detail is at once to run the risk of error. Local chronicles, family records, the booty of specialized libraries and rarely visited muniment rooms, must be left unexplored. Only by climbing to an airy vantage-point can he take in the general scene, can he follow lines of development and become aware of the far horizon. It is not now a matter of general importance to know precisely where Alesia stood, nor to be able to produce proofs that the boy Dauphin did or did not escape from the Temple. It is enough that we should be able to establish with certainty that Gaul was a gainer from the Roman conquest, and that France led the world in the age of the Augustans.

To follow the course of history means to do something more than merely trace the pattern made by battles and treaties, by reigns and revolutions. It means also the ability

to record the advances in technical achievement; to follow
the movement of manners and ideas, of prices and wages; to
plot the curves of purchasing power and living-standards;
to show how men and women lived at different times. The
history of economics and finance is complementary to the
history of politics. Not that it in any way diminishes the
importance of politics, for it would be as ridiculous to ignore the essential part played by statesmen, both good and
bad, or to neglect the wars that brought both gain and ruin
in their train, as to say nothing about the material conditions of production and consumption.

To take this wide and somewhat remote view of the history of France is not to reduce its significance in either
space or time. In space, it is one with the history of the
world; in time, we have, to quote a contemporary writer,
"got beyond believing that our history ends with the Revolution." We have also got beyond believing that it begins
with it. We are inclined nowadays to think that as much
happened between 1200 and 1300 as between 1800 and
1900. If we are to see history in its true proportion, we must
remember that as many years separate Cæsar and Charlemagne as Hugh Capet and Napoleon III.

In writing this bird's-eye view I have made no attempt to
"tell all." My object has been to provide the necessary
framework for "all." The airman does not try to identify
each tree and ditch over which he passes, for the reason that
he moves quickly and flies high. But he can at least recognize the forests and the plains, can even get a glimpse of his
native village nestling among its vines. The shapes of the
hills, the jutting bulk of the mountains, the courses of the
rivers, make it possible for him to understand why roads
were driven across country in such and such a way, why
cities were established, and why they developed in this place
rather than another. *An Outline of French History* should
enable the reader not only to follow the facts, but to under-

stand both the causes and the consequences of those facts, to see how and why France came into being, and how and why she grew and lived, prospered and suffered.

It is but natural for all men to think of their own country as being more important than others, and the French are especially prone to take this distorted view. They can put forward a plausible plea in its defense, seeing that France has played a leading role in more than one period of world development.

That France has been peculiarly blessed by nature is a geographical fact. Her physical situation is one of the most highly privileged to be found anywhere. Her boundaries are set within the hemisphere where civilization first flowered— at the extreme point of the peninsula of Europe, at the precise spot where the trade routes of the Mediterranean (cradle of the ancient world) cross those of the Atlantic (which has conditioned the development of the modern world). Because she has no fewer land than sea frontiers, she has been open to influences alike from the Continent and the wider world. She has had to maintain an army and a fleet. She has known invasion on land, and faced the threat of it from the sea. On land and sea she has built thoroughfares for her extension.

Blessed with a fertile soil and an agreeable climate, France has long been regarded as the garden of the West, and as such has aroused the envy of her neighbors. She has known many different aggressors, ranging from the broad-headed warriors of prehistoric times to the Germans of the twentieth century. Her peoples have a mixed heritage of blood, and from such compounded elements alone are great nations fashioned. Finally, France, like China, has always been able to assimilate both her conquerors and her immigrants.

It follows that the French, far from showing the dead

level of a single racial type, are as varied as is their country's scenery. It is a land of mountains and valleys, of rain and sunlight, of roofs both flat and pointed, of round-backed tiles and flat slates, of apples, grapes, and olives, of butter and oil, of a hundred different fruits and a hundred different cheeses. It is a melting-pot in which many civilizations draining from Asia and the isles of Greece, from the marshy plains of Italy, the forests of Germany, and the northern fiords, have been merged.

Take, for instance, the French language. Its basic structure is Roman. It is significant that the word *guerre* (war) entered it from Germany, the word *mât* (mast) from Scandinavia, *brigue* (intrigue) from Italy, *matamore* (braggart) from Spain, and *vote* from England. Or, again, her peoples —some tall, some short; some with long skulls, some with wide; some pacifically minded, loving a settled life round their own firesides, others daring and aggressive, who can be found the wide world over, discovering distant islands, piercing isthmuses, conquering empires, or dying for lost causes. Some live by reason, and hold law and order in respect; others value feeling above expediency, ideals above common sense. Classics and romantics, Cartesians and revolutionaries, Christians and pagans—all alike can claim the name of Frenchmen. And because they are so diverse they are not seldom at odds. As one or another type takes the lead so do political loyalties change. From respect for hierarchy and authority they pass to indicipline and anarchy, only in the end to return to their former loves. But through all these changes and chances they remain French.

It is possible, however, in all this pattern of divergences to point to certain constant traits and dominant characteristics. Generally speaking, it would seem that the French are born grumblers (differing in this from the Germans), that they are willing to endure the bondage of the soil (differing in this from the English), that they are concerned only to hoard the product of their labor (differing in this from the Spaniards). They love liberty to the point of license, but prefer privilege, gerrymandering, and favoritism to that Equality which they include in their national motto. They are inventive and optimistic. They believe in their destiny, and this makes it possible for them, on the morrow of every catastrophe, to keep their hope undimmed and to find again the source of that vitality which is the prerequisite of resurrection.

One thing, above all, is certain of them. They are determined to be French. Not one of them could say with certainty whether his own heritage is Celtic, Latin, Frankish, or whatever. Not one of them would any longer claim autonomy for his province. All Frenchmen think of themselves as belonging to France. But this cohesion in diversity is the result, not of natural endowment, but of history.

All things have their causes. It was not inscribed upon the tables of destiny that France should become what in fact she has become. Her unity, her frontiers, her glory, have all of them, to a very large extent, been artificial products. Anyone who sits down to write a history of France must show what part has been played in her development by nature, and what part, through the centuries, has been the handiwork of man.

CONTENTS

MAPS

AN OUTLINE OF

French History

Chapter I

THE FIRST STIRRINGS

(the beginning to the fourth century)

The Land of France
Takes Shape

ᴇᴛ us begin at the beginning. Not, to be sure, with the beginnings of matter, nor with the beginnings of the universe, nor even with the beginnings of the planet, but simply—and this in itself means going back a very long way—to the earliest formation of the earth's crust. In those days—three thousand million years ago—the small tract of land on our round globe which was later to be known as France was no more than a bubbling welter.

And now, in a single stride, let us span a thousand million years. At the period in which we next find ourselves the first rocks are taking shape. The outer skin of the earth's surface is becoming solid. We are entering the geological ages, which range through 1,900 million years. A vast ocean covers the planet, in which the first bacteria are stirring. Under the oceans the earth puckers up and a great chain of dry land emerges from Canada to Scotland. France is still beneath the waves.

Hundreds of millions of years pass. The first range of solid land crumbles away and a second rises from America to Ireland and to Siberia. France is under water, in which the first fish have now appeared.

But with the third convulsion of the primeval world (geologists call it the Hercynian fold, from a word that embodies the German *Erz*, meaning "ore") part of the land of France rises from the sea; the Vosges, the Ardennes, the Massif Central, Armorica, form islands of granite and crystalline schist, during the age of reptiles and ferns.

Everything in France is young compared with those great primeval masses which had been shaped and scarped and molded and smoothed by thousands of millennia. The torrents with which the land was seamed carried down trees in their tumultuous course and deposited them about the high plateaus, thus laying the foundations of future coal-fields.

We may as well accept the arbitrary divisions that scientists have performed on the earth's history. We have reached the second one: a world of sandstone, calcareous rock, and chalk. The Vosges sink temporarily under the sea; the backbone of the Pyrenees emerges. The climate is hot and dry. Cedars, pines, and firs appear, ahead of the oaks and poplars, the beech and birch, which later become the familiar trees of the French countryside. But the animals living on these plateaus are still strange, monstrous reptiles, in the main. Some animals, the marsupials, have teats.

The tranquillity of the Secondary age is followed by the convulsions of the Tertiary—a mere fifty million years ago, scarcely more than the day before yesterday. The land areas of the future France join together. The Pyrenees take on their final form; the Alps and the Jura, fragments of an immense range extending as far as the Himalayas, spring up in their turn. There are shocks and disturbances. Between the Vosges and the Black Forest a plain is hollowed out through which can run the Rhine. The Massif Central splits up, belching fire and lava. The bed of the Atlantic is defined; the waters recede, though not far, leaving uncovered in their wake the principal river-basins. The Rhone Valley, however, is still occupied by a vast inland sea. In this way the foundation of France is blocked out.

The elephants now share the forests with bison and ante-

lopes, monkeys and wild boars; later come giraffes and
horses. The climate grows less and less hot—80° Fahren-
heit at the beginning of the Tertiary age, a bare 60° Fahr-
enheit at its end, a million and a half years ago. We have
now reached yesterday.

Studying the alluvial deposits of the Quaternary age, we
no longer reckon in multiples of a thousand million years
or even of millions, but of thousands. France acquires its
familiar shape: the Mediterranean withdraws; the Channel turns England into an island. But these changes do not
take place without backwash. Snow, accumulating on the
high Alps, produces enormous glaciers, which plunge down
to the plains in several thrusts. They cover part of Europe,
and in France spread west of the Alps and north of the
Pyrenees, in the direction of the Massif Central. Dreadful
cold drives the elephants and rhinoceroses southward.
When the weather finally becomes mild, the reindeer have
to take refuge in the north. The melting ice produces huge
rivers—the Rhone and the Garonne. Erosion does its work,
smoothing the contours of the land, taming the old fierce
nature. The fauna settle down: there are deer in the brush,
and wild boars in the forests, squirrels leaping among the
branches. In the fields buttercups are growing.

The First Inhabitants of France

In this newborn world, where is man? At first, nowhere. In
a universe of monsters there is no room for human beings,
unless they too are monstrous. Shall we seek our first ancestors among those simian beings whose bones have come
to light in China and in Java, and who seem to have lived
at the very beginning of the Quaternary? In France there is
no trace of them.

There can be little doubt that when glaciers still covered
the earth, no country any more than France sheltered our

race. If her soil has proved to be incomparably rich in the remains of prehistoric settlements, the reason is not merely that it has been dug and worked more than that of any other land, but also that it offered a natural refuge to the first men.

Before the threat of the advancing ice, which made a Greenland of the European continent, the animals had fled. Whither? Toward those districts that still were free of intense cold. Life, retreating from the heights of the continent, driven westward by the ice-caps of the Alps, northward by those of the Pyrenees, found in France, and more especially in the Massif Central, its rallying-point.

Among the beasts that sought in caverns a shelter from the cold, there were some that could already claim resemblance not only to monkeys, but to human beings. But these primitive men, herded with animals far better armed than they were, would have been condemned to extinction had they not found in the thinking brain a more effective weapon than claws and teeth. In cave dwellings it was impossible to swing from branch to branch as in the virgin forest. Nimbleness was no longer a guarantee of survival. These forerunners of our race had to stand and fight and conquer. In that moment of dire need, more than a hundred thousand years ago, what "sharp mutation" was it, or what aid from heaven, that changed the beast into a man?

Whatever the cause, the fact remains. The man whose skull was found in the cavern of Fontéchevade (Charente), with the high, narrow forehead, the man who has been the cause of so much speculation, was already doing work of a kind that presupposes tools, if only that most necessary of all tools—intelligence. He, the "oldest known Frenchman," living between two glacial periods, has left us evidences of his skill. He had mastered the secret of chipping flints into sharp points. Similarly, the inhabitants of Chelles (not far from Paris) and of Saint-Acheul (in the district of the

Somme) had learned how to flatten the two sides of a stone and so convert it into a weapon.

The next type to be found seems to have been closer to the beast than to the man, in bodily structure if not in skill. He was of small stature (just about five feet) and had a very large head. He moved upright on his two feet, though with his knees slightly bent. His hands were completely human. Examples of this newcomer, who was first discovered in a cave in the Neanderthal, near Düsseldorf, have frequently been brought to light in France. Bones belonging to him have been found at La Chapelle-aux-Saints (Corrèze), at Moustier (Dordogne), and at La Quina (Charente). He has left his traces in many places, from the Pyrenees to the Eure. Whether he possessed the rudiments of an articulate language we cannot say. We do, however, know that he was versed in the manufacture and use of the club, that he could make knives and scrapers, was familiar with the use of fire, that he hunted wild animals, dressed in skins, and buried his dead. He was, in short, the representative of a civilization in embryo.

These earliest specimens of the human race were, needless to say, crude and brutal. They numbered, at the most, a few thousands. Their race, so far as France is concerned, seems to have died out entirely. Whether they emigrated or succumbed to the attacks of the climate, the bears, or the hyenas, we do not know. Neanderthal man left no direct descendant.

The Périgord Culture

With the coming of a new glacial age, men of a different type, from Asia and Africa, chose to settle in the cave dwellings of France. Grimaldi's man (Franco-Italian frontier) seems to have measured slightly more than five feet, and to have had points of resemblance with the Negro. Cro-Magnon man (Dordogne) was decidedly taller (over six feet). The man of Chancelade (also in the Dordogne) looked like a Lapp, and barely topped five feet. All were long-headed and thickset. There is no doubt that they belonged to the human family. Their achievements are in the highest degree surprising. These cave-men were no whit inferior to us in that quality of intelligence by which we set such store. All they lacked was our accumulated knowledge.

Although the influence of this ancient culture spread throughout the district watered by the Garonne, reaching as far as the Pyrenees and the Mediterranean, its center seems to have been in Périgord. One might almost say that Les Eyzies was at that time the capital of France. The cave formations of the Monts de la Madeleine have provided us with a name for this whole period of industrial and artistic activity. We call it the Magdalenian.

The marvels of the Magdalenian culture very naturally rouse in us feelings of admiration and astonishment. It would not do for us, however, to forget that in many ways it was sunk in the most appalling barbarism. It surprises us only by comparison with the age that preceded it and, to some extent, with that which followed.

The products of man's hands were taking on a new variety. They give us some idea of the progress he was making. He had increased the number of his tools, which now included scrapers and awls, spear-points and arrowheads. From shaped and polished fragments of bone he contrived needles, fishhooks, spikes, and harpoons. He could supply himself with lamps. Reindeer sinews gave him thread. The presence of such objects is proof that he hunted and fished, that he could sew, and knew how to produce artificial light.

In art he had reached a very high level, as we can see from the objects of adornment he made—ornamented necklaces, bracelets, and pendants—from the realistic statues he carved out of stone, ivory, and reindeer antlers; from his mastery of the frieze (for instance, the six life-sized horses in the Laus-sel Cave); and, above all, from the drawings and incised designs with which he covered the walls of his dwellings. The precision and the vigor of those bison, reindeer, and mammoths show clearly that the men who produced them could observe accurately and had mastered the skill needed to record the results of their observation. The line in all these mural decorations is firm, and shows no sign of grop-ing uncertainty. The color-range extends from ocher to se-pia, red, and black (compounded on a basis of manganese salts). The forms of all these animals seem to move and live before us on the rock.

Why is it that animals play so large a part in the decora-tions of this period? The answer is not far to seek. The art is the art of a race of hunters. So long as the earth had been rich in vegetation—during, that is, the climatic interludes of warmth and moisture—man had been vegetarian. It was the cold that turned him into a meat-eater. He learned to track the game with which the open steppe was filled. Hunting was no sport for him, but a way of life. So large a part did meat play in his diet that the chase of its victims came to be the central feature of his superstitions. That he might the more surely strike the bison down, he pictured it pierced by an arrow. Magic was the stimulus to art.

The culture of Périgord was religious. In its worship of gods and of animal totems it gave a leading role to sorcery and voodoo. The bones of some of its buried corpses were painted red, and men tattooed themselves in the same color. These practices must have had some occult significance. Funeral ceremonies, which were strictly observed, involved blood sacrifices. There were occasions, too, when the "civ-ilized" folk of Périgord indulged in feasts of human flesh. It is perfectly possible to be an artist and a cannibal at one and the same time.

The Magdalenian people did not live in a closed econ-

omy. Occasionally they made contact with the outer world.
A man from the Dordogne might sport a necklace of Mediterranean seashells. Someone from the Mediterranean
might own a trinket from the Indian Ocean. A wandering
tribe might peddle yellow amber from the Baltic. It has
been assumed, a little too readily, that these facts prove the
existence of a system of international trade in its infancy.
Actually such interchanges were more in the nature of theft
than barter.

We naturally feel surprised at the spectacle of these early
achievements of mankind, but we should be careful not to
indulge in an excess of enthusiasm. The then inhabitants
of France (numbering a few tens of thousands) had still almost everything to learn. Besides, the age of the cave-
dwellers was drawing to its close. The ice withdrew, this
time for good. The climate grew warmer. Many of the fauna
withdrew, with the cold, toward the north. The reindeer
made their home in Lapland: the mammoth vanished into
the empty spaces of Siberia.

In this scene of revolutionary change what became of
Magdalenian man? He abandoned his now unnecessary
caves and was tempted to follow in the track of the reindeer. Perhaps he has left descendants in the Eskimos, who
have a similar appearance, similar customs, and similar harpoons. But most of the ancient troglodytes stayed on in
France, migrating to the newly formed plains. And there,
quite simply, under the wide arch of heaven, they began to
build a different civilization.

Shepherds and Peasants

France was beginning to assume her final appearance.
What she needed she had in abundance. Her skies were
neither too blue nor too pale. The sea, never at any great
distance, gave warmth to a climate that was always mild.

She stood midway between the pole and the equator, and within her boundaries the flora of the north joined the flora of the south. Hers was a happy land, in which it was good to live.

But such privileges held peculiar possibilities of danger. They attracted the invader. All through the ten thousand years of history which are about to unroll, France was to pay dearly for her advantages. Invader followed hard on invader. They came, nearly all of them, from the east, where the winters were too cold, the summers too hot, and where the soil was unrewarding. The first newcomers began to arrive from the east, doubtless from Asia, by way of the Danube: hordes of brown-skinned men, small of stature, broad of head, in strong contrast with the long-headed Magdalenians.

An age of battles followed between the new arrivals and the occupiers, though nothing on so grand a scale as a war of races. Local collisions were the rule, and the stronger won. Armed with bows and skillfully pointed arrows, they had at their disposal that superiority of armament which is the mother of victories. Where they conquered, there they settled. At long last their enemies concluded peace. There was mingling and intermarriage and a welding of peoples. Thus did the French blend begin, between the long-headed artists and the broad-headed men of practical genius.

How large was the population? At most, a few hundred thousand. A specialist in prehistory has given half a million as the probable figure of the fifth millennium before the beginning of the Christian era. But with a developing economy the birth-rate increased rapidly. By the third millennium it had reached three million.

Let us try to see how all these people lived. The hunters, when they left their caves for the freedom of an open world, became shepherds, and this meant that those whose lives had once been sedentary and settled were transformed into

nomads. They still hunted small game. The larger, fiercer
beasts were now more rare. France still had her share of
wolves and foxes, of bears and boar and deer — in sufficient
quantities to keep fully occupied the descendants of the enemies of reindeer and mammoth.

If they wanted meat for food or skins for clothing, they
could get them from the livestock that they reared. They
had learned how to tame the horse and the ox, the goat and
the sheep, the dog and the pig. They had become breeders.
They had discovered milk and butter and cheese. They
knew how to spin wool and to weave. In order to keep their
cattle in food they moved from one grazing-ground to another, themselves living in tents, except when they built
cabins of brushwood.

About the same time as they learned the art of breeding
they invented agriculture. They could fell trees with their
flint axes. In the clearings thus made they found out how
to sow and reap. Was it mere chance that inspired them?
Did they understand the rhythm of the seasons? The cereals that they grew were many—wheat, barley, rye, oats—and
they made thin cakes of unleavened bread, grinding the
grain between flat stones. They were familiar with flax,
from which they wove linen, and with grapes, from which
they made wine. Strawberries, apples, pears, and wild cher-
ries were not unknown to them. They had a fondness for
chestnuts, hazelnuts, and plums. They liked eating acorns,
pine cones, and beech mast. Theirs was the age of the earliest agricultural triumphs. The good soil of Alsace, of the
Sarre Valley, of Angoumois and Savoy, was already being
put to the plow.

Unlike the shepherds, who moved with their flocks, the
peasants had a fixed habitat. Sometimes, true to the traditions of their ancestors, they hollowed artificial caves wherever the earth was friable (as on the chalky hillsides of the
Marne), or built huts of turf and logs, or, on the shores of

lakes, in Savoy and in the Jura, constructed pile dwellings
to protect themselves against unwelcome visitors. For, as
man had fought against the forests, so too did he strive to
master the waters, making canoes from tree-trunks, throwing bridges across the smaller rivers, fishing with nets, lines,
and spears.

Under the open heaven, as formerly within his caves, he
lived in groups. His dwellings coalesced into villages, and
families united into tribes. Man has always been a social
animal.

The Polishers of Stones

When they changed their way of life the inhabitants of
France changed their industrial methods too. They were
still working stone, but they were working it differently. In
the old days they could do no more than chip and shape,
but now they were learning how to polish. This change
brought about a complete industrial revolution.

By using flint and sandstone for rubbing, and later by in-
venting the grindstone, they manufactured many different
kinds of tools—hatchets and sickles, shears and hammers.
Some of their workshops went over to mass production, like
the establishment at Le Grand-Pressigny, in Touraine,
which exported to considerable distances its special brand
of flint saws and daggers. And because these polishers had
need of many stones, they opened up what it is no exaggeration to call mines, one example of which is a gallery at Bas-
Meudon, not far from the future site of Paris.

Pottery was another of their discoveries. Vases of many
shapes, and all of a rough-and-ready design, were made by
hand, before the wheel was known. Clay, baked and hardened in the fire, made it possible for them to store water,
oil, and wine.

These peasant shepherds were shrewd, and traded with
foreign lands. With their caravans they could travel the

roads of trampled earth; in their canoes they could risk
short journeys by water. They exchanged their weapons and
tools of stone for the raw materials, the jewels, and the pigments of which they stood in need. The proof of this is in
the hundreds of turquoises found in Morbihan, in the
hoards of seashells far from any beach. How, unless in terms
of trade, can we account for the fact that some of their ceramics are adorned with the designs found on vases that
have been unearthed in Cyprus? The West was already
learning something of the fascination of the East.

But this polished-stone culture, concerned with supplying a utilitarian demand, cared little for the things of the
spirit. Its craftsmen were not artists. They were no longer
inspired by the genius of their hunter forebears. The new
age produced no rock paintings. There were no more painters and no more paintings. It is possible to explain this in
many ways: by the disappearance of the reindeer and the
mammoth, in whom their ancestors had found their inspiration; by the coming of a more active life, with little room
for leisure; by the influence exerted by the broad-headed invaders, who had little thought for art. Whatever the reason,
the regression is too obvious to be ignored. The peasant
shepherds could leave us no more than a few crude drawings, some pendants of strung shells, some pieces of talis-
manic jewelry.

Still, they did leave us other things—giant monuments,
some of which are sixty feet in height and weigh three hundred tons. But these objects are innocent of art. The dolmens, enormous tables marking the sites of tombs, the menhirs, huge stones set up to commemorate some heroic exploit, are no more than monstrous boulders that can have
been moved only on tree-trunk sleds, and raised at a vast
expenditure of human labor. Sometimes they are set in
lines and circles as though designed to be the scene of pro-
cessions and fantastic ceremonies.

In France, between Brittany and the Cévennes, 4,500 dolmens have been catalogued, and 6,200 menhirs. They have survived, for the most part, where there is heath and moorland to protect them. At Carnac alone there are close to 2,000 menhirs. To what form of sun-worship, to what fetish cult, these stones bear witness, we do not know. The Frenchmen of the age of polished stones have not delivered up the secret of their gods.

The Smelters of Metal

The reign of stone, stone, and nothing but stone was drawing to a close. As soon as the virtues of metals were apprehended by the human mind, the weapons of war and the tools of peace were revolutionized, and the face of civilization changed.

It has been generally agreed by men of science to accept a convenient chronological arrangement in which bronze succeeds stone, and iron bronze. It is simple, and on the whole it represents the main facts accurately enough. All the same, it is quite obvious that stone must have continued to play an important part in the age of bronze, and bronze in that of iron. Nor should we limit ourselves too strictly to these two metals only. Even before the Bronze Age the inhabitants of France had known and made use of gold, silver, and copper.

Considerable quantities of gold were to be found in the Pyrenees and the Cévennes, as well as in the rivers flowing from them. Grains of it were brought down in the waters of the Rhone and the Rhine. Gold was king even in that remote period. It was used for personal adornment and in the decoration of weapons. Silver, too, though more rare and less brilliant, served as jewelry for the living and the dead.

Copper, the poor man's gold, was skillfully handled. The

peoples of the Orient had long possessed the secret of smelting it and turning it to useful purposes. This knowledge reached France by way of the Danube. The ore came from Spain. The metal was hammered out and made into flat hatchets. But copper in its native state is soft. Combined, however, with a small quantity of tin, it can be made to produce a tough bronze. This precious recipe, too, came from the Orient. For centuries past, in Mesopotamia, an alloy had been made from Caucasian copper and Afghanistan tin. The Ægean had furnished bronze to all the lands abutting on the Mediterranean. France was conveniently placed midway between the sources of Cornish tin and Spanish copper. Thus was her trade in worked metals born, and it prospered.

2500
B.C.

The ores were smelted in crucibles of sand or clay. The molten stream was then run into molds, which were at first made of stone, but later of bronze. The metal was used for the manufacture of hatchets (which entirely superseded their flint prototypes), bows, spears, maces, and daggers, which grew gradually longer until they turned into swords. But other objects were turned out as well: the furniture for shows and festivals (helmets and musical instruments), objects of luxury (vases, and circlets for wrist and ankle), tools (sickles, knives, pins, files, saws, hammers, and anvils). In every field bronze was king.

Its reign lasted for sixteen centuries, and ended only when it was dethroned by iron. Iron was much stronger. It, too, came from the countries of the East, and it entered France by way of the Rhine. Later it became evident that France was to be peculiarly favored. Iron ore was found in Lorraine, in Normandy, in Berry, and in the Alps. The forests provided all the fuel necessary for its smelting. The output of the French forges led the way for the whole of the West.

At first, iron was not taken very seriously. It was em-

ployed chiefly for purposes of decoration. Only later did
men begin to realize the uses to which it could be turned.
Its growing popularity brought about a revolution in tools
and equipment of every kind. Nails made their appearance
in carpentry, caldrons, andirons, and spits in cooking. Warriors went to battle now armed with strong swords of iron.
The whole technique of warfare was changed.

Simultaneously with this improvement in armament, the
fighting man made two more discoveries, which added to
his mobility: that of the horse as an animal to be mounted, **1000**
and that of the wheel. Western man became a rider—and **B.C.**
iron enabled him to fit his heels with spurs. The introduction of the wheel (already three thousand years old in the
lands of the Euphrates) made possible the wagon and the
chariot, and here again iron provided the means of strength-
ening the wooden disks so that they might better resist the
strains of jolting. The combination of horse and wheel led
to the introduction of harness, which in its primitive form
was faulty and of little use, until, many centuries later,
a draft system based on breast-pull superseded the earlier
yoke with its effect of strangulation. Horsemen and chari-
ots were new weapons of offense, which the defenders
sought to counter with movable shields (still made of
wood) and permanent fortifications.

Iron, harness, wheels—these things wrought a fundamental change in man's economy. The manufacture of vehicles
became one of the great industries of France. For work in
the fields, the plow was now furnished with an iron share,
and reapers with iron teeth. Agriculture improved, and the
work of forest-clearing was more readily undertaken. Those
who sailed in ships had now the use of chains and anchors.

New trades arose in response to the new hunger for luxuries. There were workshops specializing in tin-plating; others in gold and silver; still others in amber, coral, and ivory.
There were glassmakers producing beads; and somewhere

an anonymous Frenchman discovered the formula for enamel.

We have moved far from the era of the early shepherds with their tools of polished stone. The age of metals marks a stage on the road that led to comfort. France was still far from developing a great civilization, but already she was the home of an awakening barbarism.

New Peoples

New peoples as well as new technical methods had entered the country. Infiltration, both peaceful and warlike, continued for over a thousand years. The newcomers arrived from two main directions: the vast plains of the east, which contributed quantity; the Mediterranean south, which promised quality.

Basically the population of France was still a mixture of the long-headed folk, heirs of the Périgord cave-dwellers, and the broad-headed invaders from the east. Both these elements were reinforced during the age of metals. Fresh hordes of the broad-headed Aryan stock joined up with their advance guard. It has become customary to refer to them as Ligurians, though we have no means of knowing whether the word should be used to designate an original and autochthonous race or a people of migrants. The point is of no importance. Whatever their origins, the "Ligurians" of France were happy to exchange their Baltic mists for the French sunshine. What contribution did they bring? Strong arms, and the will to work. Apart from that, nothing. They were primitive, and devoid of any form of social organization. At first their skill showed itself in brigandage. Later they learned to plow, to fell, and to work bronze.

Nothing of them remains, or almost nothing, because,

ignorant of writing, they have bequeathed to us no record of their history or their customs. Since, too, they burned their dead, not even their bones have come down to us. No doubt they worshipped everything that roused their minds to wonder—sun, and warm water, hatchets, and wheels. Of their language we know nothing. All that remains of it are certain word-roots caught up and petrified in place-names.

The oldest of these place-names belong, almost invariably, to rivers and mountains. Rivers flowed and peaks glittered before ever a single village was built. The traveler, coming on a watercourse, gave it a name. More often than not, he said: "There is water," and no more. Long before the arrival of the Ligurians, water was known as *ar*, and we find the *r* perpetuated in such names as Hérault, Isère, and Arve. But who can penetrate the mystery of such names as Loire, and Rhone, and Seine? The Ligurians called water *onn*, whence Garonne, and *dor*, which gives Dordogne. The word *alp*, meaning high pasture-land, seems also to have been Ligurian. Similarly, a few of the names of inhabited places, such as Toulouse and Toulon, may well derive from the same language.

The Iberian legacy is richer. The Iberians were not of Aryan stock, but a long-headed folk, like the earliest inhabitants of the French countryside. Whether they could claim blood relationship with them or whether they came as entirely new immigrants, we do not know. Some of them, at least, seem to have arrived from Spain, working their way round the seaward end of the Pyrenees bastion, and to have spread over the south of France, as well as along the Atlantic and Mediterranean littorals, where their Catalan and Gascon descendants still live. Traces of them are to be found in the Basque language and in many of the place-names of Aquitaine and Navarre. But it must be confessed that it is very difficult to be sure where, in the tan-

500
B.C.

gled confusion of many tribes, there flows the blood of prehistoric man, or how much was contributed by invaders of
a later date.

Only about the wanderers from the eastern Mediterranean can we have any certainty. Their civilization was so
far in advance of any in the west that no doubt is possible.
These immigrants at first consisted of a few Phœnicians
who landed on the coast of Provence to barter ornaments
for metallic ores. Pre-eminent among the newcomers were
Greeks from Phocæa, who founded a trading-station on the
French seaboard—Massilia, later to become Marseille, and
long to outlive Phocæa.

From Marseille the Greeks spread out on all sides to
establish settlements. Inland they made their homes where
Arles and Avignon now stand, and worked up the valleys
of the Rhone and Durance, planting the olive wherever
they went. They were well received, because they were
good payers. Westward they swarmed at Agde (*Agathe
tukhe*, good fortune), and at Aphrodisias, the future Port
of Venus, Port-Vendres. To the eastward they were to be
found at Hyères, at Nice (with its presiding deity of Nike,
goddess of victory), at Antibes (*Antipolis*, the "city opposite"), and at Monaco. They crossed to Corsica. Sailors
from Marseille spied out the coast of Africa. One of them,
the renowned Pytheas, passed the Pillars of Hercules and
sailed the Atlantic and the northern seas in search of the
land of tin—Britain—and of amber—the Baltic shores. The
people of Marseille go so far as to maintain that Pytheas
discovered the mysterious Thule (Iceland?). But this was
probably one of the earliest of tall stories.

In this way were the glories of the infant Hellas revealed
to Frenchmen. The Greeks from Phocæa taught them the
delights of adventurous seafaring and were their tutors in
the joys of trading. But they did more than this. They displayed the very instruments of commerce, those beautiful

1000
B.C.

600
B.C.

golden staters which began to circulate in the valley of the Rhone. Marseille, too, with its vases of Hellenic purity of form, was soon to produce the first local experiments in beauty.

It was through Marseille that the alphabet, basic tool of culture, came to France. But the native metalworkers were not yet ripe for art or letters.

Behold, the Celts!

There is between the Phocæan immigration and the mass invasion of the Celts the same sort of difference as between the trickle of a gold-bearing stream and the muddy turmoil of a surging river. The Celts spread over the French lands in successive waves and eventually submerged almost the whole country. They were offscourings of the old Indo-European stock, and must have lived as nomads in the plains of central Europe for a very long time before they pressed as far westward as France. Their exodus was a matter of centuries, and was prolonged still further by the immigration of the Belgæ, which came to a final standstill on the lands between the Seine and the Rhine.

They were, all of them, broad-headed Aryans, blood-brothers to the Ligurians, from whom it is sometimes difficult to distinguish them. The Greeks called them *Galates,* the Romans *Galli,* the Germans *Walha* (from which the word *Welches,* barbarians, is derived). It is in this way that the Celts enter on the stage of history with the name of *Gaulois* (Gauls). The country where they settled came to be known as *Gaule* (Gaul). They threw the Iberians back on Aquitaine, and one group of Ligurians to the Alps. They pinned the people of Marseille to their trading-centers on the Mediterranean. They were everywhere victorious.

It is almost impossible to speak of the Celts without arousing controversy. For a long time historians ignored

500 B.C.

200 B.C.

them, but later embarked upon a frantic course of "Celti-
cization." It became the fashion to applaud the virtues of
this Aryan folk, to see in them the true ancestors of the
French people. According to the teaching of these enthusiasts, the Celtic language was the mother of all tongues. It
was reinvented for the sheer pleasure of finding in it the
etymology of every French word. To the Celts went the
honor of having been responsible for the flat stones and
standing stones to which the Celtic names of *dolmen* and
menhir were given. To the Celts went the glory of having
been the instructors of the Greeks and the founders of civilization. Infected by the prevailing fever, scholars of high
repute swelled the population figures of Gaul, which they
reckoned at twenty or twenty-four million before the Roman conquest.

So far as it is possible to judge, the Celts deserved neither
the oblivion to which at one time they were condemned
nor the excessive adulation by which they have since been
overwhelmed. Certainly they are to be numbered among
the ancestors of the French, but to no greater and to no
less a degree than the many other immigrants who preceded
and succeeded them. Intermingling with earlier settlers on
the soil of France—of whom there were already several million—they swelled their numbers and waxed fruitful, bringing the total of the population of Gaul to something in the
neighborhood of ten million—a very reasonable figure. The
part they played as civilizers was necessarily small, as was
that of all the invaders from the east. The Celts were no
more than barbarians who, when they became sedentary,
developed a species of organized society and on occasion
succeeded in imitating their more highly cultivated neighbors. Left to themselves, they were incapable, in the domains of art and of the human spirit, of producing anything either personal or lasting.

That scholars should have made mistakes about them is

but natural. Error began even with the description of their physical appearance. "They were tall and full-fleshed, white-skinned and fair-haired," wrote Michelet. That was a bad blunder. The Celts were small, thickset, and dark-complexioned. If they were later thought to be fair, that was because they indulged in bleaching. The modern French who most resemble them (and who, for that matter, most resemble the Ligurians and the broad-headed men of prehistory) are those of the Massif Central, of Morvan, and of Savoy. The Bretons are no more than their nephews.

It is impossible to say for certain whether the Celts brought the iron sword and the chariot with them to France or whether they found them already in use on their arrival. It seems probable that, as nomads making contact with settled peoples, as herdsmen coming upon farmers, as northerners swarming along the frontiers of Greece and Rome, they gained more from invasion than they gave to the invaded.

The Celtic Flow and Ebb

If the Celts had one talent more than another, it was that of warfare. They were astonishing horsemen, and skillful with the sword. They moved more rapidly and were better armed than most of their contemporaries. They feared nothing, for their priests taught them to be brave. But they imposed fear on others because they had the cruelty of a primitive people. Their enemies knew that they sacrificed their prisoners, that they cut off the heads of conquered chiefs, that they used human skulls as drinking-cups.

Scarcely were they established in Gaul when the old nomad itch once more awoke in them. Their passion for being always on the move was irresistible, as was their love of fighting. France had increased their taste for both. They penetrated into Britain, they spread over Europe toward

the countries where they could find sun and a highly developed civilization. Their goals were Rome and Athens.

They crossed the Alps and the Po. They thundered down
toward the Latin lands. They made themselves the masters
of Rome. If we are to believe Livy and the voice of legend,
they massacred the Roman senators after first provoking
them by laying impious hands on their beards. They tried
to storm the Capitol, from which they were driven only by
the intervention of the sacred geese of Juno. They agreed
to raise the siege of the city in return for a golden ransom,
and their leader flung his sword into the scales while the
precious metal was being weighed, with the words "*Væ
Victis!*"

**390
B.C.**

All that these heroic tales amount to is that the Celts
pillaged Rome and then took their departure. They turned
up elsewhere too, inseparable as ever from their horses, galloping toward Greece. They ravaged Macedonia, pressed
down through the pass of Thermopylæ, and brought destruction to Delphi, Apollo's sanctuary. Halted by the city-
states of Hellas, they crossed the Bosporus and established
in Asia Minor a distant colony, the inhabitants of which
were later known as Galatians.

We should not take too seriously these "raids" on Rome
and on the eastern lands. The Celts sought booty and ransom rather than conquest. It is nonsense to speak of a
"Celtic Empire" stretching from the Atlantic to the Balkans. It was an empire without an emperor and without
subjects—or rather it was an empire only in the sense that
the jungle is an empire of wild beasts.

Ebb followed hard on the heels of flood. The best of
warriors grow weak when they are too widely dispersed.
Wherever the Celts settled they were saved from extermi-
nation only by becoming assimilated. From northern Italy
they gradually disappeared. In Spain, which they had also
reached, they mingled with the Iberians. In Britain their

settlements were confined to the south. They were flung
back from the Danube by the German tribes, and when,
in Gaul, they seized Marseille, the Romans came to the aid
of the Phocæan Greeks, chased the Celts as far as the Isère,
and appropriated a large extent of territory, which included
the whole of the Mediterranean littoral in that part of the
Continent, Languedoc, and the Alps. Rome quickly Latinized her *Province*, from which was born Provence.

Were the Celts just unlucky? Not at all. They merely
paid the price of anarchy and lack of discipline. To conquer and to endure, bravery is not enough. Organization is
essential.

The Anarchy of Gaul

In Celtic Gaul there was authority at the bottom, but none
at the top. The nation rested on a patriarchal basis. The
head of each family had powers of life and death over all its
members. When he died, his wife was often sacrificed upon
his grave. Outside, but in close proximity to the family,
were the vassals (the word is of Gallic origin)—that is,
those who were dependent on it for their livelihood. Nor
must we forget the slaves. On many of the great holdings
they could be counted in the thousands.

At the top there was nothing: nothing in the nature of
an administration, nothing that could be called the State.
Consequently there were no public services. It was nobody's business to see justice done, to arbitrate in quarrels,
to maintain the roads, or to raise an army. When, as occasionally happened, one of the clans managed to exert its
authority over others (at first the Bituriges, later the Ædui
and the Arverni), its supremacy was short-lived. The Celtic
world became easily scattered. Its component parts much
preferred liberty to government.

This marked feature of anarchy was also to be found, on
a smaller scale, within the clans themselves. Except in case

of dire necessity, the idea of a chief was hateful to them. They were little more than loose agglomerations of families, and could ill endure the presence of a king, even if he were elected. The richest and most powerful heads of households, much like the later feudal nobles, were jealous of sovereign rights and did their best to stultify all attempts at setting up a central authority. In this they succeeded well.

The political picture of Gaul is that of a multitude of rival tribes and, within each, of warring clans. But the names of some of the tribes are worth remembering, because they later passed to cities and to provinces which became famous in the history of France. At the center of the Celtic world, on the Eure and the Loire, lived the *Carnutes,* who gave their name to Chartres. Around them were the *Eburovians* (worshippers of the yew, *eburo*), from whom we get Évreux, the *Lexovians* (Lisieux), the *Turons* (Tours), the *Andes* (Angers), and the *Bituriges* (Bourges), whose name modestly signifies "kings of the world." Westward were the *Namnetes* (Nantes), the *Veneti* (Vannes), the *Pictones* (Poitiers), and the *Santones* (Saintes). In Aquitaine, Celts and Iberians lived in close proximity to one another. The Alps were the home of the *Allobroges* and the *Helvetii.* The Massif Central was held by the *Arverni* (Auvergne), the *Cadurceans* (Cahors), and the *Lemovices* (Limoges). The *Ædui* were masters of the Saône, the *Senones* (Sens) of the Yonne, the *Parisii* (Paris) of the Seine. To the north, in the land of the Belgæ, were the *Remi* (Reims), the *Bellovaces* (Beauvais), the *Ambieni* (Amiens), the *Trevires* (Trèves), the *Mediomatrici* (Metz). These are but a few specimens chosen from the confused pattern of the numerous tribes, small and great, which formed the loose-knit nation of the Gauls.

Forests played the part of frontiers and neutral zones. The names of localities formed from the Celtic word *randa* (limit)—such, for instance, as *Icoranda* (limit of the waters? limit of the woods?)—often lay thick upon the dividing line between tribe and tribe and were later adopted by Roman cities and Christian dioceses. All the *Ingrandes, Ingrannes, Aigurandes, Eygurandes, Yvrandes,* derive their names from this source.

Centers the Celtic tribes may have had, but we should be making a great mistake if we thought of them as in any way resembling permanent capitals. Of what value was a settled town, seeing that the Gauls knew nothing of social administration? The towns, so called, were, for the most part, no more than strong-points to be used in times of danger, or temporary markets for trade. The former were situated on high ground: *Bibracte, Alesia, Gergovia.* Of similar character were towns with the word *dunos* in their names, meaning primarily a hilltop, secondarily a citadel: *Lugdunos* (Lyon), *Virodunos* (Verdun), *Mellodunos* (both Melun and Meudon), *Uxellodunos* (Issoudun), and those too in which the word *duros* (fortress) occurs: *Brivoduros* (the fort on the bridge—Briare), *Nemetoduros* (the fort of the temple—Nanterre), *Turnoduros* (Tonnerre), *Auteciodurum* (Auxerre).

The markets, on the other hand, belonged to the valleys and the rivers. The Gallic word for them was *magos,* the first meaning of which is field—*Catumagos* (the field of battle—Caen), though it was later used to designate a fairground. Thus we find *Rotomagos* (Rouen), *Turnomagos* (Tournon), *Noviomagos* (Noyon, Nogent), *Divomagos* (Gien), *Argentomagos* (Argenton, Argentan). Other centers, such as *Genabum* (later Orléans), *Avaricum* (later Bourges), *Tolosa* (Toulouse), *Burdigala* (Bordeaux), similarly served as the meeting-places of tribes for purposes of trade.

Some towns were both citadels and markets, at once *dunos* and *magos—Magodunos,* for instance (Meung, Me-

hun). In the same way the small Lutetia, capital of the unpretentious tribe of the Parisii, was both a fortress, because
of its strong position on an island, and a market, because it
stood on a waterway. But Lutetia was more a village than a
town.

The Religious Bond

In this fine disorder, this perfection of disunion, the Gauls
were bound together by the customs and ideas they had in
common. Their attitude to life and death was the same.
Their daily existence was one of extreme simplicity. Shepherds and peasants alike sheltered in round huts of clay and
wattle, roofed with stones or thatch. Their furniture was
limited to tables and chests, with sometimes a mat. They
were by nature hospitable, loving good food (they invented
the ham). Wine, too, they loved, and contrived the cask,
which is more practical than the jar.

In common with all the Indo-European peoples, they
believed in three major gods. As the Hindus acknowledged
Brahma, Siva, and Vishnu, the Germans Wotan, Tiwaz,
and Donar, the Greeks Zeus, Poseidon, and Hades, the Romans Jupiter, Neptune, and Pluto (and as the Christians,
too, had their Trinity?), so, too, did the Gauls worship a
triple deity: *Teutates, Hesus,* and *Taran.*

In addition to this supreme trio the Gauls had a multiplicity of demons and elves, gods and goddesses of a lower
rank: *Lugos* (venerated at Lyon, Laon, and Loudun), the
god of crafts and trades, a Celtic version of Mercury;
Epona, patroness of the horse; *Belen,* god of the sun
(whose memory persists in all the Beaunes of France);
Borvo and *Illixo,* the twin deities of warm streams (source
of Bourbon and Luchon). Also they gave a divine character to small rivers (the Diva, the Divonne) as well as to
great (the Rhine, the Seine, the Marne). *Vosegos* was the
god of the Vosges.

In spite of these local variants the religion of the Gauls maintained its unity through priests and ceremonies, and it was this bond that saved their society from utter dissolution. The priests called themselves druids, a name that embodies the word *deru,* meaning the oak; and one of their functions was to cut the sacred mistletoe, in solemn rite, with a golden sickle. They were at once sorcerers, doctors, astronomers, and judges. They organized human sacrifices to win the favor of the gods or to thank them for the gift of victory. They transmitted orally, and in the utmost secrecy, the magic formulas of their incantations. They worked cures by means of herbs. They acted as arbitrators in serious cases of litigation.

Each year the druids met together on the banks of the Loire, in the land of the Carnutes, the geometric center of the Celtic realm. There they did honor to the gods with copious hecatombs, and dispensed justice. The metaphysics of their religion was simple. They taught that fire would one day destroy the universe; that men's souls do not die; and that the dead have an afterlife in a distant island beyond the western seas. The Bretons, however, heirs of the Celts of Britain, placed it nearer home, identifying it with the little isle of Aval, in the district of Lannion.

This religion had already freed itself from the primitive cult of animal totems. It was not without a certain ethical character, for it enjoined the virtues of piety, honor, and courage. It seems even to have attained to a fairly high degree of abstraction. Its gods were not, as a rule, represented by images, unless the great trunks of trees may be held to have served as such. This abstention may have been due to respect for the divine symbol. It may, however, have resulted from ignorance of the arts of carving and painting.

A Rudimentary Economy

Brought into contact with the rich soil of Gaul, the Celts, whose fathers had been herdsmen, quickly developed an excellence in farming. If they continued to breed cattle in the hedged meadows of the west, they were not slow to clear the land elsewhere, and to plow the earth thus freed. Great areas of the country were still covered with forests, but these were slowly being conquered. From Flanders to the Cévennes, France is thickly sown with place-names that recall the labors of these Celtic pioneers. The world *ial* (which became the Gallic termination *oialos*) bears witness to this early work of clearing, of the turning of brushwood into plowland. It has given us innumerable *Mareuils, Mareaus, Marvejols* (the "great field"), *Verneuils* (the "field of the alder"), *Vineuils, Vigneaus* (the "field of the vine"), *Jargeaus* (the "field of the oak"), *Limeuils* (the "field of the elm"), and *Nanteuils* (the "valley field"). In this way the map of France still preserves the traces of the men who opened up her countryside.

In these fields, which were held as private property (no doubt by single families), the Gauls cultivated the various cereals, as well as flax and hemp. They worked with wheeled plows (*charrues*), each drawn by a yoked pair of oxen (the word *charrue* is of Gallic origin, as is *arpent*, a unit of land measurement). They had different types of harrow, and long scythes. They strengthened the soil with marl and lime. They let their fields lie fallow every third year. Most of the land-workers were miserably poor.

They had little in the way of industry, apart from metallurgy: a few saltpans, a few mills (turned by hand), a few workshops where pots were made (also by hand). Their weaving was somewhat less primitive. Good woolen fabrics were produced in Artois, in Franche-Comté, and in Saintonge. They manufactured trousers (*braies*), cloaks (*saies*), and short tunics with sleeves. All their materials were colored with vegetable dyes. Their leatherwork was excellent.

Commerce was confined to a few primary objects. But, even so, Gaul was already exporting wheat, livestock, wool, and slaves, in return for bronze, jewelry, ceramics, and oil. Berry and Burgundy found a market for their iron swords.

Sea communications were but little used. The Celts left the joys, the dangers, and the profits of navigation to the Iberians, the Ligurians, and the Phocæans, turning sailor only through necessity. The Veneti alone delighted in spreading their leather sails and venturing to sea in their potbellied craft. There is no Gallic place-name which has the meaning of "port." Nantes, Rouen, Lutetia (which later carried a ship in its arms) were no more than river harbors.

Land travel was undertaken on horseback or in two-wheeled and four-wheeled vehicles. The tracks were rough. Distances were reckoned in leagues (the Gallic *leuga* was the equivalent of about one and one-third miles). There is no Gallic word actually meaning a road, though there are several associated with fords (*Niort*, the "new ford"; *Chambord*, the "ford on the curve") and with wooden bridges (*Brive, Brioude, Salbris*).

Business transactions were always conducted by barter. The current value of a slave was a measure of wine. But the idea of money was already beginning to make headway. Ingots of copper may have served as units of payment. Marseille was not far distant, and there the marvelous coins of Greece were current. By way of that city, and by the Danube too, gold and silver money entered Gaul. The Arverni set to work to imitate these masterpieces, and little by little all the Gallic peoples, who never suffered from any lack of metal, took to minting coins, each copying its neighbors. This crude currency, issued piecemeal, and controlled by no central authority, was the very sign and symbol of the Gallic anarchy.

The Legacy of the Celts

What, taking all in all, did the Celtic age leave as its heritage to France? In its own way it certainly contributed to the improvement of the soil and the furtherance of certain technical processes—especially in the field of metallurgy. It led to an increase of population, and set up a human pool on which future invaders could draw. No trace remains of Gallic families. They knew nothing of hereditary patronymics, and used only individual names.

Certain traditions outlived their Gallic founders—for instance, the superstition that mistletoe brings luck, and the custom of lighting festival fires at the summer solstice. The habit of reckoning in units of twenty, common among the Gauls, persisted. It has always been customary in France to say *six-vingts* (six twenties) for 120, and *quatre-vingts* for 80. This vigesimal counting persisted; much later, the livre and the franc were each to contain twenty sous.

Probably the outstanding contribution of the Celts, however, is the French love of liberty and independence—even at the risk of falling, at times, into anarchy and civil strife.

Of the Gallic language nothing remains. No single verb, no single adjective, became embedded in the French tongue. We do not even know how a Gaul said "I am hungry." Still, with the help of a few dozen inscriptions, and the dialects—such as the Breton—which derived from Gallic originals, it is possible to reconstruct something of their vocabulary—enough to prove that the language was Indo-European, built on a rather primitive system of assonances. Place-names, and especially the names of mountains, are our surest guides (*Cévennes* comes from a root meaning "back"; *Jura* signifies a wooded height; *Ardennes* means high ground), and the names of rivers (*Doubs*, the black; *Bièvre*, the beaver stream; *Marne*, mother; the Saône and the Rhine). Later arrivals could do no more than ratify these names. Scarcely a mountain-peak or a strip of running water remained to be named.

The Celtic contribution to literature is nil. The reason for this is not that the Gauls were lacking in intelligence, but that they did not possess the indispensable instrument of literature, which is writing. Only very late in their career did they discover the Greek alphabet and the wonders it had made possible. They preferred eloquence and spoken narrative. The druids talked. The bards sang the exploits of the warriors, after the manner of Arab story-tellers. They may, for all we know, have had poetic genius, but only their immediate audiences were in a position to enjoy it.

In the arts they could do little more than stammer. They made necklaces, it is true, and bracelets and leg-ornaments of bronze, and carved beads from amber. Those, however, were activities demanding only minor talents. In architecture they produced nothing.

Such, then, was the legacy of the Celts. It was rich by comparison with that of the nomad peoples, though poor when set against the wealth of the Mediterranean civilizations. When the Gauls were living in huts, forging iron and felling trees, Phidias was carving the Parthenon friezes, and Plautus writing comedies for a Roman public. Even within the Gallic frontiers the "Province" was enjoying benefits that flowed from Phocæa and from Rome. In terms of organization and comfort it was centuries ahead of illiterate Gaul.

Illiterate or not, however, Gaul was a tempting prey. It would have been asking too much of Rome to remain indifferent to the spectacle of so rich, so well-populated a land, where was wheat and gold in abundance, and wealth

lay unexploited. It seemed marked out by destiny to provide Rome with what she lacked—foodstuffs and raw materials—for which Rome in return could offer peace and social order.

The Roman Conquest

Gaul, truth to tell, was no longer capable of safeguarding
its own independence. Not only were the tribes divided
among themselves; they had grown soft. The warlike ardor
of the earliest conquerors had cooled. The nomads had become farmers, the fighting men pacific. The spirit that
makes for victory had ebbed from Gaul. There might be
suspicion of Rome's civilization, but there was envy, too.
The Gauls, brought into contact with the Province, and
seeing it transformed, had already begun to dream of a
better life. The least contaminated were the Belgæ of the
north, because they were the latest comers and because the
temptations offered by Rome were farther removed. Most
of the other peoples were ripe for the plucking.

There were, after all, but two choices open to the Gauls:
they could be either Romanized or Germanized. The Romans were on the Rhone, but the Germans were on the
Rhine, ready to yield to the age-old lure of the West.
Caught between these two dangers, the Gauls chose the
more attractive and sought out Roman help against the
German threat.

Once before, Gaul and Roman had faced it together.
Two hordes, the Cimbri and the Teutones, coming from
the Baltic with their wives and children, had crossed the
Rhine and spread deep into the country. The Cimbri had
been seen as far away as the Pyrenees; the Teutones had
broken into the Province. The Gauls had shown themselves incapable of putting up an effective resistance—a bad
sign. Only when the Roman legions, under Marius, ap-

109
B.C.

102
B.C.

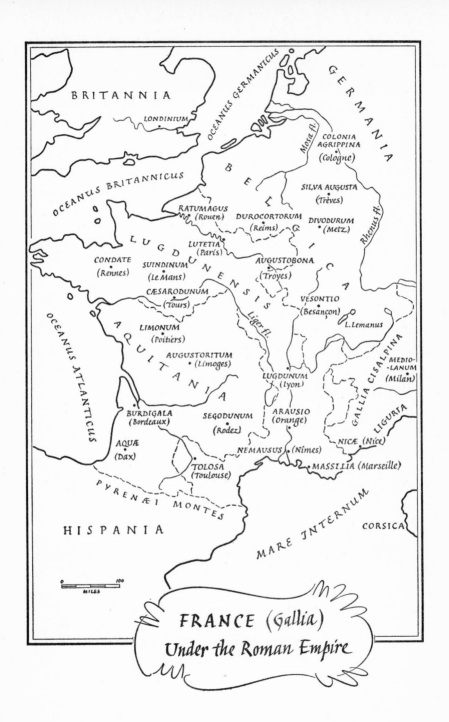

BRITANNIA

LONDINIUM

OCEANUS GERMANICUS

GERMANIA

Mosa fl.

COLONIA
AGRIPPINA
(Cologne)

OCEANUS BRITANNICUS

B E L

SILVA AUGUSTA
(Trèves)

RATUMAGUS
(Rouen)

DUROCORTORUM
(Reims)

G I C A

DIVODURUM
(Metz)

Rhenus fl.

LUTETIA
(Paris)

AUGUSTOBONA
(Troyes)

L U G D U

CONDATE
(Rennes)

SUINDINUM
(Le Mans)

N E N S I S

VESONTIO
(Besançon)

CÆSARODUNUM
(Tours)

Liger fl.

L.Lemanus

LIMONUM
(Poitiers)

A Q U I T A N I A

AUGUSTORITUM
(Limoges)

MEDIO-
LANUM
(Milan)

OCEANUS ATLANTICUS

LUGDUNUM
(Lyon)

G A L L I A C I S A L P I N A

BURDIGALA
(Bordeaux)

SEGODUNUM
(Rodez)

ARAUSIO
(Orange)

LIGURIA

AQUÆ
(Dax)

NEMAUSUS (Nîmes)

NICÆ (Nice)

TOLOSA
(Toulouse)

MASSILIA (Marseille)

P Y R E N Æ I   M O N T E S

M A R E   I N T E R N U M

CORSICA

HISPANIA

0   100
MILES

FRANCE (Gallia)
Under the Roman Empire

peared were the raiders crushed and scattered. This first
clash was symptomatic of German greed, Gallic weakness,
and Roman efficiency.

Less than fifty years later, renewed German pressure set
Rome again in motion. But this time her help was not
given for nothing. Cæsar turned the occasion to the advantage not only of his country, but of his own ambition. He
was a born intriguer, hungry for wealth and honors. Au-
dacity amounting to genius served his purpose well. To him
all means were good. He respected neither Celtic liberties
nor Rome's Republic. He destroyed the first in order the
more easily to destroy the second.

As Governor of the Province he was well placed to carry
out his plans. The Celtic tribe of the Helvetii wished to settle on the Atlantic coast. They asked him for permission to
cross the Rhone at Geneva, which was situated within the
limits of the Province. This he refused. If the ancestral
home of the Helvetii were to be left empty, it would fall
into the hands of the Germans, who would prove more
than awkward neighbors. The Helvetii crossed the Jura,
and the Ædui, in their anxiety, called on Cæsar for aid.
Cæsar fell on the Helvetii and drove them back to their
homeland. But who was to drive back Cæsar?

The Gauls did not even make the attempt, for they had
need of him. The Germanic tribe of the Suevi, led by Ario-
vistus, was advancing toward the Saône. The Gauls, thus
threatened, appealed to Cæsar, and Cæsar did not need
much persuasion. He defeated the Suevi, and Gaul was
saved—or rather she was lost. Her liberator had become her
conqueror. When the Gauls realized that they had thrown
the fold open to the wolf, it was already too late. The wolf
—it was a she-wolf, the nurse of Romulus and Remus—
showed no intention of leaving.

For seven years the Gauls strove in vain to throw off the
yoke. Cæsar, though Rome did not always show herself

59
B.C.

helpful, stood his ground. Did he really deserve all the trib-
utes that have been paid him? Writing, as he did, the story
of his own achievements, he was free to exaggerate the
numbers of his opponents, who in fact never succeeded in
bringing all their combined forces against him. When the
Belgæ rose in revolt, the Remis sided with Cæsar. When
he passed over into Britain to crush the island Celts, the
Celts of the mainland made no move. When the Carnutes
rebelled, the Armoricans came to terms. Even when a young
chieftain of the Arverni, proclaiming himself the "Great
King of the Chosen Warriors" (which is the meaning of
Vercingetorix) called on all the people to rise, the Ædui remained true to the Roman alliance. Cæsar, who was as
shrewd a diplomat as he was a clever soldier, knew well
how to pour oil on the fire of Gallic quarrels. Turn and
turn about, he used terror and leniency to further his ends,
and his subtle handling of the situation increased rather
than diminished the general confusion, so that the Gauls
no longer knew who were traitors and who were not.

The siege of Avaricum (Bourges), the unsuccessful investment of Gergovia, the storming of Alesia, and the sur- **52**
render of Vercingetorix were the final stages on the road to **B.C.**
conquest. Cæsar, writing with the calm assurance of a victorious general, was careful to have the last word. With his
own pen he described his triumph. "The chiefs appeared
before him. Vercingetorix was given into his hands. The
weapons of the enemy were cast down at his feet." The
heart had gone out of the Gallic resistance. The stronger
side had won, and not only the stronger, but the most
united. Throughout this Gallic War the Romans had held
all the trump cards in strategy and tactics. They were superior in organization, in determination, in equipment. It
was a struggle of soldiers against peasants, of legions against
guerrilla bands, of the ballista against the javelin.

All was over: Gaul had become Roman. Apart from a

few years of sporadic uprisings, she willingly accepted her
fate. She traded her liberties in exchange for civilization.

Rome the Tolerant

The scene changed. Gaul, freed from her thousand name-
less, unremembered years, now made her entrance on the
stage of history. Before Cæsar she had been a land of mystery, whose past can be guessed at only by digging in her
soil, studying her stones, consulting maps. With the coming of Cæsar, and after his death, Gaul lay revealed in the
bright light of day. A thousand written documents record
her story. We have only to choose among them, and inter-
pret what we choose. Not that that makes the task very
much easier. Instead of guessing, we must now attempt to
understand.

The extraordinary phenomenon of the sudden "Roman-
ization" of Gaul has been misinterpreted. Sudden it most
certainly was, for it took less than fifty years, whereas the
era of Gaul and Rome in close association lasted for almost
five hundred (and for longer still in the southern provinces). Such an assimilation must, one thinks, have been
due to force, or at the very least to systematic pressure. In
fact the contrary is true. Rome was not in the least anxious
to Latinize Gaul. It was the Gauls who were animated by
a fierce longing to become Roman.

The attitude of the conquerors was anything but harsh.
If Cæsar had Vercingetorix strangled after six years of martyrdom, that was merely to serve his own ends. Shrewd, or
perhaps merely contemptuous, Rome was careful not to
play the bully. She behaved as though anxious to win the
loyalty of the Gauls, and employed neither violence nor
propaganda.

Beyond a doubt, Rome brought unity into the Gallic
chaos—and, with that end in view, began by "Celticizing"

46
B.C.

the country, at the expense of the Iberians and the Ligurians. Those areas which were to be known henceforward as the "states" (*civitates*) were regrouped into four solid blocks: the *Narbonnaise*, covering the ancient "Province"; the *Lyonnaise, Aquitaine,* and *Belgium*—the three latter districts forming "Gaul of the Long Hair," as distinct from the southern part of the country, where, as in Italy, men wore their hair short. On the left bank of the Rhine, Rome constituted two frontier provinces facing the Germanies. **27 B.C.**

Within this general framework the "Long-haired" Gauls were left free to possess their own lands and to live under their own laws and their own magistrates. If they wished to retain their ancient customs, they were at liberty to do so. Rome's military control was confined to the placing of garrisons at strategic points, and to settling communities of colonists in convenient localities. But garrisons and colonies alike were soon far more Gallic than they were Roman.

The occupying legions could scarcely have been drawn from Roman or even Italian sources, since Romans and Italians were adamant in their refusal to perform military service except in a few privileged corps. In fact, the troops stationed in Gaul, to a total of 100,000 men, were recruited from many different places—primarily from the Narbonnaise, secondarily from other parts of Gaul. As representatives of Rome, wearing Roman uniforms, the Gauls were now employed in occupying their own country.

The colonies established by Rome in the Celtic lands could scarcely, in any true sense, be any longer called Roman. They numbered about thirty, and were situated almost exclusively in the south and on the northeastern frontier. In theory, they consisted of former legionaries saddled with the pacific duty of "representing" the power of Rome. But very often these veterans had no drop of Latin blood in their veins.

To sum up, Rome had neither the means nor the wish

to turn Gaul into a replica of herself, even to the extent of
enforcing the use of her own tongue. Schools were taught
in Greek. In the country at large the people were left free
to speak Latin or not as they wished.

The conquering power did not even persecute the druids,
whose subversive teachings it might well have feared. It
took no steps more extreme than forbidding their annual
assemblies and the practice of human sacrifice. It left the
Gauls at liberty to worship what gods they pleased, merely
superimposing, or adding, its own, beginning with the cults
of the Emperor and of the Eternal City. The Gauls, who
scattered divine attributes widely, but had no clearly defined or established religion, found little difficulty in including the Emperor in their pantheon. They entertained
for Rome so undying a passion that no *force majeure* was
needed to impose upon them the obligations of loyalty.

Collaboration

Far from resenting the presence of the conqueror, the
Gauls wanted nothing more than to be Roman in law and
in fact. They claimed the right to be styled Roman citizens,
and were naturalized by the thousand. Rome badly needed
all the external support that she could find, and dared not
A.D.   refuse them the privilege of citizenship. When, ultimately,
212   she accorded it as a blanket concession to all the free peoples of the Empire, she was doing no more than giving legal recognition to an existing situation.

Some historians may feel inclined to throw doubt on this
assertion by pointing to the occasional uprisings that set
Gauls and Romans at one another's throat. But these were
never serious. Either they were the result of German agitation or they were devised to further the political ambitions
of various competitors for the Imperial purple. In no true
sense were they national movements. They were local dis-

orders of the same general pattern as those which occurred in Italy.

At no moment did Gaul really contemplate breaking with Rome. At no moment did her peoples genuinely seek revenge upon the Roman world. On the contrary, throughout the centuries of the Gallo-Roman collaboration, the confessed ambition of the Gauls was so successfully to imitate the model offered by their Roman conquerors as to be indistinguishable from them.

The Gauls of the north and center were at pains to abjure their former fashion of wearing the hair long. They cropped their heads in the Roman mode. Similarly, they abandoned the use of breeches, which they regarded as a sign of barbarism, and took instead to the flowing robes of the civilized world. Personal and place-names underwent the same process of reformation. Repudiating the old Celtic tradition, nobles and peasants alike adopted the Latin system, by which every man had a surname, a personal name, and a family name (*cognomen*). Away with the *Atepomaros* or *Caturix*, which smelled of savagery a mile off! A Roman would be called *Claudius Cornelius Scipio*, which, being interpreted, meant Claudius, of the tribe Cornelius, and of the Scipio family. In much the same way the Gauls proceeded of their own accord to give to their cities names redounding to the glory of their conquerors. *Augustonemetum* (later Clermont) and *Augustodunum* (Autun) may quite genuinely have owed their names to Augustus, but there were others—*Cæsaromagus* (Beauvais), *Cæsarodunum* (Tours), *Juliomagus* (Angers), *Dea Augusta* (Die), *Augustodurum* (Bayeux)—which received those appellations as a free-will offering from inhabitants intent on pleasing the Romans.

Snobbery? Flunkyism? Perhaps. Tacitus, who witnessed with his own eyes a similar conversion, tells in his *Agricola* how the Britons became Latinized: "Not only did they will-

ingly adopt our language, but they made it a matter of
pride to speak it with elegance. They went so far as to ape
our manners. The toga became the fashion." The Gauls
did not feel that by collaborating they were in any way in-
curring a charge of cowardice or were wallowing in servility.
They were proud to think that they belonged to the Roman world, that they had stepped out of the ranks of barbarism and were now to be numbered among the peoples
who enjoyed an orderly form of government. They did not
pretend to be Romans, they *were* Romans. They had no
lack of patriotism, only they were *Roman* patriots. Let us
listen for a moment to Ausonius, the poet of Bordeaux:
"Bordeaux is my home, but Rome is a greater home. I love
Bordeaux, but I worship Rome." There is this hymn, too,
written by Rutilius Namatianus of Toulouse, in honor of
Rome: "Rome, of the starry company of heaven, Rome,
mother of men and of gods . . . we sing thy glory and, so
long as Destiny permits, will sing it still. To many thou
hast given a fatherland. Once they resisted thee, but by thy
victory have been the gainers. Thou reignest, and, what is
more, deservest so to reign. While earth continues and the
great sky holds the stars aloft, thou wilt live on." In these
passages the poets were giving expression to what their
countrymen felt.

Gaul was becoming what Rome had ceased to be—Roman. With the loss of her virtues the Eternal City had seen
something else go too—her own faith in her destiny. Her
population was diminishing, in quality no less than in numbers. Her citizens were becoming degraded, were being
transformed into a proletariat. Enslaved to leisure and to
luxury, they no longer had the will either to work or to
fight. Their patriotism was slipping into internationalism.
In the end Gaul became more Roman than Rome herself.

In peace she outdid the exploits of her warrior forebears,
and conquered Rome. A time came when all the highest

offices of state in turn were occupied by Gauls, at first in
their own provincial cities, but latterly in the very capital of
empire. They won the right to sit in the Senate (under
Claudius); they could become consuls (after the reign of
Tiberius), and even wore the Imperial purple. Antoninus
was a native of Nîmes; Caracalla was born in Lyon. Nor
was it only that individual Gauls occasionally occupied the
throne. More than once the capital itself was moved to
Gaul. Julian ruled from Lutetia; Valentinian from Trèves.
The conquerors had been conquered. Not Rome had colonized Gaul, but Gaul Rome.

Gaul's Gift to Rome

In acting as they did, the Romans were prompted by no
feelings of philanthropy. They laid hold on Gaul in order
to use her as a buttress against the German peril. They
knew—none better—what sources of wealth the country
had to offer; they intended to exploit it to their own advantage, and they did so.

Rome badly needed food and raw materials, and Gaul
was in a position to give, or rather to sell, both. Her soil
was fertile; she had rich mines and a vast reservoir of manpower. It was an arrangement of give and take. Rome stimulated production and paid good prices. Gaul found in the
Empire an enormous market for her goods. Her economy
developed—an economy based on agriculture and manufactured articles. One of the results of that development, however, was that her mineral wealth—which became an Imperial monopoly—was gradually exhausted. No longer did
the rivers roll down gold-dust in their current. The seams
of silver were worked out. Iron ore was recklessly extracted
in order to satisfy the demands of her own metallurgical industries and those of Italy.

The natural wealth of Gaul has covered the map of

France with telltale names: *Laurière* and *Auriol* (gold-fields), *Largentière* and *Argentière* (silver-workings), *Mignières, Ferrières* (iron-workings). Other names crystallize the memory of those districts which were devoted to live-stock-breeding: *Armentières* (*gros bétail*, major herds), *Achères* (bees), *Asnières* (donkeys); or to the cultivation of crops: *Fromentières* (wheat), *Favières* (*fèves*, beans), *Lignières, Lignerolles* (*lin*, flax), *Chennevières* (*chanvre*, hemp). These names remain as evidence of Gallic activities in the time of the Romans.

Gaul also supplied Rome with soldiers. She began with the *Alouette* (Lark) legion, went on to raise auxiliary co-horts of both cavalry and infantry, and, by the end of the Empire, was supplying all the contingents necessary for her own defense.

Finally, taxes. These flowed into Rome from Gaul. Cæsar had inaugurated the fiscal era by levying a tribute on the country when first he conquered it. Under one name or another, these payments or contributions served to supply the needs of the State and made it possible to run the public services cheaply. The barbarians had known nothing of either State or taxation. As soon as the State appeared, taxation followed.

It took, in Gaul, the form either of services rendered or of contributions in kind—usually the latter. There was little in the way of indirect taxation: a few customs dues (the Gallic "fortieth"—that is, the fortieth part of the value of imported goods), city tolls, road charges, and duties on transfers of property (a twentieth on sales of land, on the enfranchisement of slaves, and on all inheritances not in the direct line).

Direct taxation already took many forms. There were the poll tax, which struck heavily at all those in Gaul who were not possessed of real property; a professional tax on profits; and, above all, the land tax, for the levying of which Rome

undertook an exhaustive survey of all estates. It accounted
for perhaps a tenth part of the total revenue. Property-
owners had to make a declaration of acreage and estimated
yield. The Gallic taxpayer strongly resented these demands.

The tax-registers of the Roman administration played no
small part in the fixing of French place-names. If a Gallic
landowner was called *Eburos*, his property was entered as
Eburiacum, Eburos's holding; and from this source was derived *Yvrac*, in the southwest; *Ivry*, in the center; *Ivré*, in
the west. Owners, for the most part, had Latin names—
Florus or *Paulus*, and in these cases the estate was officially
known as *Floriacum* or *Pauliacum*, whence *Florac, Fleurat,
Fleury, Fleuré, Pauillac, Pouilly, Pouillé*. This explains how
it is that all over France, from Brittany to Auvergne, from
Saintonge to the plain of Paris, the land is dotted with
thousands of names terminating in *ac, y, é*, with variants
in *at, is*, or *ieux*, all of which commemorate Gallic holdings
of the Roman age. Even when the Roman system fell into
decay and vanished, when the land tax was no more, the
name stayed on: *Vitrac, Vitré, Vitry*, Victor's land; *Al-
bignac, Aubignat, Aubigny, Aubigné*, Albinus's land; *Cam-
pagnac, Champagnat, Champigny, Champigné*, Campa-
nus's land. From the estate the name passed to the village
or the town. After the shipwreck of the Roman civilization, centuries later, men had forgotten the meaning of the
words, but the words still floated on the surface of forget-
fulness, unshakable evidence of a long-vanished land-survey.
France is, as it were, paved with these territorial assessments
of the Roman fiscal system.

A time came when, as a result of taxation, Gaul poured
into the Roman treasury more than all the rest of the Empire. Rome, on the other hand, had worked her appellations
into the fabric of the Gallic lands, thereby enriching the
heritage of French place-names.

Rome's Gift to Gaul

Rome's real gift was that of an organized society. It may not, like that of the Greeks, have been possessed by a love of the beautiful and a sense of perfection, but at least it had a passion for the useful, which enabled it to construct paved roads, build cities, raise aqueducts.

The Romans were a practical folk, with an eye for security, prosperity, and comfort. The roads that they engineered through the length and breadth of the Empire were primarily designed to serve the purpose of military arteries. Their object was to make it possible for the legions to move rapidly from one point to another, so that internal order might be maintained and peace assured on the frontiers. Consequently, as soon as a country was conquered, roads were the conqueror's first concern. In Gaul, after a century of intensive labor, the network was completed, and it remained only to keep the thoroughfares in a state of repair. For the same reason the roads were designed to take the shortest route and therefore the straightest, climbing hills, skirting plateaus, and not bothering overmuch about gradients. That they might stand up to the wear and tear of wheeled traffic and the damages of bad weather they were laid on concrete foundations. The technique was far from perfect, as may be seen from the fact that the top-layer flags had a tendency to crack. Nevertheless, the Roman roads outlived the centuries and were for a very long time the only known means of communication.

The backbone of the Gallic network was the *Via Aurelia*, which thrust up from Italy, continued from Nice to Fréjus (*Forum Julii*), on to Aix (*Aquæ*), and ended at Arles, from which place its task was taken over by the *Via Domitia* in the general direction of Narbonne and Spain. From Arles another road ran north, via Lyon, to Colonia Agrippina

(Cologne) and the mouths of the Rhine. Lyon (*Lugdunum*) was a great traffic center. Three roads led from it to the Atlantic, one ending at Bordeaux (*Burdigala*), one at Saintes, and one, after following the course of the Loire, in Armorica. Branch roads provided links with the Channel by way of Rouen and Boulogne. The Alps were turned or straddled in three places, one road running along the coast, the other two by the Great and Little St. Bernard Passes.

Fragments of this spider's web still exist. All over France there are innumerable *Chemins de César, Chemins levés, Chemins pavés*, places called Perré, others Pierrelaye. But that is not all. The Roman name for an arterial road was *via strata lapide* (stone-paved road), which in its abbreviated form became *strata*. All the way along the line of these thoroughfares we meet such reminders as villages called Estrées or Estrade. In German-speaking lands *strata* became *Strasse*, whence Strasbourg. There are evidences too of the halting-places, known to the Romans as *mansiones*, which were responsible for the many *Maisons* on the map of France.

The roads had to cross rivers. The Celts had known how to construct only primitive bridges of wood. These the Romans rebuilt of stone. Roads and bridges, designed to serve the political purposes of Rome, were of even greater value to the economic life of Gaul, for they provided links by which people from various parts of the country could communicate and so escape from their former isolation. Gaul was in direct contact with the rest of the Empire, and this fact meant enormously increased activity throughout the country.

The cities ceased to be mere seasonal places of refuge and occasional markets. They assumed administrative importance. In them the public services functioned. They centralized information about supply and demand, and were soon performing a truly urban purpose. In the great provincial capitals a man would have been hard put to it to recognize the miserable Celtic townships of an earlier day. For the most part the Romans established their metropolitan settlements in former Gallic district centers. If they abandoned Marseille for Fréjus the change was dictated by political sentiment only, Marseille having sided with Pompey. If they preferred Clermont and Autun to Gergovia and Bibracte, that was because the latter sites were inconvenient. The Romans liked to build their cities in valleys rather than on hilltops—the sign of an expanding, and no longer contracted, civilization.

The most densely populated cities were in the south. Narbonne, Arles, Nîmes, Vienne, each contained close on 100,000 inhabitants. Lyon reached the 200,000 mark, and, standing at the point of exit from the Alps, on the very threshold of Gaul, succeeded to the role of capital, at the expense of Narbonne. It was a long time before she, in her turn, had to yield her position of pre-eminence first to Trèves, later to Arles. Every city tried hard to copy Rome in the pattern of its magistracies and senates, but above all in its monuments and dwelling-houses.

The Gauls learned the art of building from the Romans, and, hand in hand with their teachers, took pride in planning on a great scale. They showed a fondness for triumphal arches (Orange, Saintes, Reims, Autun), for commemorative trophies (La Turbie), temples (Nîmes, Vienne), and magnificent tombs (Saint-Rémy de Provence). But even more than display they liked convenience—public baths, centers of health treatment, massage, and conversation; aqueducts, which brought water from a great distance (Pont du Gard); basilicas, which served the purpose of law-courts, covered markets, and council halls; theaters and amphitheaters (Arles, Orange, Nîmes); circuses and arenas (Vienne, Fréjus, Lutetia), where, as in the Colosseum at

Rome, the mob was fed on tragedies and comedies, on races and gladiatorial shows.

Private houses were built on the Roman model, with a central atrium on which all the rooms opened. Every effort was made to achieve comfort. Walls and floors were adorned with mosaics, the windows were glazed, there was a system of central heating, and the furnishings included couches for rest or for use at meals. These, of course, were the homes of the rich. The poor, even in the cities, knew no comparable luxury. Their dwellings were of wood, as those of their ancestors had been. Splendor rubbed shoulders with poverty.

In this Romanized Gaul, in which the country estate still figured so largely, the cities exercised a powerful attraction. They interpreted the law, administered justice, determined prices, and provided entertainment. The *civitas*, which in its original sense was the designation of a people, tended to become identified with its urban center, so that the word *cité* was soon applied to it. The very names of the forty different peoples who together made up Gaul came to be confused with those of the forty metropolises. That was how Lutetia, the city of the Parisii, came to be known as Paris.

The Gallo-Roman Fusion

It would be a mistake to regard the Roman conquest as an invasion. Italy was never sufficiently prolific to settle the whole of her Empire. On the contrary, she drew into herself inhabitants from among her distant subjects. The number of Romans in Gaul was never large, except in the south. Elsewhere their cosmopolitan garrisons did not greatly modify the racial elements of the local populations. Intermarriage resulted in a certain amount of crossbreeding, but inevitably the blood of the original settlers remained in the ascendant.

Celtic or pre-Celtic by race, but Romans at heart, the Gauls ardently desired to become Romans in speech as well. They found no great difficulty in achieving this ambition, since the Celtic and Latin tongues, springing from the same Indo-European root, were related. Two centuries after Cæsar, Latin had become the common language of Gaul and was as widely spoken in the depths of Armorica as in Narbonne. The great schools did not much contribute to this process of Latinization, since it was in Greek that they passed on the accumulated treasures of rhetoric and taught men how to become brilliant orators and efficient civil servants. It was through the "lower schools," where children had their education, that the Latin language spread, and also as a result of the constant contact maintained between the country-dwellers and the city administrations. Peasants went into town to discuss their affairs with the tax-collectors, to applaud the games in the circus, to sell their produce in the markets, to gossip at the cattle shows. The Army, too, furthered the use of the Latin language. Troops were drawn from the barbarians of many different countries, and it was therefore necessary to have one official language, that of Rome. Men learned Latin in the camps—a debased, barrack-room jargon. The veteran when he returned to his village talked as the centurion talked, and all the villagers tried to talk like the veteran. Latin was no longer the local tongue of Latium, but the international speech of the Empire.

That was why the Gauls, when they learned to write, wrote naturally in Latin. Celtic had never been anything but a spoken language. It was in Latin, therefore, that the earliest Gallic authors expressed themselves, those poets who sang of Cæsar's victories and hymned the praises of Augustus. It was in Latin that the orators, haunted by the fame of Cicero, pursued their calling, though sometimes it was in Greek that the Gallo-Roman scholars, fired by the example of Longus or of Marcus Aurelius, chose to write. We should do well to remember that the first French novelist was Petronius Arbiter of Marseille; that the first French poet was Ausonius of Bordeaux; that the first French dramatist was the unknown author of *Querolus* (*The Grumbler*). They belong to the tradition of Latin literature.

Was it the existence of this common tongue that helped in the diffusion of the Christian religion, or was it that Christianity served to spread the Latin tongue? Religion and language helped each other. Jesus worked for Rome, and Rome for Jesus.

The Gauls had begun by accepting, in the most casual manner, the Roman gods. Their own triad of deities had yielded to Mercury, Mars, and Jupiter. With their submission to Rome had gone submission to the gods of the whole world, from the Egyptian Isis to the Persian Mithras. This, however, did not prevent them from continuing to revere the objects of their own mythology, or from maintaining their cult of stones and streams, or from living on familiar terms with sprites and goblins.

But now, by the roads leading from the Alps, and from the ports of the south, came Eastern merchants peddling the "good news," the Gospel of Christ. It had taken it a hundred years to reach Gaul. Rome at first had reacted violently against a doctrine that committed the unforgivable sin of not being Roman and of repudiating the worship of the Emperor. In Gaul, as elsewhere, she persecuted the first Christian communities. Holding that the followers of Jesus were dangerous criminals, she threw them to the wild beasts in the arenas, to the delight of the populace. The young slave Blandinus was crucified at Lyon, delivered to the beasts, scourged, racked, set on a red-hot chair, and finally torn to pieces by bulls. Pothinus was stoned. Denis was beheaded on the Hill of Mercury,

which was later to become the Mount of the Martyrs,
Montmartre.

And then the Emperors yielded. First they tolerated,
then rallied to the new religion. Finally they imposed it. As
the Gauls had become Roman, so did Christianity. After
all, did it not prolong the eternity of Rome? After first persecuting the early Christians, who had been recruited from
the proletarian underworld of the big towns, Rome set
about persecuting the pagans—that is, the peasants who
had remained bogged down in their old fables (*päien,
paganus, paysan,* peasant—the word is the same). While
Martin of Tours was busy evangelizing the countryside,
paganism was outlawed and the temple revenues were confiscated. Willingly or as the result of force Gaul became
Christian like the rest of the Roman world.

An Expanding Economy

On what did the Gallo-Romans live? On the products of
their rich soil, on the labors of their skilled workers, on the
profits earned by trade.

The soil needed no coaxing to give an abundant yield. It
was reclaimed by the slaves belonging to the great estates,
which were rapidly getting the upper hand of the small
holdings. The Beauce had already been brought into cultivation and had become one of the granaries of Gaul, with a
great grain market at Orléans (*Genabum*). Hemp and flax
were grown in all districts. The country round Narbonne
bred sheep with a particularly thick growth of wool. Belgium was engaged in the fattening of pigs and geese.
Cheeses were made in the Alps. Vineyards extended northward, even as far as Flanders.

The Gallo-Roman industries were flourishing. The various metallurgical enterprises turned out weapons of war
and plowshares. The ceramic craftsmen were mass-produc-

ing domestic crockery. The looms were making quantities
of cloth, linen, and wearing-apparel. The tanneries were
supplying leather containers for oil and wine. Each trade,
as at Rome, grouped its constituent members in a "college," which had its own charter and its own budget, and
figured with its banner in all professional and religious ceremonies.

The forum, or central square of the city, was the scene of
assemblies, speech-making, and amusement. It was surrounded by administrative buildings and shops. There beat
the heart of local commerce.

A few fairs, at Narbonne, Lyon, and Nîmes, brought together businessmen from the provinces at stated intervals.
Traders journeyed to them from a great distance along the
roads, with their regular milestones, and by the rivers, on
which traffic was organized and controlled by the various
guilds of watermen.

Beyond the frontiers Gallo-Roman trade, moving by road
and adventuring on the sea from the Channel to the Mediterranean, found agents and customers in plenty. Italy exported marble and manufactured goods. Spain sold her oil.
Britain made deliveries of tin. From Gaul itself came salted
and cured foods, edibles of every description, and the output of her workshops. On the whole, she exported more
than she imported. With a trade balance in her favor, she
was becoming richer and richer.

Banking made its appearance and prospered rapidly.
There were loans and mortgages, exchange operations and
speculative transactions, brokerage and commissions, miracles of credit, and all the squalor of usury. The world was
already beginning to know the triumphs and the misery
which were to mark the reign of money.

For money now was the normal instrument of trade and
investment. By taking from the cities the right to mint
coinage and by turning it into an Imperial monopoly,

Rome was not slow in teaching Gaul that money is no laughing matter, but the concern of the State, and of the State alone. The mints of Lyon, Trèves, and Arles were issuing gold, silver, and bronze currency.

But it does not follow that because Gaul from now on was to benefit from a uniform and coherent monetary system, there was no devaluation. In obedience to a seemingly inexorable law, the unit of payment became progressively more and more debased. The bronze *as*, which weighed half an ounce (13.64 grams) when Gaul was first conquered, had fallen to the twelfth of an ounce (2.27 grams) three centuries later, and eventually was no longer minted. Similarly, the silver content of the *denier* was adulterated by frequent admixtures of copper, fell to the level of a silver-coated bronze tally, and ended its career as an item of small change. The *aureus* too, the fine gold coin that Constantine called *solidus* (from which comes the word *sou*), weighed the fortieth part of a pound in the time of Cæsar (8.18 grams), but only the fiftieth part under Caracalla (6.55 grams), and the eighty-fourth part (3.89 grams) under Valentinian.

It should be noticed, however, that this debasement was a slow process. In the course of four centuries gold money lost scarcely more than one half of its metal content, and during the first two centuries of the Empire showed a remarkable stability, which it was never to recover later. The world was not soon to forget that advantage.

If depreciation grew worse in the last period of the Empire, the reason is to be found in the fact that Rome, consuming more than she produced, was exhausting her resources of metallic ore and emptying her treasury to the growing profit of the Orient. Shortage of metal meant that the weight of the coinage had to be reduced. The amount of currency in circulation no longer met the needs of trade, with the result that prices rose. A terrible dearth of the means of payment had the Roman Empire by the throat. It was an evil from which the West was to suffer for many centuries to come, though it disappeared temporarily after the Crusades, and again after the discovery of the Americas. It was not to vanish altogether until paper money filled the gap caused by a deficiency of the precious metals.

This famine was responsible for most of the world's difficulties over a period of two thousand years. At the point in history we have now reached, it was a contributing factor to the decadence and fall of Rome.

The Decadence

The Roman Empire was in a bad way. Politically, economically, financially, it was on the point of capsizing, and drowning the whole of civilization in a common shipwreck.

The truth of the matter was that it had grown too large. It extended from the Atlantic to the Caucasus, from the northern seas to the sandy deserts of Africa. How was it possible to administer such a vast tract of territory and so many different peoples? Rome centralized with the courage of despair, but, do what she might, she could not arrest the movement of disintegration. Centralization meant bureaucracy, and the bureaucrats, formalist and oppressive, always ready to obstruct private enterprise, in Gaul as elsewhere, reigned as uncrowned kings.

Disintegration began with rivalry for the supreme power. The Empire was no more than a *de facto* institution, and despotism served only to mask a deep-seated weakness. There was no law governing the succession to the purple. The throne was the center round which struggle and assassination flourished. Soldiers and party men made and unmade emperors. There were periods during which Rome had two and sometimes four supreme rulers. In one year

there were seven emperors in Gaul, of whom six were murdered. Ultimately the Empire was divided into two parts,
395   the Eastern, with its capital at Byzantium, the Western,
centering at Rome.

Gaul, formerly well administered on a system of four
provinces, ended by being cut up into seventeen, compris-
ing one hundred and twenty cities. Each province had its
governor, and in each of the cities the Emperor established
a personal friend (one might almost say a pal) who was
invested with the title of *comes* (whence *count*). Officials
sprawled over the country. Disintegration was proceeding
rapidly.

In the sphere of economics state control was universal.
State socialism interfered with every activity. The State
was landowner, in so far as the mines and vast agricultural
estates belonged to it; and factory-owner, producing woolen
and linen goods, which it alone might dye with purple. The
State controlled the banks and all foreign trade. It pro-
hibited the export of cereals, wine, and weapons of war. It
was in charge of production, and could order the uprooting
of "redundant" vineyards. Under Diocletian it went so far
as to freeze prices and wages, under pain of death for infringement: sixty deniers for a brace of chickens, forty
deniers for a rabbit, two hundred and fifty deniers for a
lawyer's fee. The black market and the rise in prices made
hay of Imperial decrees.

The admirable system of professional "colleges" became
rigid, too, and degenerated into a closed caste organization.
Membership in these colleges was made obligatory by law.
Each enjoyed the monopoly of its own special trade, all
breaches of which were forbidden. Sons were compelled to
follow their fathers' calling, and since all employment came
under the direction of one or other of the public services,
there was no worker who was not, to some extent, a state
employee.

As the cost of administration increased, the burden of taxation proportionately grew. The taxpayers were bled white to maintain the luxury of a court, which was coming more and more to resemble that of an Oriental potentate, to satisfy the Emperor's "clients" (or hangers-on), and to keep the huge machine of the State turning. The evil was all the greater since it was always the same people who paid. No mercy was shown to landowners, still less to the rich, more especially if they were senators. Bureaucrats were exempt, the friends of those in authority, and all who were necessary to the regime—that is to say, soldiers and proletarians.

It is scarcely an exaggeration to say that the later Empire was the proletariat crowned and anointed. Members of the plebeian order paid no poll tax. The slaves, it is true, remained, but that was because the state economy could not do without them, since there was no other form of manpower. But they had become a particularly valuable form of property, because, now that Rome was making no more conquests, their numbers could not be increased. They were far better treated than formerly. They were allowed to have "colleges" of their own. The flood of freedmen swelled, and these newly enfranchized citizens were judged capable of occupying the highest positions in the State, not excluding the throne.

In this way it came about that Rome eventually suffered from a shortage of human material as well as of precious metals. Under this double lack her economy crumbled. A fall in the birth-rate, combined with the fact that an ever increasing proportion of the populace was growing lazy and was concerned only to enjoy state pensions, aggravated the manpower crisis. There were too many children and too many unemployed. The gap could be filled only by bringing in barbarians, and that meant the end of Rome.

The Roman Legacy

But we should do wrong to underestimate the achievements of Rome. Tragic though her death-throes were, they must not blind us to the incomparable benefits she conferred on the future France. To get some idea of what she accomplished we have only to compare the state of Gaul before and after it became Latinized, the Gaul of the Celts with the Gaul of the Gallo-Romans. Five centuries of co-operation had completely metamorphosed the country. Five centuries—a period rather longer than that which separates the birth of Jeanne d'Arc from the building of the Eiffel Tower.

Five centuries of freedom, it may be argued, would have produced precisely the same results. The story of the Germanies is the answer to such a view. They had succeeded in forcing back the legions of Augustus to the Rhine. But the triumph of their arms spelled the misery of their peoples. When they drove out the Romans, they lost the advantage of sharing in an organized society. They remained uncivilized, illiterate, and scarcely more than a collection of wandering tribes. Nor did they ever make up for the time thus lost. The Rhine, which from south to north united the countries through which it flowed, irremediably divided those to east and west, which it separated.

France, on the other hand, drew in deep draughts of Rome. Through her it learned the lesson of Greece, which is the lesson of beauty. More directly, it received instruction of a less elevated but more useful kind—that of the ordered life. First and foremost, of ordered life within its own frontiers. The Gauls had known nothing of such things as law and justice and a settled monetary system. Rome turned their hovels into houses, their places of refuge into cities, their tracks into roads, their barter into trade, their anarchy into a State. It gave them lessons in everything—not excluding excess. But in the savage centuries to come they never ceased to feel a homesickness for the organization that had once been theirs, nor ever knew real peace of mind until they had found Rome again.

The Romans, it cannot be denied, were themselves no better than former barbarians who had made the journey to civilization earlier than other peoples. But that can be said of all societies, since their origins, without exception, have been the same. Under the skin of the most sophisticated Roman the savage still lurked, as can be seen when we are brought face to face with their frequent acts of unexpected brutality. This explains how it came about that, though Rome freed Gaul from the appalling tradition of human sacrifice, she herself still slaughtered captured enemies, and had a passion for the bloodstained games of the circus. We must accept Rome as she was, her vices as well as her virtues.

Order beyond the frontiers was the other side of the same medal. The troubles and agonies of the dying Empire should not make us forget that Gaul knew three full centuries of peace and serenity. The Pax Romana is no myth. Sheltered behind the frontier of the Rhine, with its double line of fortified ramparts, its ditches and its palisades, its camps and watchtowers, Gaul for three long centuries could snap its fingers at invasion. It is difficult to imagine the marvel of that achievement. Three hundred years of peace. Three hundred years during which Gaul never ceased to prosper and to grow. Not for a long time did Roman Gaul feel that evil of a falling birth-rate under which Italy suffered. There is good reason to believe that her population rose from ten to something like fifteen million.

But now the good years were over. All along the Empire's crumbling dikes the waters were mounting. Once more the land of France was to become the prize of nomad races. It is time to say good-by to the centuries of peace. Never again was France to know immunity for so long a period of time.

CHAPTER II

THE DARK NIGHT OF BARBARISM

(the fourth to the tenth century)

*The Germans
at the Gates*

THE ROMANS had taken only seven years to conquer Gaul. The Germanic invasions were spread over three centuries, and the barbarian inroads into France, taken as a whole, occupied more than six hundred years. This new attack was far from being an example of blitz warfare, the issue of which can be determined by the outcome of a few battles. To say this is not to say that the Huns and the Norsemen did not stage a number of spectacular assaults, but only that the onward thrust of the invaders more closely resembled the slow movement of whole peoples.

The Germans did not wait until the last Emperor of the West had fallen, to trespass on Roman territory. Throughout the last two centuries of Roman history they had been violating the frontiers, and were already beginning to settle in Gaul. Who were these Germans? The ethnologist would answer that question by saying that they were dolichocephalic Aryans; in other words, that they were a long-headed, fair-haired race, belonging to the same Indo-European branch as the Celts and the Latins. The historian would add that they were born fighters. Tacitus, who was intent on singing their praises, with the object of humiliating his Roman compatriots, made no bones about defining the nature of their vocation:

Tranquillity they find intolerable. It would be more difficult to persuade them to plow the fields and wait for the coming of the harvest than to set out in quest of enemies and wounds. One might go farther and say that they think it a sign of meanness of spirit and of cowardice to win by the sweat of their brows what they may just as well obtain by the spilling of blood.

These were the neighbors beside whom the Gauls were fated to live. Life and death meant nothing to them. To kill was an act of war and nothing else. A murderer might be pardoned if he merely indemnified the family of his victim. Nor was the price of ransom excessive. It was foolish to waste pity on the dead warrior, for he had been received by Wotan into Valhalla, which was the place of all places reserved for heroes.

The Germanic peoples fought one another with passion. Pretexts were never lacking among so many neighboring and rival tribes, all seeking to find somewhere to settle between the Rhine and the Vistula. Jostling shoulder to shoulder were Franks and Alamanni, Saxons and Vandals, Lombards and Burgundians. There were the Suevi, to be known at a later date as Swabians; there were the Goths of the West, or Visigoths, and those of the East, or Ostrogoths; there were the Saxons and the Angles; there were the Scandinavians. Some of these peoples—the Burgundians and the Vandals, for instance—could lay claim to a Slavic rather than a Germanic origin. The Alans, certainly, were Slavs, as well as the Sarmatians. Many of these barbarians, who seemed good for nothing but hunting, pillage, and war, were the fathers of future nations.

For the moment, the Roman world was attracting them as the lamp attracts moths. All they wanted was to singe **256** their wings. One band carried out a successful raid into Gaul, through which it swept, leaving panic in its wake. The Gallic cities hastily entrenched themselves. But the Germanic pressure showed no sign of diminishing.

These early exploits were followed by a period of peaceful penetration. The barbarians showed themselves to the Romans no longer in the light of invaders, but of auxiliaries: "You need soldiers? You need manpower? Well, here we are." Rome was not sure whether to rejoice or to panic at the prospect of aid thus offered. But in the long run she accepted, and settled large numbers of the Germans in Gaul. The Roman army willingly enrolled these mercenaries who loved fighting and did not meddle in politics. Nor had it any reason to repent this decision, for the barbarian troops, officers and common soldiers alike, served Rome faithfully.

The agricultural laborers recruited from beyond the Rhine, and likewise settled as colonists, came precisely at the moment when they were most needed to work the great estates. These immigrants served both as soldiers and as plowmen. They cultivated the soil, and kept a watch on the roads in the interest of Rome. The map of France is covered with evidences of this peaceful infiltration. The Frankish settlements have left behind them many a Francourville and Francorchamps; the Alans, Allones and Allainville; the Goths, Gourville and Gueux; the Sarmatians, Sermaizes; the Alamanni, Aumenancourt; the Vandals, Gandalou; the Marcomanni, Marmagne; the Saxons, Sissonne and all the villages in the countrysides of Boulogne and Bayeaux with names ending in *tun* (English *ton* or *town*).

These, however, were only scattered colonies, which the Gallo-Romans managed to assimilate without much difficulty. But round the mouths of the Rhine and the Escaut the Franks drifted across the frontier in very large numbers and settled. These were the Franks from the salt-lands, the Salic Franks, and before long they swamped the Gallo-Roman inhabitants. The Latin language had to give ground, and it was in this way that the future dividing line between Flemings and Walloons took shape.

The Huns

This slow trekking of diverse barbarians had not yet seriously begun to threaten the security of the Empire, and
Rome might perhaps have continued for a while her policy
of carefully controlled immigration, had not a human cata-
clysm burst upon the world.

It is impossible to understand what happened without
taking into consideration a sudden drama that had long
been taking form at the other side of the Continent, in that
Chinese Empire which was, as it were, Rome's twin. Both
these vast and settled civilizations, unable to defend themselves behind their Great Walls, were tempting prey for the
barbarians. In northern China, already in process of decom-   318
position, the Huns had gained a footing, and there they remained until the Mongols, coming from the land of the
Manchus, forced them to withdraw. The Huns, thus driven
out of China and pressed back into the Asiatic steppes,
were now on the lookout for some new plundering-ground   350
and began to roll westward. It was their irruption that,
thrusting the Germans from their path, forced them up
against the frontier of Gaul.

These Huns were authentic nomads of the true Mongol
blood, ancestors of the later Hungarians, of the war bands
of Genghis, and of the Turks. They knew no homes but the
backs of their horses, and these they never left, even to
sleep. From the saddle they discharged arrows tipped with
bone. They pillaged every place through which they passed,
and even the Germans, intrepid warriors though they were,
trembled at their approach. The German peoples, disunited
and terrorized, took to flight—as usual—toward the West.
There they hoped to find the security and the food they
now sought in vain in the devastated prairies where they
had been living. Fear and famine drove them on. Rome,

though aging and enfeebled, remained their only hope.
Surely she would take them under her wing?

Thus it was that, while the Huns drove forward as conquerors, the Germans entered the Empire in the guise of
suppliant refugees. For the Huns, Rome was a prey; for the
Germans, a place of safety. But if the prey was still magnificent, the place of safety was precarious. Rome had little
left but the shadow of her former might. Though her prestige remained, her greatness had departed.

What proves that the Germans came as friends and not
as enemies is that they offered to stand shoulder to shoulder
with the Empire against the Huns. As guests of Rome they
consented to place themselves under the orders of a Roman
official, Aëtius, who at that time governed Gaul in the name
of an emperor without authority. Aëtius gathered together
an army of Franks, Visigoths, and Alans, of Burgundians
from Savoy, of Saxons from Normandy. There were only
barbarians now on whom to call for the defense of Roman
Gaul.

Opposed to Aëtius stood Attila, the self-styled "Scourge
of God." In order to become the undisputed leader of the
447 Huns he had had his brother assassinated. Byzantium had
been blackmailed into paying him tribute. From the Danube he led his forces to the Rhine, and thence to the Seine.
On the way he had swelled his numbers by including in
their ranks all the wandering Germanic bands which, having failed to flee in time, had rallied to him. Gaul lay wide
open, incapable of resistance. What he did not pillage he
burned. He destroyed Metz and besieged Orléans. It was
near the latter place that Aëtius appeared suddenly, barring
his path.

Rarely can there have been a stranger meeting of opposing armies: one leader ostensibly the representative of
451 Rome, the other attacking her, but both with only bar-

barians under their command. With Aëtius were the Visigoths, with Attila the Ostrogoths. There were Franks and
Burgundians on either side. Attila, taken by surprise, retreated toward Troyes, where the ghost of Rome won a
final victory. But the Huns had no intention of making a
stand to the last man. They had already collected a handsome booty, and there were plenty of places in the wide   **453**
world for their exploits. They recrossed the Rhine, made a
descent on Italy, and pursued their nomad career until they
finally disintegrated. Gaul had had a narrow escape.

Nothing remained of Attila's raiding expedition but the
memory of an appalling fear and the spectacle of smoking
ruins. Nothing, that is, except the presence of the Ger-   **476**
mans. While the last of the emperors was dying obscurely
at Rome, the Germans, both those who had entered the
country ahead of Attila and those who had followed in his
train, succeeded in settling within the Gallic frontiers. Not
all of them, however, remained. The Vandals continued
their exodus in the direction of Spain and Africa; the Ostrogoths pushed down toward northern Italy; the Angles and
the Saxons carried out landings on the coast of Britain. But
the Visigoths found a new home between the Pyrenees and
the Loire, the Burgundians between the Loire and the
Rhine, the Franks between the Rhine and the Somme.
They had taken a liking to their place of refuge, and there
was nobody now to dispute their presence.

The Franks in the Ascendant

Between the Germanic immigrants and Rome there had
never been any question save of alliance and collaboration.
The possibility of rupture had never so much as been
hinted. What rupture could there be, now that Rome was
dead? The Frankish, Burgundian, and Visigoth leaders,

decked out with the titles of Imperial officers, enjoyed among themselves the idea that they were perpetuating the Empire.

All that happened was that the anarchy of barbarism triumphant succeeded to the anarchy of Rome at her last gasp. It is not hard to imagine into what a state of utter prostration the wretched land of Gaul had fallen. She had become, at one and the same time, the battleground of warring tribes and the prey of their rapacious greed. Her cities were destroyed, her countryside was abandoned. As soon as the German occupants had exhausted the resources of any one region, they moved on to another. The soil no longer produced enough food to keep the population alive. Famine and destitution were everywhere. The immigrants, who were ignorant of even the most elementary rules of hygiene, brought with them the most terrible diseases. It was at this period that leprosy, the Frankish contribution, began its ravages.

To what authority could men rally in such a general state of disruption? Franks, Burgundians, and Visigoths were at one another's throat. Their kings were no more than war chiefs, without any wide prestige or power, and incapable even of imagining what an organized state was like. They were elected rulers whom their followers raised upon a shield in acknowledgment of their choice. But a shield is not a throne, and tribal traditions could not replace the discipline of an empire.

There was one way only of preserving order, and that was to pretend that they were carrying on the Roman system. This the Franks were shrewd enough to realize. They had chosen as their chief a certain Chlodwig (the word means "battle of glory"), who was later to be known to history as Clovis, a name that, softened in the course of centuries, became the favorite appellation of the kings of France: Louis. The grandfather of this Clovis, Mérovée, had served under

482

Aëtius against the Huns. Clovis himself was a clever, obstinate man. He entered on the stage of history as the defender of the Roman idea—and Rome was no longer in a position to call his bluff. In her name he settled the Franks between the Somme and the Loire, in a district where, at the moment, a "usurper" was claiming supreme power; and it was with the title of a Roman general that he repulsed an attempted invasion by the Alamanni. He had himself named consul at Tours, thereby aiming to prolong the fiction. He took up his quarters in Paris in what remained of the palace of the Emperor Julian. His descendants, the Merovians (or, as the German historians have styled them, the Merovingians), assumed the title of Augustus. This parody had its uses, in that it firmly established the supremacy of the Franks.

It was the memory of Rome, too, that, after the Frankish triumph, gave unquestioned power to the Catholic Church. The Germans in Gaul had quickly forgotten their barbarous gods, and adopted the God of the Christians, and of all civilized peoples. But around that God a struggle had already developed between the Arians, or disciples of Arius, who held that the Son had not existed from all eternity, and the Romans, who believed that the Son and the Father were equal. The Visigoths and the Burgundians threw in their lot with the Arian heresy. Clovis, who was still a pagan, but who knew how useful the Gallo-Roman people and clergy could be to him, declared for the God of the Catholics—in other words, for the Pope of Rome. This was another victory for the ghost of the old Empire. Clovis was baptized at Reims. Thereafter he was to fight for Rome, and the bishops of Rome were to fight for him. Both Burgundians and Visigoths were crushed, and the Franks remained supreme through almost the entire length and breadth of Gaul, which was soon to become *France*.

At this turning-point of language and of history, at this

486

496

496

500

507

moment when a name and a nation were being born, it is well to ask whence, precisely, came this appellation which was to collect about itself so much glory in the future. The Franks had brought it with them from their earliest settlements on the coast of the North Sea, though it is by no means certain whether it meant the "brave" (*freh*) or the "free" (*frei*). There is no disputing the fact, however, that those who would be free must first be brave.

Even before the Franks had spread over the northern half of Gaul, they seem to have thrown something like an advance guard into the small agricultural tract of country lying to the north of Paris. This tiny district, from which the city drew its supplies of grain, was even then called France, and it has proudly clung to the name ever since. In the nineteenth century people were still speaking of Saint-Denis-en-France, and in the twentieth there are several humble communes that carry the same suffix: Roissy-en-France, Bonneuil-en-France. It was here that the word was born, as the Franks were quick to realize, since it was at Saint-Denis that the Merovingian King Dagobert, one of the descendants of Clovis, founded the abbey in which all the future kings of France were buried; since, too, it was in Paris, standing on the very edge of the plain of France, that the Franks established their capital.

In a more general sense France became the land of the Franks, as England was the land of the Angles, and Lombardy of the Lombards. It meant, at first, all the territory north of the Loire, as distinct from the lands on which the Burgundians and the Goths were settled. The name of Romans fell into disuse. The Gallo-Romans became intermingled with the Franks, and as Franks they considered themselves. Later still, by a natural process, the name of France was applied to the whole of what once had been Gaul.

The Frankish victory, which gave birth to France, also

assured the pre-eminence of Paris. Had the Visigoths carried the day, either Toulouse or Narbonne would in all like-
lihood have been the capital. Had fortune favored the Burgundians, that role would doubtless have fallen to Lyon.
The Franks had to choose one of their own towns. Tournai
and Soissons had both been Frankish centers, but they were
too far to the north. Orléans, on the other hand, was too
close to the Visigoths. Lutetia of the Parisii, though small,
had been the residence of a Roman emperor and seemed
designed by history to be a capital. Furthermore, it fulfilled
every geographical requirement. The Seine and its tributaries made access easy. The Île de la Cité offered good protection against future assailants. No doubt about it, the
choice must fall on Paris.

Fusion . . .

The early history of France is marked by two contradictory
phenomena. On the one hand we find an astonishingly
complex mixture of blood, customs, and ideas, all the
marks, in fact, of a new country in its adolescence; on the
other, an ever present threat of disintegration.

Between Gallo-Romans and Franks, between the Roman
and Germanic legacies, fusion was rapid and easy. There
was good will in plenty. The Gallo-Romans were only too
eager to rally to the occupying power; the Germans asked
nothing better than to profit by the lessons that Rome had
to teach them. The apportioning of landed property presented few problems. The Germans, who had been brought
up in a system of collective ownership, took easily, first to
family property, and then to individual property. The Visigoths and Burgundians, it is true, laid down the general
rule that two thirds of all cultivated land and one third of
all slaves must be handed over to them by the masters of
great estates. In effect, they did not press their claims to ex-

cess. The Franks, on the other hand, merely insisted on all titles in the former Imperial domains being made over, and dismissed none of the private owners.

The Germans respected Roman law to the extent of applying their own customs to themselves and to nobody else. Each people kept its own laws. The Gallo-Roman was judged in accordance with Roman legal practice, the barbarian by the usages of his fellow countrymen. The system was far from practical, but it did engender an atmosphere of tolerance. Barbarian law was customary, not written. In essentials it was little more than a penal tariff. Thus, the Salic law, which was the law of the Salic Franks, demanded that the murder of a deacon should be punished by a fine of four hundred golden sous, that of a freedman by one of eighty, that of a swineherd by one of thirty. The loss of a thumb was held to be worth forty-five sous, of a little finger fifteen. An insult cost six sous. If the blood-price of a Salian was reckoned at two hundred sous and that of a Roman at only a hundred, the reason was that by Frankish custom the kin on both sides, male and female, were indemnified, whereas under Roman law only the male heirs were entitled to compensation. The difference in value implied no political inequality.

The Salic tradition barred women from the inheritance of landed property. At a later period the Kingdom of France was held to form part of the Salic territories. Consequently, it was argued, the crown could descend only in the male line.

Another Salic custom that was retained for many centuries was known as the "judgment of God." Accuser and accused were allowed to fight in single combat, the assumption being that God would assist the innocent. There were other versions of the same test. In one of them the accused was bound hand and foot and flung into a vat filled with holy water. If he floated to the surface, he was held to be blameless. In another he had to grasp a red-hot bar of iron; if after three days no sign of the burn was visible, he was acquitted.

Frankish custom prevailed too in the naming of persons. Not only did the Germans keep their own names, which were designed to perpetuate their courage or their strength, but the Gallo-Romans imitated them, without always understanding what the words meant. A man was no longer called Marcus Cornelius Scipio, but Dagobert (Bright as the Day), Chilperic (Sure Aid), Godfrid (Peace of God). A great many first and family names prevalent in France at later periods derived from these Germanic composites: Bertrand (Bert-hramm, Shining Crow); Baudouin (Baldwin, Doughty Companion); and all names terminating in *baud* (from *bald*, doughty), *bert* (from *bert*, shining or brilliant), and *ard* (from *hard*, strong).

But though the names of persons, which were all baptismal, followed the Germanic system, the language itself remained essentially Latin, and the barbarians, who numbered only a twentieth part of the population, adopted the common speech of Gaul. At most they added to it their own warlike vocabulary (*garde, guet, maréchal, sénéchal, heaume, bourg*). Their contributions to the French language did not amount to more than four hundred words, of which only one hundred were verbs (for example, *blesser, saisir*), and twenty adjectives (for example, *blanc, bleu, gris, brun, riche*). They gave to it also the aspirated *h* (*hache, haie, harangue*), and the transformation of the Latin *v* into the guttural *g* when used at the beginning of certain words, such as *gué* and *gâter*. Finally, the Frankish habit of counting in units of twelve persisted, and appears in the French tendency to employ a duodecimal system. The sou was worth twelve deniers (as the shilling still is), Charlemagne had twelve peers, eggs were sold by the dozen. This was a modest legacy compared with that of the language of Rome, which, modified by time and use, was to become the *Romansh* dialect.

The changes in language differed in different regions. The linguistic evolution in Picardy was not the same as in Aquitaine, Anjou, and Provence. The new France was neither homogeneous nor unified. A system of universal military service or the wide currency given to a popular book, such as the Koran, can serve as a mold in which a language takes a certain shape. France lacked both. When the people of the northern provinces wanted to say yes, they made use of the words *hoc illud* ("just that"). This became contracted into *oïl*, and later into *oui*. The southerners, on the other hand, merely said *hoc*, and, being more completely Romanized than their compatriots in other parts of the country, continued to say *oc*. As a result, the northern dialects were considered generally to form the *langue d'oïl*, from which French emerged; those of the south, the *langue d'oc*.

Between these two speech variants the Loire long served as the dividing line, just as it had marked the frontier separating the Frankish domination from the districts in which other influences were in the ascendant. But as Frankish penetration drove deeper, and the political leadership of the north became more clearly marked, the *langue d'oïl* spread up the tributaries of the Loire in the direction of the Massif Central, until, finally, the separation between *oïl* and *oc* came to be established approximately along the line from the Gironde to the Lake of Geneva. In the *oïl* districts the Gallo-Roman place-names ending in *acum* assumed a terminal *y* (*Victoriacum*, Vitry). In those of the *oc* a final *ac* became general (Vitrac). The men of the *oïl* said *cheval* and *chanter*; their neighbors of the *oc*, *cabal* and *cantar*. The north had received the largest influx of barbarians and had shown a greater willingness to settle down with them. It was therefore but natural that it should be farther removed than the south from older Roman models.

The barrier between speech-forms was also the watershed between contrasting roofing materials. French houses may, in this respect, be classed in two separate groups: in the north, flat tiles or slates; in the south, rounded or convex tiles of the Roman type. The same general line also divided the customary law of the barbarians from the written law that was part of the Roman heritage. All these variants were beginning to appear at the time of Germano-Gallic fusion.

. . . and Chaos

The astonishing thing is that differences within the racial amalgamation should have been so little marked at a time when everything else was so chaotic.

One other linguistic frontier did, in fact, develop in the far west, where the Roman tongue was overwhelmed together with the Gallo-Roman population. The Breton influx completely revolutionized Armorica. Whence did these particular invaders come? From near-by Britain, in which the Anglo-Saxons, themselves driven from the banks of the Elbe, had landed. The island Celts had tried unsuccessfully to resist. King Arthur and his Knights of the Round Table long remained the heroes of a legendary epic. Forced from their home, the islanders set forth to colonize a lesser Britain on the mainland, between the estuaries of the Rance and the Loire.

442

When the Britons arrived on the scene, this province was no less Romanized than the rest of Gaul. It very quickly became Breton, and Breton it remained. Whether the newcomers massacred the population, drove it out, or enslaved it cannot now be said for certain. It would appear from the evidence available that the Bretons remained unchallenged in their new home. Except in the sphere of religion (they had already been Christianized) they changed everything. Neither language nor customs remained the same. At a time when the Germans were busy Romanizing themselves the Celts of Armorica became fanatical isolationists. They brought with them into the peninsula even their native place-names. Armorica became Brittany, and a migrating Cornwall took root as Cornouaille. King Arthur was buried in the land of the Bretons. The handsome Tristan, who had loved the fair Iseult, was born there, and there he died. Breton villages have names that give them a strongly marked character—rough, primitive names embodying vocables that come sometimes from the Latin (*ple*, Latin *plebs*; *loc*, Latin *locus*), often from the Celtic (*tre*, parish; *lann*, church; *ker*, hamlet). Brittany formed a world apart. Only after the passage of centuries did it become part of the French system, and an even longer time had to elapse before the local language lost its position of supremacy.

The Franks were not greatly perturbed by this dissidence. Their thoughts were too much taken up with other troubles. The fragile structure of the national unity, founded by Clovis and restored by Dagobert, had soon collapsed. Only for one year had the Burgundians agreed to pay tribute to the Franks, and the Visigoths would admit the presence in their territories of no more than a few Frankish garrisons. Both peoples seized on the first opportunity to declare their independence.

The barbarian kings were innocent of even the most rudimentary notion of the State. They held their domains as personal property, to be divided among their sons at death. When there were four such sons, then the paternal heritage was cut into four pieces, Paris going to Childebert, Soissons to Clotaire, Orléans to Clodomir, Metz to Thierry. On one occasion four kingdoms were cut from a single inheritance: Neustria in the northwest, Austrasia in the east, Aquitaine and Burgundy in the south. Assassination was the rule in

511

561

the royal house. Chilperic had his wife strangled; Frédé-
gonde stabbed her husband; Clotaire delivered both wife
and son to the flames. It would almost seem as though these
barbarians were intent on copying the habits of the later
Empire, even in its worst excesses. Both the Frankish Kingdom and the Roman Empire suffered from the same inherent weakness: the absence of any settled rule by which
supreme power could, without question, be passed on at the
death of its holder.

The nation was sorely tested as the result of these territorial dismemberments, these royal murders, and the incessant fighting that followed from them. Although the
Germans had entered Gaul to the number of five or six hundred thousand, the population steadily decreased from the
effects of war, famine, and pestilence. Men and women fled
to the depths of the forests, where they reverted to a primitive form of existence. The barbarians had resuscitated the
barbaric age.

The Arabs

But chaos as yet was only in its early stages. Invasion followed invasion. The Huns had melted into thin air. The
Germans and the Bretons had taken root. It was now the
turn of the Arabs to threaten new dangers. Theirs was no
ordinary menace. They did not come seeking a colonial
empire (like the Romans) or a refuge (like the Germans).
They were animated by an ideal: they fought for a faith.
They regarded themselves as the messengers of God, who
is Allah; they believed they were entrusted with the duty
of converting all men to the true faith, according to the
Koran.

But men may have faith and yet be barbarians. Such was
the case of the Semitic Bedouins, those pirates of the desert
whom Mohammed had uprooted from their sandy home
and turned into fanatical conquerors. They seized Mecca,   **630**

and were prepared to make war on the whole world—a holy war—with the object of spreading the faith of Islam or of massacring the unbelievers. Their theological dogma was simple, and within the power of even the least educated to grasp. There is one God, the Creator of all things. Paradise is assured to the faithful who pray five times a day, observe the fast of Ramadan, give to the poor, and, so far as is possible, make the pilgrimage to Mecca.

If the Arabs had had no weapons but their exemplary fervor, no immediate danger would have threatened. But in Persia they had found a race of marvelous small horses, and they had learned from the Chinese the use of stirrups. High-mettled riders, and dexterous with the bow, they soon overran Asia and Africa, from the Indian Ocean to the Atlantic. They crossed into Spain, where the kingdom of the Visigoths crumbled before them. It took eight centuries to drive them from it.

711

France seemed to be in no condition to arrest the progress of their armies, which had now been swollen by huge contingents of Berbers already converted to Islam. Popular terror confounded Arabs and Africans alike under one single name: Saracens. After their passage into Spain they became Moors. The torrent had grown into a flood. How was it possible to resist it? The Merovingian dynasty was quite incapable of doing so. For a long time now the kings had enjoyed little more than the trappings of power, and their monarchy would have been the merest anarchy had not the controller of their household, who bore the title of Mayor of the Palace, taken it upon himself to administer their realm as well as their estates. To one of these mayors of the palace it fell to front the advancing Arabs. He was called Charles—that is, the Valiant—and nicknamed Martel, because he hammered home his blows. Christened as a German, and bearing a Latin sobriquet, he was a living example of the fusion from which France sprang.

The Pyrenees had proved to be no barrier. From Narbonne, which they occupied, and Nîmes, from which they   719
extorted ransom, the Arabs moved up the Rhone Valley.
They were seen at Lyon; they destroyed Autun. Fortune   725
still favoring them, they struck again on the Garonne. They
took Bordeaux. Their advance guards reached the Loire.
The main body of their forces marched on Tours.

The Franks arrived in the nick of time. Somewhere near
Loudun the Arab horsemen flung themselves against   732
Charles's heavy infantry. The Moslem charge failed to break
the Christian ranks. During the night following the battle the
invaders, like Attila before them, turned about. France was
saved. Europe was not to fall a prey to Islam.

Not that the Moorish menace did not still remain to
be dealt with. Driven from Aquitaine, the Arabs clung to
Provence, where they pillaged Avignon. Charles Martel had
to fight for the recovery of Nîmes, and suffered a setback
before Narbonne. Even at a much later date his grandson,
Charlemagne, was still having to wage war against the
Saracen bands, and it was in the course of his homeward
march from one such expedition in the Pyrenees that his
lieutenant Roland posed for the portrait of a legendary   778
hero.

By what miracle were the Arabs, who had been uncon-
quered since the days of Mohammed and were still strong
enough a few years later to sack Rome, driven from the
Frankish lands? Was Charles Martel's heavy infantry really
too strong for them? Had a long series of conquests weakened their enthusiasm? The true explanation is simpler.
The barbarians of the desert were at home only in their
own sandy wastes or under the hot sun of Spain; not in the
marshes of Poitou, at the oncoming of autumn. France was
no place for them.

Was their defeat, on a total reckoning, her loss? That
seems to be the view of some historians, who maintain that

in this contest between Franks and Arabs it was the latter who were the true champions of civilization. This is a mistaken view. The quarrel was merely between one set of barbarians and another. For the barbarians of France some hope of a settled society still remained. In Charles Martel they had found a savior and the possible founder of a new dynasty. With Rome still a memory, it was possible for them to build a nation.

But for the barbarians of the desert things were very different. Their case was hopeless. The brilliance of Seville and of Granada was but a flash in the pan. There, indeed, the Moslems had produced an effect of civilization, but it was no more than an illusion bred of contrast. Their outstanding talent was for destruction. From Syria to Africa they had carried pillage and ruin. Libraries burned, forests felled (which would never grow again), amphitheaters demolished stone by stone to construct hovels for themselves—such were the marks of Arab "culture." It might borrow the art of vaulting from Byzantium, arches from Persia, sugar from China, and numerals from India, but its true gift was for making the dry land sterile and pursuing the trade of piracy on the high seas. In France the Arabs left behind them nothing but ruins.

The Norsemen

France knew no respite between her battles against the Arabs and the incursions of the Norsemen. All through these troubled centuries she was forever having to do battle with Lombards, Slavs, and Saxons, or to hurl back fresh nomad bands invading from the east—Avars, related to the Huns, hot from their pillaging of central Europe, or Hungarians, a variant of the same tribe, who appeared on their swift horses under the walls of Metz, of Nîmes, of Bourges. The first of these newcomers presented but a distant threat;

the menace of the second was only temporary. The Norse peril was torrential and immediate.

They came, these men of the north, from the Scandinavian lands, crossing the sea in undecked ships with red sails, and prows carved into the image of grinning dragons. They were intrepid sailors who ventured deep into the many estuaries of the coast and then, in lighter boats, rowed up the rivers as far as they could go. Alternatively, they would round up such horses as they came upon, transform themselves into cavalrymen, and penetrate deep into the countryside. They raided cities and abbeys, pillaging and burning as they went. When they had collected booty enough, they returned to their ships, content with what the "season" had yielded. These fair-haired barbarians were of the Germanic family. They, too, worshipped Wotan and believed in Valhalla. From the Germans they had learned the art of writing. They could fashion jewelry. But their real genius was for fighting and for facing the ocean storms.

The Norwegians conquered the countries of the far north —Scotland, Ireland, Iceland, Greenland. The Swedes drove deep into the Slav territories, and settled in the country that a later age would know as Russia. The Danes, who were the most venturesome of them all, cast greedy eyes on western Europe. From the Elbe to the Tagus and as far as the coasts of Italy they roamed, leaving terror and desolation behind them. 799

Each *drakkar* (for such was the name they gave to their ships) was capable of carrying fifty men. One hundred, two hundred, would appear at a time. Sometimes as few as five ships would suffice for the launching of a devastating expedition. These Danes were as shrewd as they were fierce, and timed their descents as a rule to coincide with feast-days—Good Friday, Easter, Whitsun—knowing that thus they were more likely to find the Christians off their guard. There was no plan or pattern in their burnings and massacres. They sought only to sow terror, and would willingly renounce a warlike enterprise in exchange for a good ransom. They could be bought off for five or six thousand pounds of silver. If they were in a greedy mood they might ask as much as twelve; if they were in a hurry they might put up with less than their normal price. They were already clever businessmen, these Danes, seeking glory on the battlefield only if there was money in it.

Their usual custom was to set up headquarters on some island. Thence they would launch their raids, and thither they would return. It served them as a base harbor and as an entrenched camp. In case of necessity they would winter there. To it they brought their booty and their prisoners, holding the latter until a solid indemnity should be paid. In the North Sea it was the Frisian islands that they used in this way; in the Atlantic, Noirmoutier; in the Seine, the island of Jeufosse, close to the confluence of the Epte; in the Loire, the island of Biesse, opposite Nantes. These were the "bridgeheads" of the Norsemen, from which they preyed upon the West.

France could do little against them. She had not even the ghost of a fleet with which to oppose them on the sea or in the rivers. On land the flower of the Frankish troops were powerless against so elusive an enemy. They had been able to cope with the Arab invasion, for that had been a struggle between opposing armies; but they could never get to grips with this amphibious foe, these men who were sailors and centaurs at will, who appeared unheralded, and vanished in a twinkling, to reappear at some other spot a hundred miles away. The "Viking" strategy was disconcerting to the Franks.

Since they could neither keep these enemies at bay nor wipe them out entirely, they grew resigned, for the most part, to buying them off. A city here would purchase a respite, an abbey there would induce the assailants to withdraw—at a price. In fact nothing could have been better calculated to ensure their return. The unloading of these undesirables became a reciprocal activity between the different kingdoms of the West. The English bargained with them to turn their attention to the mainland. The Germans speeded them on their way to France. Paris smoothed their road to Burgundy. It even happened occasionally that a ruling prince would enlist one band of Norsemen under his banner, and at his charge, in order to repulse the inroads of another, though this arrangement sometimes led to awkward acts of treachery.

An attempt was made to block the rivers by erecting a series of fortified bridges—the Seine at Pont de l'Arche, the   865
Loire at Ponts de Cé—but the results were disappointing. Either because the works were never satisfactorily completed or because their defenders were careless, the Norsemen found little difficulty in overcoming them.

Their inroads went on far and wide for more than a century and a half. By way of the Rhine and the Meuse they reached Trèves; by that of the Escaut, the Yser, and the Canche they carried destruction to Amiens, Saint-Omer, and Reims. They sailed up the Seine and took Paris and Rouen, Saint-Denis, Chartres, and Melun. For eighteen years they were the masters of Brittany. From a more or less permanent settlement on the lower Loire they attacked Nantes, Angers, Tours, Blois, Orléans, and sent out flying columns in the general direction of Le Mans and Poitiers. They appeared on the Charente and the Garonne, at Bordeaux and at Toulouse. Aquitaine remained their prey for half a century. They infiltrated as far as Limoges and Clermont. They set up permanent quarters in the Camargue, whence they reached Nîmes and Valence. Only the upper valley of the Rhone escaped their attention. But since the Arabs and the Hungarians had already ravaged it, it did not get off scot-free.

In the long run, however, the Danes lost something of their dash. The Franks learned better how to stand against them. The cities rebuilt their ruined walls. Paris, after having succumbed five times, twice put up a successful resistance. In front of Metz and Laon, of Saint-Omer and Le Mans, of Auxerre and Chartres, all of them encircled by ramparts, the Norsemen were checked. Wearied at length and sated, they were in a mood to accept conversion to sedentary life and the Christian faith. Why should they not settle down somewhere beyond the islands that had served them as their earliest rallying-points? Treaties could be signed with men who had been baptized. One of their bands had already been allotted Friesland. Brittany was given to another. It was a gift the Franks could make without much sense of loss, since they had never been truly its masters. The Bretons, however, drove out the intruders. The band of which Rollo was the leader had better luck. Rollo himself was baptized at Rouen and swore fidelity to the King of France, in return for which concession he was granted a domain. This was at first confined to the country lying around the estuary of the Seine, though later it was rounded out by the addition of Cotentin and Bessin. This new-made province grew into Normandy.

Elsewhere the Danes strove for another fifty years to continue their earlier exploits. From Jeufosse they set out on expeditions. But their prime was past. They were persuaded, in return for a gift of ships and food, to shift the scene of their activities, and took their way to Spain some time before their compatriots from Normandy started off to conquer Calabria and Sicily.

Normandy itself remained a permanent entity. The fair-haired newcomers were quickly assimilated with the existing inhabitants. In the course of a few generations they forgot their Nordic tongue and learned to speak the Romansh dialect. The Norman dukes hastened to become Frenchi-

886

921

911

962

966

fied. Nevertheless, this last of the great migrations left in-
delible marks upon the country. From Denmark the Norsemen had brought many new varieties of animal—horses,
and sheep, and milch cows, the parents of a later Norman
breed. They enriched the French language with their ma-
rine vocabulary (the *mât*, or mast; the *quille*, or keel; the
foc, or jib; the *lest*, or ballast). They left traces of the place-
names of their province, so rich in terminations such as
bec (stream), *mar* (pool), *fleur* (gulf), *dal* (valley), *beuf*
(hut), *tot* (cottage).

And so, from invasion to invasion, the work of stirring
the mixture of the French people went on.

Among the Ruins

The price paid for six centuries of invasion was appallingly
high. Where now was the rich Gaul of Roman days? The
France that had succeeded to it in the rank darkness of the
barbarian night was a thing of skin and bone, almost at its
last gasp. The country was a wilderness of ruins. On the
northern plains wave after wave of invaders—Mongol, German, Norse—had broken in quick succession. The valleys
of the south had been pillaged by Arabs, and had lain for a
long time under the heel of the Spanish Moors. From those
times date the many towns called Mézières and Mazerolles,
names that come from *masures*, or hovels, the remains of
cities and houses in collapse.

Of the urban civilization of the Gallo-Romans nothing
remained. War, pillage, and fire had killed the towns; massacre and famine had taken toll of their inhabitants. Even
had it not been so, what good purpose could be served by
living on in these congeries of buildings which had long
ceased to fulfill any administrative function and could but
attract the greedy eyes of roaming pirates?

The countryside gained by what the cities lost, since the

refugees sought safety in dispersion. Once more a rural economy was in the ascendant. Each estate lived its own life, shut away from the outer world, attempting to provide the bare necessities, which were all that men now hoped for. The stock name for such estates was *villa,* a word that means both land and buildings—the whole settlement, in fact, containing the owner, his agricultural laborers, his artificers, and his serfs. Quite naturally, the villa and its villeins, or inhabitants, gave birth to later villages.

It is easy in France to identify the sites of these establishments. Their whereabouts are revealed by a multitude of names ending in *ville,* preceded, as a rule, or followed by the name of the proprietor: Angerville, Outarville, Trouville. They are most numerous in Beauce and Normandy. This does not mean that these places were first brought under cultivation during this period, but only that the villages, with their names, were superimposed on earlier estates.

Similarly to these terminations in *ville,* others, such as those in *villiers* or *villers* (from the Latin *villare,* meaning the dependencies of a farm, and later a hamlet), and, in the east, in *villé* or *weiler,* as well as names containing the word *court* (from the Latin *cohors, cohortis,* signifying primarily the farm *yard,* and then the farm itself—the same derivation that we find in the German *Hof*)—all bear witness to the scattered country settlements of the Frankish age: Auvilliers, Badonviller, Ribeauvillé, Guebwiller, Martincourt, Guyancourt, Courdemanche, and so on. The land of France is thickly sown with telltale names. The crops grown on these various estates consisted of the different cereals, beans, and vines. The soil was left fallow every third year. The fields were reaped. The trees in the near-by forests were felled, since wood was the only fuel available and provided the raw material for building.

Industry had almost entirely vanished. A few only of the

minor trades remained—smithying and weapon-making, tailoring and cobbling, weaving and clothmaking. Those who practiced them worked with what materials they could lay their hands on, to provide the needs of the small communities in which they lived. One improvement alone belongs to this period—the water-mill. Since it made the grinding of corn, on a scale suitable for local requirements, easier, its use spread rapidly and widely.

Except between neighboring estates, trade had, in the main, ceased completely. How could there be a regular exchange of goods in the prevailing conditions of insecurity? The simplest journey had become a matter of difficulty and had to be organized almost on the scale of a military expedition. The only persons who could move freely about the country were the pilgrims, for they had nothing to lose. All other travelers needed a stout escort. Moving by water was the most practicable method, though not without its dangers from wandering bands of Norsemen. Roads were far more dangerous, even where they still existed. Nothing had been done to maintain the surfaces of the old Roman highways.

Communications with distant countries had become few and far between. Kings and churches, it is true, could still obtain a few articles of luxury, such as fabrics and jewels, but the mass of the population had no contact whatever with peoples living beyond the frontiers. In the north the Danes were masters of the seas, and in the south the Mediterranean routes were effectively cut by the Arabs. Gone were the days when wines and spices had come from foreign lands! Men now had to depend on substitutes. Wax took the place of oil in the churches, and parchment replaced papyrus. The ports of Arles and Marseille were dying of stagnation. Byzantium, as a great capital city, had become inaccessible.

Banking and credit were marvels beyond the cognizance of all except a few Jews, driven from Islam, who, as a result of the ecclesiastical ban on usury, were now the only money-lenders, though this was not so serious as it might have been in an age when the flow of currency had sunk to a mere driblet. The deposits of precious metals had been exhausted, and the reserves of money, though increased by treasure taken from the Avars, had been much reduced owing to the enormous payments made to the encroaching Danes. Gold, which already in the last years of the Empire had become a rare commodity, and which the Franks knew in its minted form of the sou and the third of a sou, eventually disappeared altogether. The golden sou of the Salic law had rapidly come to be nothing but a term in accountancy, and fines were paid in silver, at the rate of forty and later of twelve deniers to the sou. The content value of the silver denier was progressively falling, and its minting, which the central power had tried in vain to control and concentrate in its own hands, fell under the control of thousands of churchmen and lay operators. Coins of different weights, of different types, and bearing different effigies were in constant circulation. Too much specie, too little real money. The rare golden coins coming from the Orient, the Arabic denier (*dinar*), and the byzant (*bezant*), were objects of curiosity and envy. Faced by this condition of monetary chaos, which was in sad contrast with the satisfying unity that had prevailed under the Roman system, the West had often to resign itself to payments in kind. The Saxons delivered to the Frankish kings a tribute of five hundred cows. Four mares (valued at three sous each) were currently bartered for one ox (valued at twelve). Bills were settled in corn or horses. All this provides infallible evidence that the country was relapsing into a barbarian economy.

Because services were rewarded by grants of land, and because obligations were settled in terms of personal labor, this absence of money was one of the complex causes that were soon to produce an entirely new social system—feudalism.

The Road to Feudalism

In point of fact there was no longer any such thing as a State: in other words, there were no taxes and no public services. The Merovingian kings, it is true, did make an attempt to levy the old Roman dues, but it was ill received by the Frankish peoples—who had not invaded Gaul for the pleasure of becoming taxpayers. But once these had disappeared in a general saraband of immunities, and as a result of administrative negligence, what resources were left to the central power? It could still reckon on booty taken in war, on tribute paid by conquered enemies, on an occasional gift, on a few fines, on toll charges, and on the products of the royal domain. But all this did not amount to a fiscal system. As the kingdom came to be more and more cut up into smaller and smaller sections, and the king received fewer and fewer of the rents due to him, all public services disappeared. The fighting forces were no longer paid. Each man armed himself and went to war at his own charge. There was no budget for state requirements. Such work as was necessary was carried out locally with forced labor. The administration no longer bothered itself about such things as education, public health, or justice, and gradually all power in the country found its way into the hands of the Crown's most powerful subjects—the Church and the great lords.

From now on, an aristocracy was substituted for a royal government. It was only natural that this should be so. In periods of insecurity the weak were forced to beg the protection of the strong. When the perils of war and invasion appeared to be part of the eternal order of things, human activities fell automatically into two groups. Production was the duty of the protected, fighting of the protector. There was no essential inequality in the two sets of functions. There was, so to speak, a form of contract between them. It was only at a later period that a rigid hierarchy took root, when the warrior had achieved social superiority over the worker.

Because the king was far away, and help, when it was needed, had to be immediate, the system came to be organized on a local basis. The great landowner's estate became a refuge in time of trouble. The protector was the *senior*, the *seigneur*; he protected the *vassus*, the *vassal*. The estate had its own economic unity, and now it tended to acquire as well a degree of political autonomy. In the name of a king without power the seigneur became all-powerful. He administered justice, minted money, recruited soldiers. In theory he was himself the vassal of the king. In fact the bond was, for the most part, symbolic only. Between the king and his people there was no longer any familiarity. They were divided, the one from the other, by the seigneurs, of whom the people had need.

The most important of these seigneurs were those who at one time as representatives of the Crown had been charged with the surveillance or administration of the provinces. Their function, by becoming hereditary, had grown beyond the power of the sovereign to control. Like the Roman emperors, the kings had come to delegate their powers to a number of *comites*, who later became *counts*—counts of Champagne, of Anjou, of Barcelona. Similarly, on the frontiers of the kingdom, on the "marches" of Flanders, of Toulouse, they appointed men with the title of *marquis*. Where they attributed a number of provinces to a single leader, he was known as a *duc*—duchies of Normandy, of Burgundy, of Aquitaine, of Gascony. The local lords swore fealty to their regional suzerain. In this way a complex hierarchy was completed.

II *The Dark Night of Barbarism*   89

This hierarchy of *men,* this chain of vassalage, slipped imperceptibly into a pattern of feudalism, a hierarchy of *land.* Men might die, but the soil remained. As the weak had looked to the strong, so now did the peasant's hut look to the castle keep, the allotment to the great estate, the great estate to the county or the duchy. Each property became a fief. France was now no more than a scattering of fiefs. If this dismemberment was, to some extent, her tragedy, it must be admitted that at one particular period it did respond to the deepest wishes of the French people.

At the lowest level of the social hierarchy there was terrible poverty and great wretchedness, not because of the new organization of society, but because of the invasions. Feudalism aimed at providing some sort of palliation for the evils brought by these attacks, and in this it was successful, though the success had come rather too late. Walls and fortified castles did, in the long run, wear down the aggressive spirit of the last of the pirates—whether Norse or Hungarian. Formerly there had seemed to be no end to the miseries of the population. The land had been outraged, and the number of its inhabitants was diminishing. Roussillon had become a desert, which had to be peopled with immigrants from Catalonia.

Everywhere the standard of living was well below the middling. The men of this age had sunk so low that they were little better than beasts. They delighted in nothing so much as getting drunk whenever the opportunity came their way. Their clothes were limited to smock and trousers. They lived in hovels of mud or huts of wood. Slaves (the sons of former slaves, or prisoners of war, or condemned criminals) were growing ever more rare. They were regarded as forming part of the estate on which they worked, and from which they could not move. From now on they were the *servi manentes,* the serfs, the churls. They shared the miserable fate of the free men, for whom, only too

often, freedom meant no more than the right to choose
their form of misery.

The Vain Efforts of the Carolingians

What could the Frankish kings do to assert their authority?
The Merovingians, descendants of Clovis, abandoned the
attempt. Indifferent to what went on around them, they
left it to their mayors of the palace to carry out their functions. Charles Martel, the conqueror of the Arabs, was never
brave enough to claim the throne, but his more venturesome son Pepin did so, thereby bringing about a change of
dynasty.

The Frankish custom was to elect a king, but choice was
limited to one of the members of the reigning family. How
would it have been possible to switch from one family to
another and make such usurpation acceptable? Pepin had
the brilliant idea of adding consecration to election. The
great lords chose, and the Church ratified their choice.
Pepin had himself anointed with holy oil, after the manner of the Visigoth and Saxon kings, and of the kings
of Israel. Thenceforward the *sacre*, or act of ceremonial
anointing, legitimized the king of France.

To make this crowning the more solemn, Pepin obtained
the oil from the Pope himself. At this time the Pope stood
in need of Frankish support against the Lombards. He
came as a suppliant to beg the "very Christian King" to
754   take in hand the cause of the See of Peter. Pepin promised
aid (and kept his promise). The Pope, in return, crowned
him at Saint-Denis. At the same time, and the more surely
to establish the royal family, he anointed both his sons.
The exchange was a fair one.

In this way was the new dynasty established. It was to be
made famous by Charlemagne, and to become the Carolian
—or, according to the Germans, the Carolingian—line.

Would it be more fortunate than the Merovingians? From the very beginning it was hampered by the same weaknesses. When the king died, both families divided the royal heritage between all the remaining sons. Under the successors of Pepin, as under those of Clovis, France was fated to disintegrate.

Pepin had two sons, who both reigned as kings at the same time, and quarreled. It was by sheer good luck that   768
the younger died. Charles remained undisputed sovereign,   771
the Great King—Charle-magne. His domination extended over a vast stretch of territory. Pepin had conquered the Lombards, the Saxons, the Bavarians, and the Saracens. But Charles did more than merely confirm these victories. He achieved new ones, and extended the frontiers of Christendom. His kingdom included Brandenburg as far as the Oder, Saxony, the marches of Austria, Dalmatia, and a good half of Italy. With the capture of Barcelona he spilled over to the other side of the Pyrenees. Fifty-five campaigns and a series of frightful butcheries were needed before he could gather all these territories into the Empire. If we shut our eyes to its fragility, we can still indulge the illusion that what he created was a reborn Empire of the West. Why, then, should he not take the title of Emperor rather than that of King? What is supposed to have happened is this: Rome formed part of his dominions, and as, one Christmas night, Charles was kneeling in prayer in St.   800
Peter's, the Pope placed upon his head a golden crown, and the people hailed him as the new Augustus, Emperor of the Romans. We are told, quite seriously, that this step was taken on the Pope's own initiative, unknown to Charles, who was as much surprised as anybody else. All this is very difficult to swallow, but so well was the game played that there are still historians who are duped by it. As a matter of fact, it is quite obvious that Charles was delighted by his promotion. It is incredible that he should not have brooded

upon and ardently desired some such event. It ranked him with the Emperor at Constantinople, who first pulled a face and then resigned himself to addressing him as "our brother." It raised him to an eminence far above the great lords who exercised their power *de facto*. It made it easier for him to establish his dynasty, to restore the central power, to revive some sort of organized state.

But was that crowning in Rome really sufficient to restore the Empire of the West? Charles tried hard to make men believe that it had done so. He organized his royal train to include a multiplicity of ceremonial officers. There was a seneschal to superintend the service of his meals; a chamberlain to guard the royal apartments and the royal treasure; a count of the stables, or constable, who, with his marshals of the household, was in charge of the royal horses and was supreme commander of the army. There were chancellors who had in their care all official documents and the conduct of the administration. There were ushers to introduce ambassadors to the presence, and counselors to frame the policies of the throne. From the palace set out the "officials on mission," whose duty it was, in theory, to control the great lords. All this elaborate setup was the result of much careful thought and many good intentions, but it was powerless to transform chaos into monarchy.

Similarly, Charles's sincere efforts to bring about a renaissance in letters and the arts succeeded only in achieving a parody of Rome. The Romansh tongue was but a rough-and-ready tool, so far removed from Latin as to make that tongue incomprehensible to the generality of his subjects, and too rudimentary in itself to produce a literature. Besides, where were the literate who might have performed this service? The Roman schools had been swept away by the storms of the Dark Ages. Outside the Church no one knew anything, and no one could teach. Charlemagne himself had received only the most elementary form of education. He spoke a Teutonic dialect, and wrote with difficulty. But he hungered after learning and knowledge. He studied Latin and Greek, and brought many scholars to his court from foreign lands—more particularly from Italy. Under pressure from the throne, Latin manuscripts were recopied on parchment, and a crop of bad imitations of good authors grew up. But nothing could raise this deliberate effort at cultivation above the level of mediocrity.

In the arts the same touching enthusiasm produced the same lamentable results. With the fall of Rome, all technical methods had fallen into oblivion. There was no one any longer who could build, carve, paint, except very badly. The nomad invaders had brought with them an art suited to their own level of civilization. They could mount stones or lumps of glass in metal settings, and this species of jewelry they used for decorating reliquaries, sacred vessels, and even furniture, as well as for purposes of wear. It appealed to their taste for color and glitter. It had its origin far back among the Asiatic peoples—the Scythians and Sarmatians.

Charlemagne wanted something better. His childish tastes, which were those of his time, led him to revive the art of calligraphy, to encourage illumination. Susceptible to music, he did his best to bring back the Roman chant. But when he wished to equip himself with a palace, all he could do was to steal antique columns from Ravenna. What possible point can there be in trying to rehabilitate this gloomy age, to glorify this abortive renaissance? Neither Charlemagne nor his companions were responsible for its failure. They were too close to their barbaric past, and were not ripe for civilization. The most they could do was to raise a few buildings, copying Rome and aping Byzantium. Their efforts were doomed to failure from the beginning. The genius of the barbarian centuries could not burst into flower. The conditions were not favorable. Durable materials were lacking; an outlet on the world was lacking; an adequate body of support was lacking. Timber is not the equal of marble; Aix-la-Chapelle was not the equal of Rome. An economy based on exchanges in kind cannot replace a monetary system, nor can works of supreme art be produced in an age of poverty and insecurity.

The Empire in Disruption

If Charlemagne has been regarded as a great man, it is because he overtops the many Merovingian kings who never were, nor ever could be, more than dwarfs. It is a legend that has transfigured him. It would be truer to say two legends. There was first the French one. It seized on the person of the Emperor a century or two after his death and turned him into the hero he never had been in his life. He was dressed in a new fashion and given a flowing beard. He was presented as a great legislator and an incomparable warrior. He was set in the midst of knights and paladins. His victories were made into the subject matter of song, because he had waged many wars. His virtues, too, were sung, because his reign had covered forty-six years. At a later date German mythology made Charlemagne its own. This time, because he had rallied the German peoples under his temporary suzerainty, the Emperor of the flowing beard was metamorphosed into the champion of Pan-Germanism.

Behind these two legends, one of them purely literary and highly colored, the other wholly political and heavy with propaganda, the historian must seek to discover Charlemagne as he really was—a man with a mustache but no beard, a constant but untalented fighter, a German, though without knowing it. Behind the Emperor and his ten wives he must reveal the King forever tottering on his throne, and succeeding only with great difficulty in getting himself obeyed. His soldiers threatened to abandon him; one of his bastards rebelled; conspiracy followed conspiracy. The great lords were not prepared to give up their prerogatives and, in the security of their domains, lived as almost independent rulers. The Carolingian Empire was terrifyingly fragile.

If proof be needed, it is this: that it collapsed. It was too large, too widely scattered, and it fell into hands that were too weak to hold it. In any case, the laws of succession in force among the Carolingians, as among the Merovingians— though there had been a short-lived effort to set up a system of primogeniture—inevitably led to its division among the dead monarch's surviving sons. One such division followed another. The son who thought himself to be the loser on the deal made war on the other members of his family. Kings and emperors, uncles and nephews, brothers and cousins—Lothaires and Charleses, Louis and Pepins—deposed one another and quarreled endlessly about their heritages. Only the professional genealogist can take the slightest interest in the dreary record of murders and treacheries. `817`

Out of all this confusion of family brawling, history need preserve only two essential facts, two important dates, which, at an interval of two years, gave recognition to a new birth—that of France. One marks the first formal use of the mother tongue, the other the first reference to the nation as such.

First fact: two grandsons of Charlemagne, Louis the German and Charles le Chauve (the Bald), signed a pact of alliance against their brother Lothaire. This pact has come down to us as the Strasbourg Oath. Instead of being inscribed in Latin, it made use of the vulgar tongue—that is to say, of Romansh. The text contains the French language in embryo. `841`

Second fact: Lothaire sought peace, and the three brothers signed at Verdun a treaty that divided the Empire into three parts. To the east, Eastern, or Germanic, France; to the west, Western France; and between the two a ridiculous slice of territory, stretching from the North Sea to `843`

Rome, and containing all the districts watered by the Meuse and the Rhone. This was adjudged to Lothaire. The result was three vertical strips carefully designed by one hundred and twenty experts so that each should have its share of the different systems of climate and vegetation obtaining from north to south. But Lothaire's buffer state, so far from preventing a strife between France and Germany, served only to whet the appetites of each and to be a bone of contention. There were to be endless struggles in the future for possession of the province lying at the heart of Lothaire's kingdom, and later to be known as Lorraine. The Treaty of Verdun carried within it the seeds of many wars.

The France that emerged from the Treaty of Verdun was very far from filling out the contours of the ancient Gaul. Its total population amounted to little more than ten million. Cambrai, Lyon, and Arles all lay in foreign territory. When the turn came for Lothaire's kingdom to be broken up, the French lands were found to owe allegiance to half a dozen sovereigns. The valley of the Meuse belonged to the Germanic King, Lorraine to its own titular holder; Burgundy and Provence formed part of still another realm; so did Savoy, so did Aquitaine—to say nothing of Navarre and Brittany, each of which had its own suzerain, or the dominions of Norsemen and Saracens, who snapped their fingers at all kings alike. Nor did these attributions take account of the various lords, both great and small, who were waxing fat on chaos, minting their own money, raising their own armies, living as absolute masters on their own estates, and less concerned than ever about the central power, now that they frequently did not even know where it lay.

Paris, indeed, which had been the capital of Clovis, had been abandoned by the Carolingians. Charlemagne, wishing to set up his machinery of administration nearer to the

895

heart of his Empire, had chosen to reside at Aix-la-Chapelle, though he never succeeded in raising it to higher status than that of a market town. Charles le Chauve, the first of the French kings, preferred Compiègne to Paris. His successors took refuge on the hill of Laon. It was as though they were frightened of Paris, as indeed they were: frightened of the river that had so often served as a highway for the Norsemen, frightened of a city that pillagers had sacked. By running from Paris they admitted their weakness, and made it worse.

One Single Star: the Church

In all this confusion there was but one unity; in the blackness of this night, a solitary gleam, and even that uncertain —the Church of Rome. Through her the radiance of the antique age still shone upon the world. She had conquered Gaul long before the appearance of the German raiders, and in the person of Clovis she had later consolidated her triumph. At a time when all in the Frankish Kingdom were at sixes and sevens, the Church was well on the way to becoming a highly organized body. For each rural domain there was a parish; for each district, a diocese, in which a bishop held sway. At first these bishops were elected by the people, though they soon came to be appointed by the king. The final stage in this ecclesiastical organization came when the Pope installed a number of super-bishops, or archbishops—Saint Boniface being the first to hold that title.

All these men of the Church shared fully in the life of their flocks, so fully, indeed, that it was by no means rare to find bishops who were fathers of families. Then a reaction set in, and Christians of a different kind sought to withdraw from the world and live very simply in monasteries and hermits' cells. Saint Martin built the first of such

retreats not far from Poitiers. Saint Honorat founded the
Abbey of the Îles de Lérins, off the coast of Provence. The
Abbey of Cluny, which came into existence as a Benedictine house, contributed a number of variants to the rules
laid down by Saint Benoît (Benedict). The monastic idea
became widely successful, and France was soon covered by
a swarm of abbeys, temples of prayer and meditation,
sanctuaries where men could take refuge from the disorders and temptations of the world.

Bishops and priests, monks and abbesses could, after their
deaths, attain to the summit of the Christian hierarchy.
Even a few laymen could sometimes join them there. The
people made saints of them. There came a time when saints
were almost mass-produced, for sanctification was a way of
giving thanks for services rendered and of honoring the
memory of the departed. It also popularized the veneration
of relics.

The title given to these saints was not *sanctus*, but *dom-
inus* (lord). For this reason we find embalmed in place-
names many of the most famous saints of France: Martin,
who has marked as his own Dommartin or Dammartin,
just as Bishop Rémy, the Apostle Peter, and the Virgin
Mary produced Domremy, Dampierre or Dompierre, Dan-
nemarie or Dammarie.

The place-names of this period bear also other forms of
Christian signature. Thus, the *chape* of Saint Martin (the
cloak that the Bishop of Tours shared with the beggar),
piously preserved in a chapel, reappears in every place called
Capelle or La Chapelle. The Celles and La Selles derive
their names from the *cella*, or hermitages. Oratories (*ora-
torium*) have left their traces at Ouzoir, Louzouer, Oradour,
and Louradoux; basilicas have given us Bazoches and
Bazoges; churches (*ecclesia, églises*) have become trans-
muted into Eglisolles and Grisolles; monasteries (*mona-
sterium*) into Montreuil, Montereau, Ménétréol, Montreux,

Marmoutier, and Noirmoutier. Bishops and monasteries were rich, as a result of accumulating the gifts and legacies of the faithful. In this way they became the foremost owners of landed property of France. One third of the whole country belonged to them. From all the peasants who sought their protection they received the tenth (or tithe) of the yearly yield.

But the Church did not sleep on her moneybags. Mindful of the fact that Jesus had been the son of a carpenter, she set herself to raise the status of manual labor. The monks gave a practical example, in obedience to the precept laid down by Saint Benoît. They were tailors and weavers and shoemakers. The religious communities turned enthusiastically to the work of clearing the land, giving back to the plow wide tracts on which the forests had encroached. All over the country a multiplicity of *essarts*, or clearings, made their appearance. Some monasteries, like that of Saint Martin at Tours, employed as many as twenty thousand serfs. The Parisian Abbey of Saint-Germain-des-Prés owned property as far distant as Normandy and the Nivernais and worked it methodically.

But the work of the Church was not confined to the sphere of rural economy. She provided almost the only stimulus to art and letters, both almost at their last gasp. She was the chief customer of jewelers, masons, and glassmakers. She ordered consignments of marbles and fabrics and mosaics. She did her best to set up schools in every city—though these were primitive enough, in all conscience —where children did, at least, learn something, if only reading, writing, and singing. She organized pilgrimages, which opened men's eyes to wider horizons and filled men's minds with less limited ideas. Such books as there were owed their existence to churchmen. Gregory of Tours wrote the first history of the Franks; and lives of the saints, in bad Latin, grew numerous.

In worldly affairs, too, the Church exerted herself. She protected the widow and the orphan, acted as arbitrator in lawsuits, and assumed the duties of an impotent administration in helping the unfortunate. She opened hostels for the poor and hospitals for the sick and inns for travelers. Her councils denounced the cruelties of war. Her consecrated buildings provided asylum for fugitives, innocent and guilty alike, who might be fleeing from the violence of kings and lords and mobs.

She waged a relentless war against every form of heresy, as well as against all the surviving vestiges of paganism. She set her face against witchcraft and the superstitious belief in omens and divinations. She condemned the practice of giving presents at Christmas and the New Year as being a relic of druidism. She imposed a new way of reckoning chronology from the birth of Christ, and this calendar, adopted by Rome in the sixth century, spread throughout France in the eighth.

In the barbarian ages there was only one solid discipline: that of the Christian Church.

Church versus Kings

The Church worked in the name of Christ the King, and not for the kings of the earth. On occasion she appealed to them for protection, and supported them when it was to her advantage to do so. But it was her own advantage that she had in mind and not that of the Frankish dynasties. And because she sought temporal power, she came, inevitably, into conflict with the sovereigns, opposing her power to their powerlessness.

The bishops owed their strength to the fact that they had in the early days been elected by the people. They were the representatives of public opinion. In later times their wealth gave them another trump card. In Clovis they had welcomed a "new Constantine"; in Pepin they had seen the protector of the Papacy; in Charlemagne, the champion of Christendom. They showed more respect for strong-fisted kings than state officials ever did; but when the kings were weak, they braved them to their faces.

At the end of the Merovingian period the Church was far more than a state within the State; she was a state in the absence of a State. So well aware of this was Charles Martel that he could not set his authority firmly on its feet without first attacking the immense landed wealth of the bishops and monasteries. Might not the conqueror of Islam do as he pleased? He was shameless in his seizure of ecclesiastical estates, treating them as a species of "national property," which he proceeded to distribute among his friends. He launched a campaign of "brutal robbery" and "national-ized" on a big scale. Nothing like it was to be seen again for the next thousand years. As a result of these methodical evictions, and making all due allowance for the partial acts of restitution set on foot by the Carolingians, the Church, for all her efforts, never again enjoyed her former wealth. **739**

She took her revenge, whenever possible, by undermining the monarchy. Twice she deposed the son of Charlemagne, that Louis who was so "pious" that he was known as the "Débonnaire"—a man so mild-tempered that he let himself be treated as a child. When she threatened Charles le Chauve with the same fate, he timidly asked that he should not be judged save by the bishops who had anointed him King. The name of the Archbishop of Sens, Ganelon, has come down to us as the very type of all traitors.

In the long run the Church played exactly the same role as the great secular lords who were masters in their own lands. Like them the Church offered protection to the humble, and the humble looked to her for aid. Bonds of vassalage were formed. The bishops and the abbeys main-tained and protected huge numbers of hangers-on, finally emerging as feudal overlords. As such they rebelled against every attempt to diminish their authority. They levied taxes, issued money, administered justice, and fortified their castles. They acknowledged the royal suzerainty only when it did not irk them.

If bishops became great lords, so, too, did great lords become bishops. Dukes and counts claimed the right to exercise the royal prerogative in the matter of appointing to episcopal sees and abbeys. Sometimes they disposed of them to the highest bidder. It is scarcely astonishing, therefore, to find bishops who were more skillful at hunting wolves than at preaching the Gospel, ready to drink deep and fight hard, ready, even, to traffic in sacred objects. The priests, appointed as were the bishops, by the great lords, were ruined by similar debauches. The Church became decadent, not through any fault of Rome's, but because of the condition of the world in which she had elected to play too great a part. She had thought to find her own advantage in the overthrow of kings, but in fact she fell with them.

Was she aware of the danger? She pulled herself together just in time by abandoning the Carolingian dynasty, which had shown itself incapable of administering the Roman heritage. She took her chance with a new family, which was to give France, for the next eight hundred years, a third race of kings. The origins of this family are obscure. The people, who saw in it the mirror of themselves, put about a tale that it was descended from a Paris butcher, and Dante accepted this version. It had grown prosperous on the banks of the Loire, where its lands had originally lain. There it developed into a powerful feudal house from the moment that Charles le Chauve, needing its help against the Norsemen, created Robert le Fort (the Strong) Count of Anjou, and later a Duke of France.

No one is in a better position to step into the shoes of a dynasty than a successful general. Had not Clovis begun his career by overcoming the Alamanni, and Charles Martel his by driving out the Arabs? Profiting by these examples, Robert the Strong held his ground against the Norsemen, and met a glorious death on the field of battle. His son Eudes was the hero of a victorious defense of Paris against the pirates. When the Carolingians proved incapable of carrying out their royal function, who more suited to succeed them than this race of strong and valiant men? Eudes was elected King. 885 887

Not that this single election was sufficient finally to unseat the dynasty. The Carolingians were still there. As yet they had not abdicated. Between the powerless descendants of Charlemagne and the sons of Robert le Fort, the feudal lords, lay and ecclesiastical alike, made their choice, and they chose the course most likely to leave the royal authority weak and to consolidate them in their privileges. In the course of a hundred years the crown passed from one family to the other, and during all that time the ruin of the central power became more and more pronounced.

The last of the Carolingian kings died at twenty as the result of a hunting accident. His uncle, who claimed the succession, called upon the Germans for help, and they marched into the country and encamped before Paris. The great-grandson of Robert le Fort, Hugues, Duke of France and Count of Paris and Orléans, took the field as a pretender in the national interest. Faced by a choice between a pro-German prince and a Duke of France, the great lords assembled at Noyon threw in their lot with the latter. Hugues was anointed King by the Archbishop of Reims. The Carolingian family faded into obscurity. 987

This incident, at the time of its occurrence, was no great matter. It cannot even be said with certainty that the alliance between Church and throne lasted for very long. Hugues was in a position to take the surname Capet, because, as Abbot of Saint-Martin-de-Tours, the old Gallic sanctuary, he possessed the most precious of all relics, the "cape" of the holy bishop—a fact that the Capet family did not soon forget.

The kings of this new line were faced by a tremendous task. They had to seek allies where and how they could, and as best suited their interests. They started from nothing, with a kingdom in fragments, a dishonored title, a nonexistent economy. In the night of the barbarians at its densest it had fallen to the house of Capet to bring the sun into the sky.

Chapter III

RADIANT DAWN

(987–1328)

The Secret
of the Capetians WITH the coming of the
Capetians everything changed, and was to change still
more. A re-establishment of authority began which would
grow progressively stronger. The national economy would
improve, and a prosperous time lay ahead for literature and
the arts. In every sphere of life France was about to turn
over a new leaf. After the centuries of invasion came the
centuries of expansion, and around its kings the nation took
on form and substance.

How came this miracle? Was it merely a normal result of
the slow passage of time? By no means. In the very same
period that saw the unification of France, Germany was dis-
integrating into fiefs, and Italy into communes, while in
England nobles, middle classes, and populace were linked
in a struggle against the royal power. What happened in
France was the work of the Capetians, and of them alone.
Before a federation can be formed, there must be a man to
inspire it. Before men can unite, there must be a center
around which unity can grow. In this instance that center
was a single family. It had no particularly outstanding gifts.
At least half the kings to whom the succession fell were
mediocre or average. What is true is that they knew what
they wanted, and wanted it with all their hearts. They had
plenty of common sense, and they were obstinate.

Their ambitions, on the whole, were sordid. At a time when there was no wealth but land, they thought only of acquiring more of it. Nor did they boggle at the means. Anything to them was good that would serve their ends— war, cunning, marriage, inheritance. Where their predecessors had failed, they must succeed. In that realization of the Capetian monarchs lay the miracle.

They understood what neither the Roman emperors nor the Frankish kings had understood, what the German Empire, where the crown passed from one feudal family to another by the chance of election, was still far from understanding. They discovered the secret of continuity, which was that there must be a law of succession. The whole inheritance would in future devolve upon the eldest son.

That secret was far from being so simple as it seems to us. The passing on of the crown in the male line by right of primogeniture was contrary alike to natural law and legal custom, both of which stood for equality of division between all the surviving children of a dead father. It meant sacrificing the younger members of a family to the elder. Before it could be adopted, the Capetians had to make a great decision. They had to make up their minds that the interests of the land should take precedence of those of the family, that national feeling should override paternal sentiment. The price was heavy, but by paying it they avoided all threat of disintegration, all danger of weakness in the structure; and they produced a masterpiece of longevity to which, without realizing what it was doing, the Revolutionary Convention paid tribute when it addressed Louis XVI by the glorious name of Louis Capet.

Fortune fought on the side of the family. A run of short reigns would have made it impossible to give the dynasty a firm foundation and to impose the new system. But the Capetians were robust. For 327 years, without interruption, son followed father on the throne, with a high average per reign of thirty years. Later, in the absence of direct heirs, the collateral branches prolonged the lifetime of the dynasty, which lasted in all for 861 years spread over thirty-seven kings, which works out at an average for each of twenty-three years, taking into account Jean I, who died when he was only five days old.

A statistical study of this family shows results that are remarkable in other ways too. More than half the kings of the house of Capet were called either Louis or Charles. Louis was Clovis, who in this way lived on. Charles was Charlemagne, who lived again. Usurpers the Capetian kings might be, but they were conscious of their solidarity with the first two reigning families. It was their wish to continue the past. When to their names was added that of Philippe—brought by a Princess of Kiev who became Queen of France—they were imitating Byzantium. They sought to bring Greece and Rome once more into union. In this way they forged a chain that linked the ages.

How many of these thirty-seven kings died a violent death? Four only, and two of these as the result of an accident, whereas murder had been as much the rule among the Merovingian and Carolingian monarchs as it had been among the Roman emperors. Was this merely a matter of chance? No, it was a consequence of that system of succession which destroyed all competition for the throne.

One danger there always was: that a minor might succeed. Regency was the weak spot in the Capetian armor, because it awoke the spirit of rivalry among princely relatives and great lords. By definition, when there is a regency there is no king. Luckily only two cases of minority occurred during the first centuries of the Capetian dominance. One pursued its course without any untoward incident; the other put power into the hands of a woman with a sound head and a good heart. Later regencies were less fortunate.

But this obscure family had a hard road to travel before

it could impose its will. By tradition the king was elected.
At the coronation of Hugues, the Archbishop of Reims is
said to have declared: "The throne descends not by right
of inheritance, but through the possession of noble blood
and of wisdom"—an absurd dictum because nobility of
blood and wisdom are matters of opinion. When he said
that, the Archbishop of Reims was speaking as a feudal
lord.

Since he was elected by his peers, the king could establish
the hereditary system only by a subterfuge often repeated.
For a century and a half the reigning monarch had his son
elected, during his own lifetime, as king designate. At the
death of his father this king designate became the king
crowned as a result of the *sacre,* or anointing, carried out at
Reims (or, by accident, occasionally at Compiègne or Orléans). Thus was the freedom of election whittled away
until such time as custom became law.

But the cleverest stroke of all was the king's proclaimed
intention of defending his people, and consequently of ensuring their support. To the symbol of the scepter he added
that of the hand of justice. According to the form of his
oath, he assumed the duty "of assuring to all and sundry
the justice that is their due, and of maintaining the people
in their lawful possessions." In the days of Saint Louis, the
Oak of Vincennes completed the imagery. The monarchs
of the house of Capet were the defenders of the weak, and
this meant, more than anything else, that they would humble the strong.

Tirelessly, through eight centuries, they carried on their
struggle against the feudal lords.

The Feudal Drama

When the crown became hereditary, the feudal fiefs followed suit, with the result that the nobles consolidated

their power against the king. Like the ancient *villa,* from
which it had emerged, each local fief formed a self-sufficient
world apart, linked to other fiefs only by those rules of
vassalage which were made up of rights and duties. The
vassal owed to his overlord the duty of giving him counsel
and, in certain specified circumstances, of bringing him aid,
which took the form of military service limited to one or
two months in each year. The overlord owed to his vassal
the duty of protection. The king was only the supreme overlord, and since he was not always as strong as his vassals, it
did not follow that he was always obeyed.

Strange customs began to take shape and gradually came
to constitute a feudal code of behavior. What was the mark
that distinguished the lord from his people in such a way
that there could be no social confusion? His function as a
warrior, which was the natural outcome of his duty to protect. This function was outwardly expressed by two of the
tools of his trade: the horse for attack, the castle for defense.

The horse was the very sign and symbol of nobility. Ever
since the Arabs had imported the stirrup, warfare had become so much a matter of mounted knights that it came
to take on the form of an equestrian sport. The villein
merely put up with war, the lord made it. For him alone
was reserved the honor of getting himself killed. As soon
as the page reached the age of fifteen he was granted the
privilege of carrying his master's shield and became a squire.
At twenty-one, if he was brave, and rich enough to buy
arms, he was dubbed knight. At first the title was secular
only, but very soon the Church took it in hand and sanc-
tioned it with a preparatory ritual of fasting, vigil, Mass,
sponsors, and oath. The knight was pledged to defend all
churchmen, as well as the poor, the widow, and the orphan.
He must be loyal and pious. But, for all that, he remained
little more than a piece of fighting machinery behind the

rampart of his breastplate or his coat of mail, his helmet, and his shield. Carrying a weight of one hundred and sixty-five pounds of armor, brandishing his sword, lance, or mace, he and his horse, likewise armored, made but a single unit. He was a movable castle keep.

The other kind of castle—the kind that could not move—was no less a suit of armor, but made of stone. The camp (*castrum*) had been metamorphosed into the fortress (*castellum*). Moated, thick-walled, flanked by towers with loopholes for the discharge of arrows, and with machicolations for the dropping of boiling oil, with drawbridges and portcullises and massive keeps, the castles of this period were designed to hold assailants at bay. Erected at strategic points, they dominated the plains and overlooked the rivers. Centuries later the trace of them could still be found in all the Rocheforts and Roqueforts, in all the Châteauneufs and Castelnaus and Châtelets and Châteauroux up and down the country, and in the innumerable place-names which contained the word *ferté* (from *firmitas*).

Thus armed, the feudal nobles could snap their fingers at the king of France. They were kings themselves in their own domains. And since they must recover the cost of equipment, arsenals, and fortresses, they looked on war as a paying industry. They set out to pillage other castles or to conquer other fiefs. They rarely fought for the pleasure of fighting, but frequently for profit.

France did not suffer much from these private wars, which bore no resemblance to the devastating invasions of the earlier nomads. The feudal lords came and went. The numbers of fighting men involved were minute. True, they left ruin in their wake, but ruin that was neither very serious nor very durable. The damage they caused was nothing by comparison with that perpetrated by the barbarian hordes. Their warfare was warfare on a small scale, a pastime for a few hundred men with nothing better to occupy their time, likely to do no more than disturb the quiet of the peasant working in the fields or shake the king's authority.

The peasants put up philosophically enough with these raiding expeditions. There was nothing they could do about them. It was always the serfs and villeins of the great estates who were the victims. Burnings and brigandage and famine —such was their lot. To the lord who protected them they had to make payment in the form of rents or statute labor. To the lord who attacked them they could oppose only their lamentations.

Could the king do much more? At the beginning of the monarchy the royal domains were laughably small. Paris belonged to a lord of Vendôme, and the head of the house of Capet possessed there nothing but a dwelling. He could call his own no more than a few villages in the environs (Compiègne), and a few towns (Orléans, Dreux, Senlis) at a somewhat greater distance. He was king only by courtesy, a king deserving of mockery. He was defied by brigands, and surrounded by his great vassals—the duke of Burgundy, who had inherited part of the Burgundian lands; the count of Flanders, busy laying the foundations of a huge fortune; the duke of Normandy, successor of Rollo the Dane; the comte d'Anjou, who made a hobby of collecting castles; the comte de Blois, whose fiefs extended as far as Troyes, Meaux, and Provins—to say nothing of the titled bishops holding Reims, Langres, Châlons, Laon, Beauvais, and Noyon; to say nothing of the great lords of the south, the counts of Toulouse, of Barcelona, and of Aquitaine, who kept royal state upon their lands; to say nothing of the duc de Bretagne, whose followers were an army in themselves; to say nothing of the territories that owed no feudal allegiance but, like Provence and Savoy and Lorraine, lay beyond the frontiers. Poor king, defied by the lord of Montlhéry, and entirely unknown to the majority of Frenchmen!

And yet it was that little king who was to be the maker of France.

The Road to Unity

The kings of the house of Capet, only too well aware of their weakness, played a subtle game. They played it according to the rules of feudalism. Where necessary, they bought allegiance with a gift of land. More often they profited by the system to round out their own estates. When they married they demanded a fief as dowry. When a great lord needed money, the king bought his lands. When a vassal died without an heir, the king invoked the law of intestacy, in virtue of which the vacant property reverted to the suzerain. Whenever a succession was doubtful, the Crown laid claim to it, and it was then that the king enforced his title, sword in hand (almost every war for the next few centuries was to be a war of succession). In these ways, by every means in his power, peaceful or warlike, by marriage, by bargaining, by purchase, or by conquest, he added city to city, fief to fief, province to province, until France became coterminous with the royal domain.

It was a labor that demanded time for its accomplishment, and sacrifices and compromises. The kings needed support to bring their efforts to a happy issue—not the support of foreigners, for if the Carolingians had been, as sovereigns, more European (or more German) than French, the Capetians desired to be rulers only of one country—their own. It was left for the rebel lords to play the ugly part of traitors, seeking aid from Englishmen and Germans and Spaniards. The monarchs of the Capet line sought their supporters within France alone, throwing in their lot with Church and people, their natural allies.

The Church, no less than the kings, aimed at keeping private warfare within bounds. Bishops and councils strove to impose the Truce of God, which forbade the feudal

armies to fight between themselves from Saturday evening
to Monday morning, then from Wednesday to Monday,
and during Lent; forbade too all attacks on cemeteries,
travelers, and livestock. These bans were more or less respected. The royal house, for its part, imposed the "king's
forty days" (the *quarantaine le roi*). Should a quarrel break
out between two feudal lords, each side was forbidden to
take up arms until forty days had elapsed. If the antagonists
ignored this rule, the king reserved to himself the right to
intervene. In this way the peacemaking efforts of the
Church and the unifying action of the Crown made common cause.

The interests of the people lay in the same direction. If
the peasants dwelling within the shadow of the castle were
at the mercy of their lord, the men of the towns, who later
were to gain the name of "burgesses," no longer sought protection under the wing of the baron, but by acting against
him. Freeing themselves from his tutelage, they formed
small local republics—in the south the "municipalities,"
conducted in the tradition of Rome; in the north the "communes," whose inhabitants decided their affairs in "common." The barons, needless to say, refused to accept these
breakaway tactics. The burgesses had to rebel and fight.
The king helped them so long as these revolts were aimed
against the feudatories, but he was careful not to do so
when his own authority was called in question. And so it
came about that in France this new development served to
strengthen the Crown, while abroad, in the Italian republics and the free cities of Germany, it merely had the effect
of prolonging the period of feudal disintegration.

Though political liberty was denied them, the communes
did obtain certain local privileges—civic rights and the
granting of city charters. Within the protective circle of
their walls they prospered. France was soon able to show
places with such names as Villefranche and Villeneuve. The

burgesses had been freed of dependence on the great lords. It was the king whom in future years they were to supply with men and money.

The policy of the Capetians was not planned on a grand scale, nor was it generous. It aimed only at efficiency, and was quick to grasp any opportunity that looked like furthering this object. Like the members of a shrewd peasant family, intent on getting hold of every scrap of available land, these Capetian kings identified themselves with their domain and worked for it alone. They were something better than French kings: they were the very incarnation of France.

For the matter of France became, with them, a living reality. Hugues Capet spoke no language but Romansh. He did not even know Latin. The fleurs-de-lis were to become the symbol and blazon of royalty. The word *French* began to emerge, first applied to the inhabitants of the country and only later to their tongue. But for these new sovereigns of theirs the French counted for less than France.

They were champions of the French idea, and of Paris too, which soon regained its old importance. The Carolingian kings had abandoned the capital; the Capetians made it once again the head and front of the realm. Not but what they had been tempted by the cities of the Loire. Was it not from Angers that their dynasty had come? Was not Tours, with its Abbey of Saint-Martin, a religious metropolis, and did not its monetary system prevail against that of Paris? Had not Orléans been the favorite residence of the first of their line? But Paris, standing at the gates of the ancient "France," commanded all the roads and waterways of their earliest domain. From Paris, by way of the Seine, the king had first gained access to the sea. It was around Paris that France was to take shape.

The Steps to Unification

Of the fourteen Capetians of the direct line who took the task in hand, none was without merit. But three were outstanding: Philippe II, Louis IX, and Philippe IV.

Philippe II, known as Auguste because he was born in August, had the most fire. He defeated his foreign enemies. **1180** Attended by unfailing good fortune, he gathered in the scattered fiefs—the western provinces by force of arms (Normandy, Maine, Touraine, Anjou, Poitou, Saintonge . . .), the northern cities by acquiring their title-deeds (Arras, Boulogne, Amiens . . .).

Louis IX, who twenty-seven years after his death became Saint Louis, if judged only by the material results of his **1236** reign, was a national disaster. This exemplary sovereign, the very type of virtue crowned, practiced goodness and paid dearly for it. When victor in the field, he loaded his conquered enemies with gifts. Instead of gathering into his own hands the French territories, he gave them away. He renounced Catalonia and Roussillon, did nothing to enforce those rights to Castile which he inherited from his mother, and restored Saintonge, the Limousin, and Périgord to their former owners. He might have compelled the King of Aragon to respect the frontier of the Pyrenees, but did not. He might have driven from French soil the English King, whom he defeated at Saintes, but did not. The country was to pay a high price for his policy of fair dealing. Without knowing it, this most peace-loving of all kings laid the foundations of many future wars.

Had all the sovereigns of the house of Capet copied the scrupulous unselfishness of Louis IX, the Kingdom of France would quickly have broken up. But in the long run the dynasty turned his amazing reign to good account. It was no small advantage to be able to lay claim to such an ancestor! All the French kings to come acknowledged the paternity of Saint Louis. All of them were bathed in the radiance of the pious legend of a king who had been as good as he was beautiful, as loyal as he was golden-haired, the friend of the poor, the arbiter of princes, the servant of God. Saint Louis's gift to his descendants was a halo.

Philippe le Bel (the Fair) seems, by comparison, a monster. But he was a useful monster. He, too, had his legend, but it was the legend of a cruel and greedy tyrant, of a thief and a counterfeiter. He certainly was no saint, but he was a man, and that, in the circumstances, was to be preferred. He brought the realm more solid advantages than any other of her kings. He repaired the ruinous legacy of his grandfather's generosities. He bought Chartres, he occupied Lille and Lyon. By legal agreement he acquired Bigorre; by confiscation, La Marche and Angoumois; by marriage, Navarre, Brie, and Champagne. He outfaced all the enemies of France, the Pope included. In his reign France, for the first time, was no longer content to walk in the footsteps of Rome. She was greater than Rome.

When the direct line came to an end with the three sons of Philippe le Bel, the royal domain was forty times larger than it had been in the days of Hugues Capet. It stretched now to the very coastline of the Channel, from the district of Caux to Mont-Saint-Michel. In La Vendée it touched the Atlantic. It lay along the Mediterranean from the Aude to the Rhone delta.

In the course of these three centuries of acquisitions patiently planned and carried through, many a conspiracy had had to be scotched, many an intrigue contrived. It had been necessary to start in a small way, so as not to put the frightened on their guard—to gather in Melun when it was left masterless, to purchase Gien or Mâcon, to give away the fiefs that had become too heavy and unwieldy—Burgundy, for instance. Some secondary fiefs—Valois among others—had had to be alienated as marriage portions; char-

1285

1326

ters had had to be granted to certain provinces, such as Normandy, which were only loosely linked to the realm. And always it had been essential to stand firm, essential to make the royal authority felt.

Moments of stress there had been, the most serious of which had almost split the kingdom in two as the result of a schism in Christendom. The Catharist heresy, starting in Albi, had reached a degree of intensity at which it threatened the unity of France. It had begun as a minority religious movement, but it took on the appearance of feudal rebellion when the counts of Toulouse gave it their support, and of treason when its leaders appealed for help to the King of Aragon. Soon Frenchmen were fighting Frenchmen with a fanaticism that gave a foretaste of the atrocities which accompanied the later wars of religion. Northerners were ranged against southerners, *langue d'oïl* against *langue d'oc*. The Capet monarch, thinking ahead of the immediate moment, was careful to take no part in the repression. He appeared on the scene only when the issue had been decided, to gather in the gains and firmly to attach the whole of Languedoc to the royal domain.

Expansion in Europe

Simultaneously with the rounding out of the realm, Frenchmen were beginning to move outside their frontiers. Their turn had come at last. For centuries they had endured wave after wave of invaders; now, under the lead of the house of Capet, the time for expansion had arrived.

But the kings were careful not to dissipate their young strength in foreign wars. For the most part they confined themselves to encouraging the daring of others, and to drawing profit from it. Once more it was the great lords and the Church who took the initiative; and this time the lords were little more than the Church's strong arm.

These enterprises, near or far, were carried out in the name of the Cross. They are known to history as the Crusades. There is a tendency, however, to reserve this title for the expeditions that had as object the deliverance of the Holy Places. In point of fact, Rome set herself to organize Crusades of quite a different kind, her intention being to use them for the purpose of imposing her discipline and propagating the faith. The war against the Albigensian heretics was really a Crusade preached by order of the Pope. So was the campaign in which the chivalry of France hastened to the help of Spanish Christians threatened by the Moors, an undertaking that ended in the foundation of Portugal in the interests of a Burgundian dynasty. A Crusade, too, was the capture of Sicily from the Moslems by the men of Coutances, and, at an earlier date, the Norman assault on England.

The Duke of Normandy, William the Bastard, had claimed succession to the English throne. The Pope had excommunicated the English King, made common cause with William, and given him a consecrated standard and a ring containing one of Saint Peter's hairs. For this holy war, adventurers from all parts—Bretons and Burgundians and men from Aquitaine—had taken service with the Normans 1066 in return for promises of booty. Fourteen hundred sailing ships put sixty thousand troops ashore on the island. Their equipment was superior to that of the defenders. William's knights and bowmen crushed the Saxon infantry, whose armament consisted of little more than axes. Nor did they know anything of the art of building castles. London was taken. William, now the Conqueror, seized the English crown, expelled the Saxon clergy, rewarded his followers with gifts of land, and turned them into the new nobility of England. A French dynasty was installed in London, and the French tongue became throughout the island the language of the court and of the law.

This victory may have increased French prestige, but it very soon proved itself to be a thorn in the side of the French King. His Norman vassal had been crowned at Westminster, and though for the moment England had become a Norman colony, it was soon obvious that the roles might be reversed, and Normandy become an English dependency.

The situation was worsened by a number of feudal marriages. Maine and Brittany, Anjou and Touraine, then Aquitaine and the provinces of the Massif Central fell into the hands of the English King, who was also Duke of Normandy. The French empire of the Plantagenets was twice the size of the Capetian realm. It stretched unbroken from the Somme to the Pyrenees and, closing all outlets to the Atlantic, was in a position to stifle the Kingdom of France.

It was but natural that the Capetians should fight to free themselves from this asphyxiating pressure. For them it was a matter of life and death. They could not even rely upon the loyalty of the inhabitants of the occupied provinces. No tide of national feeling drove the Frenchmen of the west to rebel. These feudal quarrels left them unmoved, nor was there any reason why the English suzerainty should be a cause of outrage, since, after all, the Anglo-Norman King was no whit less a Frenchman than the King of France. What would have happened if the Plantagenets had finally carried the day against the Capetians? One may play variations forever on the theme of what never happened. A Franco-English fusion under a common scepter would no doubt have turned to the profit of France, which was the more highly civilized of the two countries and had a larger population. But history cannot be changed by hypotheses.

In spite of appearances, it was the Capetians who held the trump cards. Their power was firmly based, whereas the English dynasty was fragile. There was a considerable risk that it might be still further weakened owing to the fact that, by English law, women might succeed to the throne. Barons and clergy alike did all they could to undermine the royal authority. In short, one after the other the provinces of the west returned to the French allegiance. Philippe Auguste recovered Rouen, Tours, and Angers. Philippe le Bel

1152 reconquered Angoulême. In the French body politic only one open wound remained: Aquitaine. Bordeaux, which a Princess had brought in dowry to an English King, remained for many years to come a British trading-center. Such a situation was heavy with possible consequences. Would the King in Paris acquiesce in this foreign intrusion? Would the King in London remain permanently content to be the French King's vassal and to swear fealty to him? The feudal system, faced by such a problem, looked like sheer lunacy. Something, some time, was bound to go wrong.

For all of one hundred years wars between France and England had become more or less the rule. Wedded to a policy that was never to vary during the centuries to come, England was contriving incessant coalitions on the Continent, all of them directed against the power of France. She was already turning to account the passions of the Germanic races, and the Germans were only too ready to answer the call of the west. Already the plains of Flanders, the natural thoroughfare of every European invasion, were well on the way to becoming the cockpit of the Continent.

At Bouvines, Philippe Auguste, with twenty-five thou-

1214 sand French knights, shattered the onward march of Anglo-German armies three times as strong. Paris went wild with

1217 joy over this first great victory of the national forces, and acclaimed the King. Next, the French landed in England and agreed to return home only after the payment of a war indemnity. But neither Bouvines nor the expedition that followed it could resolve a problem that was by its very nature insoluble.

Expansion in the East

The Crusades proper had the Orient as their objective.
Those who took part in them wore a large cross woven on
the shoulder. Their purpose was to deliver the Holy Sepul-
cher, long profaned by the Moslems. It mattered little that
Turks had succeeded Arabs, or that soon Egyptians would
drive out Turks. Whatever the enemy's name, he remained
the "infidel." Having endured the holy war of Islam,
Christendom was ready now to switch to the offensive.

The initiative in this matter of the Crusades was taken
by the Church, and all Europe combined to carry them   **1095**
through. Primarily they were a French adventure. Pope
Urban II, who first summoned the West to arms, had been
a Cluniac monk. It was from Clermont-Ferrand that he
launched his manifesto, and it was the French who answered it. The bulk of the forces enrolled consisted of
French knights. The Orientals were never in any doubt of
this, and used the name "Franks" to include all Crusaders,
no matter what their nation.

The First Crusade consisted of no more than a mob of un-
disciplined fanatics, who pillaged, and got themselves killed,   **1096**
in the name of Christ. But the army of feudal barons which
followed on its heels was more fortunate. They caught the
Moslems when the latter were disorganized by internal
strife, took Jerusalem, and set up four governments: the
Kingdom of Jerusalem, the Principality of Antioch, and the
two counties of Edessa and Tripoli. For close on two centuries French dynasties ruled in Syria.

But their position was weak in the extreme. The Christians occupied no more than a coastal strip. The Moslems
were on every side and constituted a permanent threat.
When Edessa fell a second Crusade had to be dispatched,   **1187**
and when Jerusalem succumbed, a third. The Kingdom of
Jerusalem was now no more than the Kingdom of Saint-

Jean-d'Acre. Crusade followed Crusade in a vain endeavor
1204   to recover the Holy Places. On their way to Palestine the
knights turned aside. One body wandered aimlessly to Con-
1217   stantinople, where they forced the Greek emperors to give
way to Latin emperors. Another sought in Cairo the keys to
Jerusalem. It was no longer faith alone that pointed the
way. The Crusaders were not fighting now for religion, but
in the hope of winning fiefs and amassing booty. They
thought less of God than of trade. They colonized; they
bought and sold. In the long run, instead of driving Islam
out, they came to terms with it. The great adventure ended
in alliances and compromises and mutual tolerances. The
two religions shared the same buildings. Allah and Mohammed were acknowledged in return for spices and cotton
goods. The holy war had turned into a financial enterprise.

But the financial enterprise, too, ended in failure. The
Crusaders by losing their ideal had lost their unity. They
squabbled between themselves under the very noses of the
infidels. First it was the barons at loggerheads for local lord-
ships; then sovereigns at odds beneath the walls of Jerusa-
1191   lem. Philippe Auguste, who had more important work to do
in France, abandoned the English Richard Cœur de Lion.
The Germans of Frederick II turned their arms against the
French knights, who at long last drove them off. Orders of
warrior monks, founded in the Levant, attacked one an-
1261   other—Hospitalers against Templars. The Genoese restored
the Greek emperors at Constantinople at the expense of
their Latin rivals, whom the Venetians supported. The
brawling stopped at last only when the Turks and Mame-
lukes gained the day. They succeeded in patching up the
quarrels of the Westerners by the simple expedient of turning the whole lot of them out.

The sum total of the movement was that the French succeeded in establishing footholds, making contacts, and gain-

ing a lasting prestige throughout the Levant. If the Crusades, on balance, ended with a setback for the Church, they were rich in consequences, both political and economic. French culture, bursting from the old constriction of its national frontiers, swept over the East. The soldiers of Europe took with them their manners, their fashions, their codes of behavior. Saint Louis went on two of the Crusades in person, and this quite improbable monarch managed to accumulate a store of military disasters and moral victories. He was defeated in Egypt; he was taken prisoner, and later   **1252** released on payment of an enormous ransom; he lived for four years in Syria and left behind him the memory of incomparable virtues. Then, eager to strike at Islam where it could most easily be reached, this crowned and sceptered saint landed at Tunis, and died in Carthage of the plague.   **1270** In this way it came about that the whole of the Mediterranean area bore the marks of the later Crusades, which were, all of them, exclusively French.

There had never been any question of providing the French colonies with settlers. At Jerusalem, Godefroy de   **1100** Bouillon had with him a company of three hundred knights, and no more. There was no mass emigration. The French and the armies of the West supplied no more than nucleus establishments to the Levant, barons and monks; but that was enough to ensure that a French imprint would be left upon it.

In France itself the Capetians managed to turn the Crusades to account. Except for Philippe Auguste, who was ab-   **1191** sent for just a year, and Saint Louis, who followed the beckoning finger of his faith, they all preferred to stay within the kingdom and draw advantage from the departure of the feudal lords. And in this matter they were in luck's way! The most turbulent of the barons took wing, either because the Pope had promised remission of sins to all who took

part in his holy war, or because the bait of new lands to be
won and easy booty to be accumulated drew them from
afar. The cause of internal unity was the gainer.

The cost of armament and traveling was borne by the
Crusaders themselves, and often, in order to obtain the
1100   necessary resources, they were compelled to sell their lands
or to give them as securities for loans. Bourges, for instance,
was ceded to the King by a lord who took the road to the
Holy Places. Those who returned were, by definition, those
who had failed, and they too had to borrow or sell. The absent were always the losers, and those who came back were
not necessarily the winners. The true winners were those
who had never budged—the kings who gathered in the fiefs,
the burgesses who gained their civic freedoms.

The Crusades stimulated French unity in yet another
way. They had recruited and mingled men from *oïl* and *oc*,
men from the north and men from the south, vassals alike
of the kingdom and the Empire, Auvergnats and Burgundians, soldiers from Aquitaine and Champagne, Flemings
and Provençals. As a consequence the frontiers set up by the
Treaty of Verdun were broken down, and the way was made
smooth for the brotherhood of Frenchmen.

The Monetary Revolution

By gaining a foothold in the eastern Mediterranean and
blasting a hole in Islam's Iron Curtain, the Crusaders restored the contacts that had once existed between the
nearer Levant and the Far East. They—which is as much as
to say, the West in general—had access to the silks of Tyre
and Antioch and Tripoli; to the oil and sugar-cane, the
oranges, lemons, and figs of the Lebanon, the carpets of
Damascus. Theirs for the asking were the muslins of Mosul,
the dates of Arabia, the spices of the tropic seas—pepper,
nutmeg, cloves, and cinnamon—musk from Tibet and per-

fumes from the Indies, balm, camphor, sandalwood, as well
as the silks and incense of China, ivory and precious stones,
and all the many dyes for staining textiles—indigo, saffron,
redwood, lac. What did they sell in return? At first very
little: salt, fish, furs, wood, iron ore and wrought metal,
weapons of war. But a day came when they could offer what
was commonly known as Flanders cloth, but should be described, more accurately, as the incomparable woolen goods
of Artois. And since only the Western peoples transported
merchandise across the Mediterranean, whether going or
coming, the profits of the carrying trade were all for them.
It was in this way that the cities of Italy and Catalonia grew
rich, and not only they, but Marseille and Montpellier as
well. Europe's balance of payments, which in the eleventh
century had shown a loss, drew level in the twelfth, and in
the thirteenth was on the right side. As a result the West,
rapidly accumulating wealth, began to import the precious
metals and rediscovered what had been unknown since the
heyday of the Roman Empire—gold.

The King of France resumed the minting of coin, lagging
in this, though only slightly, behind Sicily, Florence, and   **1266**
Venice. To Saint Louis goes the glory of having been the
first to issue the *denier à l'écu*. This monetary revolution
was pregnant with consequences, for the great feudatories
had never managed to arrogate to themselves the right to do
more than mint silver pieces. Now, at a blow, they found
that they were in a position of inferiority to the central
power. The king's money, which circulated freely through
the country, was bound, sooner or later, to drive out the
barons' money, which was legal tender only within the confines of the various fiefs. This meant a serious setback for
the whole feudal system.

But, attractive though the king's money was, it lacked
stability. From century to century and reign to reign it fell
almost continuously in value. The reason for this was that

the State, in the absence of any genuine system of taxation, was without regular resources and had to do its best to defray the cost of national unity by way of devaluation. Each province conquered meant a little less metal in the coinage. This explains how it came about that the more efficient the king, the more did he have to debase the currency, and that only the peace-loving monarchs who followed in the footsteps of Saint Louis could allow themselves the luxury of a stable currency.

At this period the unit of account was quite distinct from currency used in cash payments. For accounting purposes, men reckoned in livres, sous, and deniers (the livre being worth 20 sous or 240 deniers). Cash transactions, on the other hand, were carried out in an enormous variety of coins, all of different weights and face values—*gros*, *mailles*, *écus*, *agnels*. This system made possible a relative stability of prices expressed in units of account. All that changed was the quantity and quality of the actual money in the housewife's slender purse. Roughly speaking, in the course of the three centuries that covered the reign of the Capetians of the direct line, the royal money became three times lighter, and the livre of Tours, which was an accounting unit, was finally the equivalent of only 77 grams of silver, or 5.63 of gold. All that history has recorded of this progressive debasement is the unfair legend that Philippe le Bel was a "coiner" king. It is true that, unlike his ancestor Saint Louis, he did manipulate the currency in every conceivable way. But public opinion was aroused only when, as the result of an excessive revaluation, the debtor found himself in difficulties. Philippe le Bel had to face a movement of popular disaffection only because the money he had "coined" was too good. Slander has turned the facts upside down.

The fact remains that Philippe, having first *devalued*, was foolish enough to embark on a policy of *revaluation*. Currencies are no more capable of flowing uphill than are rivers.

1329

1306

It is their natural tendency to drop to a lower level. Devaluation enabled the peasants to free themselves from a load of debt, and it was because of the enormous increase and variety of coins as a result of the flood of new metal that trade was in a position to revive and a wage system once more to come into existence.

Thus it was that the monetary revolution marched side by side with another revolution, which was both economic and social.

The Economic Revolution

The West had found in the East new products that changed its whole way of life. Gone was the tasteless food of the barbarous ages, the narrow uniformity of the feudal centuries. New crops were being raised in the southern districts of France—rice and buckwheat, as well as the apricot, the orange, the lemon, and the saffron. Cotton had been discovered, though as yet no great use was being made of it. But the marvel of marvels was silk. Men were beginning to acclimatize the mulberry tree, on which the silkworm lives. Sugar was beginning to take the place of honey, and paper was replacing parchment. The world was learning comfort, and dreaming of luxury.

At about the same time, certain innovations were completely altering the economic structure. The whole technique of transport, for instance, was undergoing change. The magnetic needle, imported from China, and the invention of the tiller were revolutionizing navigation. It was possible now to build bigger ships and so open vaster horizons. On land, the horse's power of endurance had been increased by the use of the iron shoe, and his pulling-power much improved by a new type of harness. From the beginning of time the strain had been designed to fall upon his neck, and this had produced strangulation. The new system

transferred the weight to his shoulders. The rigid halter increased the draft-power of the horse six times. Teams were
no longer arranged abreast, but tandem-wise, and a pair
thus harnessed could draw a load fourteen times heavier
than they could have managed under the old system. Formerly they had been used almost entirely for riding and pack-
saddle work, but now they could shift a much greater mass
of freight. By thus conquering the horse, man had provided
himself with the most useful of helpers.

New means of payment, new outlets for trade, new products, and new motive power—in these things lay the secret
of prosperity. Agriculture, industry, commerce, and banking
had come to a new birth. It was as though everywhere life
was exploding with the forces of its pent-up vigor.

Farming was now on a greater scale and better conducted
than ever before—better conducted because the soil was being enriched by the introduction of new crops. The acreage
of grassland was much increased, and more livestock was
being bred. The windmill brought much-needed help to
the miller. The cultivation of the vine was being extended.
The English, for whom wine was a luxury, did all they could
to develop the vineyards of Gascony, whence came the Bordeaux vintages. In Burgundy a farmer leased for ten sous
a few hectares of plowland "on condition that he planted
vines," and in this way Clos Vougeot was born. Everywhere
forests were falling to the ax. Heathlands were brought under cultivation, marshlands were drained—for instance, in
Poitou. Causeways were built in the valley of the Loire to
save the fields from flooding, and all along the coast of
Picardy dikes were constructed to keep the sea at bay. The
whole map of France was, as it were, in flux.

Industry was conducted, for the most part, on a craft
basis. But already certain regions were breaking loose from
the old closed economy, and specializing. The first papermills were set up in Languedoc. In the valleys of the Pyre-

nees ironworks prospered, arming the Crusaders, equipping the knights. In the north, first in Artois, later in Flanders and Brabant, wool from England was being spun and woven. Lille, Douai, Cambrai were the first centers of industry on a grand scale.

As a result of this division of labor and of expanding markets, trade flourished. Traffic arteries within the frontiers were restored. Roads were remade, if not with the old Roman paving, at least with pounded chalk. Such were the highways that filled the country with new place-names— Cauchy and Chaussade. Bridges were built—the famous bridge of Avignon, Pont-l'Évêque, Pont-Audemer, and Pont-Saint-Esprit. Foodstuffs and manufactured articles circulated far and wide by road and river. Merchants—those middlemen who buy to sell again and who serve as intermediaries between producer and consumer—swarmed over the country after long centuries of absence. *Regrattiers* they were called, or hucksters, but soon *merciers*, or peddlers.

The frontiers were easily crossed, and this made for a rapid extension of foreign trade. The feudal age, in spite of its walls and tolls, was more liberal than we are inclined to think. The idea of customs dues, as between countries, was in its infancy, and currencies were interchangeable. Never had trade been more truly international.

The Crusades had bred in men a taste for taking risks. Trade followed in the footsteps of the warring barons. Marseille, Avignon, and Lyon equipped fleets that sailed to Egypt in search of fortunes for their owners. Montpellier concluded agreements with the dealers of the Levant. Narbonne and Arles became the clearing-houses for the spices that were endlessly in demand for cooking, for medicinal use, and for the making of wine. Saint-Jean-d'Acre became a trading-station for the Marseille merchants. Cyprus, where the house of Lusignan set up in business, supplied the Provençal ports. There were French businessmen in Alexandria.

On the Atlantic seaboard the wine trade brought wealth to all the scattered harbors from Bayonne to Bordeaux. La Rochelle and Nantes specialized in salt. Rouen supplied London with the wines of Burgundy. Dieppe was the center of the herring fisheries. Saint-Omer, until Bruges outclassed her, was the main outlet for wool.

Most of the trading was done at the fairs. These took place at different localities on the great highway that linked the cloth-producing districts with the seaboard towns importing spices from abroad. Flanders merchants and Italian businessmen met within the territories of the French isthmus. So long as the Saint-Gothard route remained impracticable, the north-south traffic was unable to make use of the Rhine and was diverted by way of the Great St. Bernard to the Rhone and the Seine. In Languedoc a regular fair was established at Beaucaire, and one at Le Lendit (not far from Paris). But it was Champagne, with its many fairs —at Troyes, Bar-sur-Aube, Provins, and Lagny—that became the main center of European trade. There goods were unloaded and sales made. There ledgers were balanced, debts settled in cash or carried forward on credit. And there, when business had been concluded, the bales were corded up once more and the traders separated. The four fairs of Champagne, working within the framework of this ritual, were so spaced as to cover between them the four seasons of the year, and each lasted for almost fifty days. Visiting foreigners were furnished with safe-conducts, and toll dues were waived on all consignments intended for the fairs. Just as the needs of the sea-borne trade in wines from Aquitaine produced the first rough sketch of a future maritime legal code, so were commercial rules and usages elaborated at the great exchange gatherings in Champagne. They were a magnet too for all the motley riffraff of the West. Drinking and rowdiness went hand in hand with trade.

Such a deal of complicated business could not be transacted without having recourse to banking and exchange operations. As the Church still set its face against the lending of money at interest, Jews undertook such matters. Driven from Lyon, they conducted their financial activities in Bordeaux, Montpellier—and elsewhere. Their only serious rivals were the Italians (known for convenience as "Lombards"), with whom business took precedence of Christian edicts. True heirs of the Greeks, and past masters in the manipulation of credit, they made of France their chosen field of speculation. A number of them settled down in Cahors. Grouped in trading companies, they dealt in all the complexities of commerce—wholesaling, insurance, the issuing of loans on security, and investment. On occasion they even acted as tax-collectors and controlled the financial operations of kings and barons. Like the Jews, when they were plundered of their wealth they built it up again with infinite patience. When they were turned out of the front door, they slipped in again by the back. They knew that they were indispensable.

Thus was capitalism reborn, which the barbarian invasions had destroyed along with capital. Bills of exchange and the operations of the clearing-houses set money briskly circulating. To the soil, which remained the basic source of wealth, now came to be added the earliest type of transferable security. The first joint-stock companies were floated for the exploitation of mills. There were dealings in ground-rents, in prisoners' ransoms, in legal fines and penalties. In all these new activities it was not the great lords who were the gainers. In order to keep themselves in arms and armor, in order to carry on their wars, they borrowed more often than they lent. It was the peasants and the town-dwellers who became the creditors. This turning of the tables was one of the aspects of the social revolution.

The Social Revolution

For as long as shortage of money had made a wage system impossible, for as long as four-legged animals had not replaced two-legged men as beasts of burden, slavery had been a necessity. Never, throughout the barbarian centuries, had money been regarded as a commodity. Any kind of traffic in capital had been forbidden. On the other hand, human beings (as though it were the most natural thing in the world) had regularly been used as merchandise, and the trade in men and women had been a generally accepted fact.

From the moment that capital became mobile, from the moment that a more practical type of harness had made a new form of energy easily available, slavery became an anachronism. It began to be seen as more advantageous to accept ransom for prisoners of war, and to use those members of the population who had been born serfs wherever manpower was needed, instead of keeping them bound to one piece of land without right of movement. A liberal economy had no use for these petrified, and often lazy, helpers. What it needed was a labor-pool that could be drawn upon when and where it was needed. Employers were now in a position to pay for work done and to reward initiative. If there was land to be cleared, the obvious way to go about the work was by freeing the serfs and giving them a piece of land (*rupture*) for which they paid rent. In this way the slave of yesterday became the tenant proprietor —the *rupturier*, or *roturier*, of tomorrow.

Just as the kings had urged the city communes to emancipate themselves from feudal bondage, so now they encouraged the enfranchisement of the serfs—though more readily on the fiefs of their vassals than on the royal domains. They even went so far as to claim moral sanction for the step. "Natural right ordains that every man should be born free"—so runs a proclamation issued by Louis X. More often their generosity was dictated by political or financial considerations. The freeing of serfs weakened the great lords, and the newly enfranchised were a source of income to the State as soon as they became taxpayers. Whether exercised in the interests of communities or of individuals, such freeings substituted for a system of slavery inherited from antiquity a new system in which farming for rent, and working for wages, took the first place. All that remained of the old feudal dominance were a few "rights," and even these were shorn of much of their importance by the new invention of rent (whether in money, kind, or services). A few of the new freedmen did, it is true, regret their ancient servitude, which had given them an assured livelihood without any corresponding responsibility. But most of them rejoiced in their liberty and were prepared to face the possibility of being less materially well off than they had been in the past.

But the "people" of the twelfth and thirteenth centuries were by no means poor. It may be true that the peasant's dwelling was still a rough-and-ready affair (though chimneys and tallow candles were becoming much more general), with thatched roof, daub and wattle walls, and timber frame. But against that must be set the fact that rents were low, and tending to become lower still. The clothing of the field-worker consisted of close-fitting trousers (*les chausses*), a tunic belted at the waist (*le bliaud*), and a cap tied under the chin (*le béguin*). At night he still slept naked on a mattress stuffed with chestnut leaves, but in the daytime he already had a linen shirt. Such early steps on the way to progress, taken in conjunction with an improvement in the quality of food, all gave evidence that life was coming to be less and less precarious.

In the cities comfort was increasing all the time. Mer-

chants and craftsmen swarmed in the urban centers, proud
of their emancipation and of their newly won privileges.
Each trade had its own quarter, as in the Arab *souk*. There
is still a rue de la Boucherie in Limoges, a rue des Tanneurs
in Amiens, a rue des Chaudronneries in Dijon. Paris has
its Pont au Change, its Quai des Orfèvres, its rue des Lombards, its rue de la Ferronnerie; Marseille its Cannebière
(where the makers of hemp ropes carried on their business);
Bordeau its rue Judaïque. Painted signs announced the nature of each shop: Au Chat qui pêche; Au Plat d'Étain;
A la Poêle percée; Au Lion d'Or (by which we should understand *"au lit on dort"*). For the time being, only a few
streets were paved, only a few stone houses were rising above
the more modest buildings with their exposed timber fram-
ing. But the citizens were daily growing richer. They began
to follow the fashions, and wore the long-skirted tunic, and
later the short doublet. Fantastic modes, such as pointed
shoes with toes two feet long, and women's hennins almost
a yard in height, gave evidence of how easily the citizens
were adapting themselves to the new life of plenty.

The population of France was increasing. People from
the various provinces were intermingling more and more.
Consequently they were feeling it necessary to acquire a
more fixed identity than the mere use of their baptismal
names could give them. Of nicknames they made surnames,
and these became hereditary within the family. These might
derive from distorted Christian names (from Pierre: Péret,
Perrot, Piérard; from Nicolas: Colet, Colin, Colard, Collot,
Colson); or from some physical oddity (Calvet, bald;
Leroux or Rousseau; Lesourd, the deaf; Legrand); from
place of origin (Picard, Lescot, Dupont, Desgranges); from
occupation: the typical manual worker, *forgeron* (*faber* in
Latin, Schmidt in Germany, Smith in England), gives
Lefèvre in the north, Lefeuvre in Brittany, Fèvre in the
center, Faivre in Franche-Comté, Fèbre or Febreau in

Poitou, Favre in Charente, Fabre or Fabri in Provence, Faure in Guyenne.

But they were far from living sheltered lives, these Duponts and Lefèvres. In the countryside there was always the threat of local famine, in the cities of fire. Such dangers were unavoidable. But the life of every day was not too harsh. The purchasing power of the working population was rising, since prices increased less rapidly than wages.

High prices were the inevitable complement of a debased currency. In terms of the weight of precious metals they were actually falling (by twenty per cent between the beginning of the thirteenth century and the middle of the fourteenth), thanks to increased production. On the other hand, so great was the demand for labor that, in spite of a rising birth-rate, wages had risen. The humblest day-laborer in the reign of Saint Louis could earn the equivalent of eighty bushels of corn in the course of a year, which the numerous festivals of the Church reduced to 250 working days.

The conditions of the laboring population were the better in that its organization was not left to the mercy of employers. Trades were grouped in corporations—much like the old Gallo-Roman "colleges," though in addition they had many rules and regulations which may have been borrowed by the Crusaders from the corporations of the East. Fear of overproduction gave strength to these groupings, which were designed to protect producer and consumer alike. The apprentice became a journeyman, the journeyman might become a master, and a master might be elected head of his corporation (*juré, prudhomme, syndic,* or *capitoul*). There were many trade rules. Work at night and on Sundays was forbidden. The number of apprentices was limited, and the length of their apprenticeship fixed. The wages of a journeyman must not fall below a certain minimum. The regulations governing manufacture and sale were meticulously drafted. So rigid did this system very soon become that abuses were inevitable. For the time being, it provided a frame within which the newborn French economy could develop swiftly.

The Political Revolution

The master achievement of the Capetian dawn was the revival of the idea of the State. It grew up under the twin threats of the old feudal dominance and the new power of money.

Since the days of Rome the very idea of what the State was had vanished. The illusion bred of the bad Carolingian caricature had not long endured. The patient building carried out by the kings of the Capetian house had restored a true system of administration, which at the level of local politics was now strong enough either to oppose or to supplant the feudal authority, and, in the wider sphere of the nation, to establish the pre-eminence of the king.

At first, in the provinces, the kings could rely only on their stewards, whose duty it was to administer the royal domains, to render justice, and to maintain order. These officials were called *prévots*, or provosts. As the royal authority grew, new officials were added who took priority of the provosts. They were called magistrates (*baillis*) or seneschals (the name was interchangeable). Finally, at one step higher, came the *enquêteurs*, or commissioners. To avoid the danger of the *baillis* or seneschals themselves becoming feudal lords, they were forbidden to acquire land, and even to marry their sons and daughters without royal permission.

In Paris the chancellor was responsible for the legislative, the grand seneschal for the executive, authority. The king was surrounded by his twelve peers, who were the greatest of the feudal lords, only on the occasion of his coronation. For the rest of the time they were associated with the burgesses

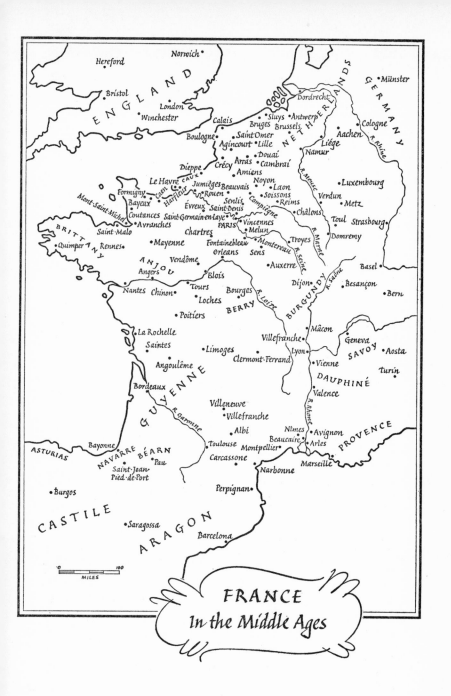

FRANCE
In the Middle Ages

who formed his council. The lawyers took precedence of the lords.

A time came when the council, overburdened with duties, had to split into special commissions. One of these, responsible for the administration of justice, took the name of Parlement. It was the highest court of the realm, accompanied the king wherever he went, and held its sessions at Orléans or Melun before finally fixing its headquarters in Paris, in the Île de la Cité. The second commission was styled the Grand Council. Its duties were purely political. The third, which looked after the national finances, took the title of the Chambre, or Cours, des Comptes.

For the newly revived State had, from now on, a true system of public finances—in other words, a budget and regularity of taxation. The budget, which was very much like that of any private householder, could still be regarded as modest: 45,500 livres in the days of Saint Louis for one whole Crusading year: 53,000 under Louis X. There was no civil service. Two hundred officials sufficed for the running of the central administration. The treasury derived its resources from the normal income of landed property—the profits of farms and forests. These were later swollen by "grants in aid" demanded from his subjects by the king for the maintenance of an army. Such "grants" took the form of irregular taxes, very inequitably levied. Even in those days the French regarded them with marked repugnance. All who could plead privilege or right did so in order to escape from having to pay them. Philippe le Bel had to discontinue the tax on sales of wine and corn, but tried to make the amount up by extorting a levy on incomes, amounting to a hundredth, and later to a fiftieth, part. Louis X devised a tax on salt, which became known as the *gabelle*. Those liable for taxation were on occasion called together in a special assembly, in the hope that they might be prevailed upon to consent to the demands made upon them. In this assembly

1251

1316

nobles, clergy, and commons were all represented. This was
the origin of the States-General. And so it was, by a process
of timid fumbling, that the outlines of a fiscal system took
shape.

Who was responsible for the royal treasure? The sovereigns, since they had no confidence in the security of their
own strongboxes, entrusted it for safekeeping, on current
account, to the most prosperous banking-house available—
the Order of the Templars, which had been founded in the
Levant and had established its "registered offices" in Jerusalem, using for the purpose a palace close to the ancient
Temple of Solomon. These Templars had at first been an
order of soldier monks, but had soon developed into an
organization of financiers. Many gifts and many legacies
had come their way, with the result that before long they
were the richest property-owners in the world. Sums on de-
posit, jewels, and precious metals flowed into their vaults,
which had the advantage of being situated in buildings that
were sanctified and therefore inviolable. In Paris the fortified keep in which they kept their treasure came to be
known as "le Temple." Throughout the West they lent
money at interest, in open defiance of the precepts of the
Church. The laws of God were not for the likes of them,
nor, for that matter, the laws of the kingdom, seeing that
when Philippe le Bel was at odds with Rome they sided
with the Pope. Was this, strictly speaking, treason on their   1307
part? Philippe was more inclined to show his power than
to indulge in argument. He had the Templars tortured and
burned, and a great part of their wealth "nationalized."
France, no doubt about it, was a State at last. From now on,
it was in the Louvre, the very stronghold of her kings, that
the royal money was stored.

In this way did the State emerge triumphant from its
struggle with the world of international finance, and it intended to do no less in its battle with the great landlords

within its own frontiers. These, in the security of their fiefs
and walled castles, were still forces to be reckoned with.
But they had lost something of their earlier arrogance. They
no longer had serfs and citizens at their command. They
had been compelled to accept the king's supremacy, to be
bound by his justice, to recognize his currency, to give up
their ancient privileges of banditry and private warfare.
Nothing of their former glory now remained but luxury.
They could command a numerous retinue of household
servants, in which jesters, doctors, and heralds rubbed
shoulders with grooms and men-at-arms. They possessed
rich wardrobes of gold brocades, suits of shining armor, and
large arsenals of weapons. But they were bored in their remote worlds of splendor, and whenever the opportunity
came their way of accepting posts in the royal household,
they gladly exchanged their independence for attendance
at court. Thus were the proud nobles tamed. Tamed?—
appearances are not seldom deceptive. When the king was
firm they bent the knee, but at the slightest sign of weakening they raised their heads. These feudal grandees, who
never ceased to mourn their ancient privileges, took advantage of every chance that came their way—even the misfortunes of their country—to win them back again.

France had become a State, but still she had no legal system. The old Roman law, rediscovered by the gentry of the
robe, might serve as a written code for all the south, but
the northern provinces were still entangled in three hundred and sixty customary rights. Centuries were still to pass
before Roman and common law could settle down in happy
married domesticity under the overruling authority of the
royal power. The rise of the house of Capet was accompanied by revolutions in the economic, the social, and the
political spheres, but not in the legal. All that showed there,
for the moment, was the shadowy beginning of slowly evolv-
ing change.

The Church and the Faith

In so far as it was a feudal institution the Church, too, had
entered on a period of decline. The more the Papacy aspired
to play a part in politics, the more at odds did it find itself
with the kings. Four of them it excommunicated, and for
a brief period placed the whole kingdom under an interdict.
But, outfronted by Philippe le Bel and compelled to leave
Rome for Avignon, the Holy See capitulated. Only in matters of faith did the Church maintain itself as a power without competitor.

Though in the temporal sphere Christianity might have
to withdraw before the forces of nationalism, as a spiritual
influence throughout the countries of the West it remained
supreme. Men believed with a fanatical ardor, venerating
the relics of the saints, the Blood and the Tears of Christ,
the Crown of Thorns, the fragments of the True Cross and
of the Holy Cradle. Witches were burned and heretics persecuted. But the highest proof of piety lay in the making of
pilgrimages.

Whether undertaking these journeys of their own free
will or as penitents, the pilgrims played a very large part in
the national life. They passed in an unbroken concourse
along the great roads. Those whose objective was Jerusalem
followed in the footsteps of the Crusaders. Others went to
Rome. The less adventurous contented themselves with visiting Saint-Martin-de-Tours. The majority took the route
that led either to Mont-Saint-Michel or to Galicia, whither
they traveled to worship at the tomb of Saint James.

Saint Michel (Michael) was, to some extent, the Christian successor of the Gallic Belen and the Roman Apollo,
and at times seemed almost to figure as the heir of Mercury.
Guardian angel and slayer of the dragon, he was the patron
saint of all the centuries of chivalry. Respect was paid to

him on inaccessible heights—the rocky needle of Le Puy,
and Mont-Tombe, soon to be renamed Mont-Saint-Michel.
On the road leading to this latter shrine the pilgrim from
the south would come on no less than seventeen "mounts"
dedicated to the saint before reaching the true end of his
journey, which lay on the very edge of the "dangerous sea."
Like children rummaging on the beach, the pilgrims would
gather cockleshells, and take them home as proof that they
had traveled to their goal. In this way the cockleshell became a sign, originally of return, but later, when a few
shrewd tradesmen took to making shells of lead, of departure. All the pilgrims acquired them, even, and especially,
those who were bound for Santiago de Compostella. In this
way the cockleshell from the bay of Mont-Saint-Michel was
transformed into the *coquille Saint-Jacques.*

The road to Santiago de Compostella became so famous
that it was called "the Road" and nothing more (*el Ca-
mino*). Staff in hand, and with the cockleshell as mark of
identification (perhaps, too, as a useful object to eat from),
the pilgrim—a new nomad—made the whole long journey
on foot. At many places along the route, gates and streets
of cities assumed the name of the saint—Porte-Saint-Jacques
(at Saint-Jean-Pied-de-Port) or rue Saint-Jacques (in Paris,
1327   as in Pau). At the beginning of the fourteenth century it
cost no more than nine or eleven livres to make the pilgrimage from Arras to Santiago.

The Church did more than merely organize these vast
movements of men and women. She maintained the roads,
built or repaired the bridges (there was an order of "*frères
Pontifes*"). She established a system of staging-posts and
hostels (there was another order of "*frères Hospitaliers*").
She set up shelters at difficult spots on the mountain passes
(at the Great St. Bernard, at Roncevaux, at Somport). She
issued a guide for the use of travelers which gave information about where drinking-water and sanctuaries could be

found. She guaranteed the safety of the pilgrims by issuing decrees making it an act of sacrilege to attack them, and by insisting that their baggage should be exempt from all toll dues.

It is true to say that the pilgrims blazed a trail for commerce. But that was far from being the only service the Church rendered to the economic life of the country. The abbeys were enthusiastic supporters of the great fairs—for instance, at Le Lendit, where prospective customers could venerate a nail from the True Cross and buy a "nail" of clove almost at one and the same moment. As landowners the monks were tireless in their endeavors to clear more ground for the plow. The monasteries, acting as bankers, advanced money to peasants who wanted to buy equipment and livestock. As educators they organized schools in which Latin was taught, so that in time the word *clerk* came to be almost identified with *scholar*. As tenders of the sick they increased the numbers of hospitals—*hôtels-Dieu* and "lazar-houses." The Church and the faith sanctified the whole of the calendar. Two great annual feasts—those of Saint Jean and Saint Michael—set the rhythm of the rural laborer's year, one marking the summer solstice, the other the autumnal equinox, ushering in the sowing and the harvest time, and serving as terms in all agricultural labor contracts. Lesser saints became the patrons of the smaller local fairs and, caught up in the popular vocabulary, gave their names to seasons and to weather cycles.

On the trade guilds religious fraternities were grafted, within which masters, journeymen, and apprentices met to do honor to their own especial saint—Saint Joseph for the carpenters, Saint Éloi (Eligius) for the goldsmiths, Saint Crispin for the cobblers, Saint Fiacre for the gardeners. These fraternities, enriched by subscriptions and professional dues, acted also as friendly societies, paying out sick-benefits to their members, and taking part, with banners flying, in the ceremonies of the different feast-days. Some of their rituals were a mixture of Christian and pagan, and foreshadowed the Masonic lodges of the future. The Church, fearful of seeing them break loose from her control, did not encourage such manifestations, and by five of the councils they were condemned. But they reflected the wishes of the common folk, and the monasteries—less rigorous in this than the councils—were, for the most part, on good terms with them.

These monasteries were now thickly sprinkled over the length and breadth of France. To the ancient Orders of Saint Benoît and Cluny new ones had been added—Cistercians, from Cîteaux, Franciscans, and Dominicans. Each order swarmed, spreading in much the same way as a multiple-branch business. Clairvaux, first founded by Saint Bernard, had eighteen hundred houses scattered over the world, Cluny two thousand, Cîteaux three thousand. The abbeys of Jumièges, of Saint-Wandrille, and of Mont-Saint-Michel were famous throughout the West.

It was about this time that France began to be covered with a pattern of new parishes, the patron saints of which were to give their names to future municipalities. Saint Saturnin, as the result of local variants, became Saint-Sorlin, Saint-Sernin, or Saint-Satur. Saint Benigne of Dijon was distorted into Saint-Blin or Saint-Bérain. From Saint Hilaire came Saint-Hélier or Saint-Chély; from Saint Maxime, Saint-Mesme; from Saint Ferréol, Saint-Fargeau; from Saint Cloud, Saint-Claude—while, as for Saint Étienne, Saint Pierre, and Saint Denis, they were everywhere! More than two hundred localities were destined to commemorate Saint Michel, and the places named after Saint Jean (John), especially in the southeast, are too numerous to mention. But the most popular saint of all, particularly in the west and southwest, was Saint Martin. In our own twentieth century there are 3,700 French churches dedicated to him,

1115

and 485 towns, villages, and hamlets which perpetuate his
memory.

But better than all these names, the superb monuments
of stone which civilization was beginning to put forth as her
visible buds of life and beauty began now to bear witness to
the fervor of faith.

The Budding Grove of Civilization

That the great cathedrals were born of faith there can be no
doubt. Nobles and commoners shoulder to shoulder dragged
the materials for these magnificent edifices, stone by stone,
from quarry to site. But such miracles of architecture would
have been inconceivable in the centuries of poverty and
chaos. They were the product not only of piety, but of peace
too, and of wealth.

It is not so much the supreme manifestations of Romanesque and Gothic that deserve attention as the thousands
of small country churches. From now on, the solidity of
their outlines, the thrust of their bell-towers, were to domi-
nate houses and fields and plowland, so that for a thousand
years the shape and pattern of the French village would be
unalterably fixed. High above townships and cities the stone
lacework of towers and turrets was to bear witness to man's
striving to draw near to heaven.

Romanesque. This was a squat version in stone of the
elementary timber constructions of the barbarian centuries.
The name comes from the fact that it attempted to revive
the achievements of Rome. The countries of the *oc* had
kept the secret of the Roman vault and, thanks to their
new wealth, had been able to employ it in their buildings.
Churches of one general type sprang up all along the
pilgrim route from Saint-Martin-de-Tours to Santiago de
Compostella, by way of Limoges, Conques, and Toulouse,
whence the influence of the school of Languedoc spread far

and wide. Each region adopted a style largely dictated by
prevailing influences and the types of stone easily available.
The pattern of Notre-Dame du Puy and the Auvergne
school, with its wealth of multicolored ornament, spread
as far as Clermont-Ferrand, Royat, Issoire, and Brioude.
1089 The monks of Cluny, who had built a church with five
clock-towers and over five hundred feet high (the largest in
Christendom until St. Peter's in Rome), provided a model
for all who wished to raise a house of God. Under their
tutelage emerged the Burgundian school, which left its
mark on Autun, on Vézelay and Paray-le-Monial. The Provençal school, which exerted an influence on Arles and its
neighborhood, was more severe, darker, more mysterious.
In Périgord domes made their appearance, inspired by the
example of Byzantium, in Cahors as well as in Périgueux.
The school of Poitou was responsible for the façades of
Bordeaux and Poitiers. Building in Normandy, with its
stress on lantern-towers, combined architecture with shipbuilding, naves having the lines of ocean-going vessels:
Rouen, Caen, Jumièges, Avranches—many variants, but one
single type expressing solid strength and calm forcefulness.

Gothic. After the solidity of the Romanesque a new style
of soaring perpendiculars took form which the Italians of
the Renaissance later called Gothic in mockery. Between
Romanesque and Gothic is all the difference between
prayer kneeling and prayer with arms stretched heaven-
ward. Gothic leaps frantically to the sky—a medley of pillars, arches, spires. It turns stone to lace—whittling, piercing, tapering, climbing higher and ever higher—a thing of
light and dizzy adventure.

Gothic was a French art, an art from the Île-de-France. It
began to flower on the morrow of Bouvines, in a world of
peace and prosperity. Everywhere the white cathedrals began to rise, poems in stone and painted glass, forming a
garland all about Paris and Saint-Denis—Meaux, Reims,

Laon, Senlis, Soissons, Noyon, Amiens, Rouen, Chartres, Bourges. . . .

The monasteries and their monks had financed the Romanesque, but it was the new municipalities, their bishops and their merchant princes, who found money for the splendors of the Gothic. City competed with city, each intent on raising the largest, tallest, loveliest cathedral to the glory of God and Our Lady. Architecture ran to excess, became outsize. A work begun needed more than a whole generation to bring it to completion, on so vast a scale was it often planned. It would be begun in one style and finished in another, or more often never finished at all. Sens is short of a tower, Strasbourg of a spire. The whole of the nave at Beauvais is missing.

But Gothic art was not confined to these colossal works of stone. It found expression in the smaller sanctuaries, such as the Saint-Chapelle, designed as a reliquary to contain the Crown of Thorns; in slender-columned cloisters, as at Mont-Saint-Michel; in jewels of secular construction, such as the Conciergerie in Paris, and all those belfries which served city watchmen as lookout towers and contained the bells to call the citizens together in times of trouble, material evidence of a new freedom; in walled castles, the Louvre, Coucy, Carcassonne, Aigues-Mortes; in deeply thrilling statuary, ranging from grimacing gargoyles to smiling angels and pensive Virgins; in carved woodwork, church stalls, and chests in private houses to serve the purpose of wardrobes and dressers, writing-desks, benches, and beds.

1245

Never has there been, never will there be, a civilization so sure of itself as the Gothic. Greatness was its intention, greatness and durability. America of the twentieth century, for all its feats in building, has not achieved a comparable solidity. The Egypt of the Pharaohs never ran riot in such extravagance of fancy. France, and France alone, of the twelfth and thirteenth centuries set herself to build in all

her provinces, well-nigh in all her hamlets, on the scale of
giants. To win so high a stake prodigious wealth had to be
set to serve the purpose of prodigious hope.

French Language and Literature

That science should lose its way in the pursuit of vain chi-
meras, should let itself be dazzled by the visions of astrologers
and alchemists, was the fault of an age of poets. But, even
so, the makers of horoscopes did at least learn something
about the heavens at which they gazed, and the alchemists,
dreaming of the philosophers' stone and the elixir of life,
did discover antimony, zinc, and phosphorus. In the matter
of transmuting gold they were born seven or eight centuries
too soon. In medieval medicine there was an element of fan-
tasy, but so has there been in the medicine of all ages. Al-
bertus Magnus maintained that amethysts could make a
man eloquent, that the emerald brought victory in battle.
Far sillier things have been said in more modern times.

The introduction of Arabic numerals, which aided calcu-
lation; the invention of optical lenses, which opened the
way to scientific research; the construction of a practical
compass, which made possible the exploration of our planet
—all these things went to show that the sterility of the barbarian darkness had finally vanished. For all that, it was not
in such positive contributions to knowledge that the true
glory of the Capetians lay. The age of which they mark the
dawn earned its lasting renown by giving birth to the
language and literature of France. The Romansh tongue,
henceforward to be known as French, not only overcame
the competition of the local dialects; it actually came to
challenge the predominance of Latin as a literary medium.

The earliest story-tellers were, in part, mountebanks. Poetry partook of trickery. The wandering minstrels who entertained the great lords in their castles were as deeply

skilled in sleight of hand as in the singing of songs. More
often than not they would begin their entertainment by
telling a fortune, but, that done, would go on to tell of the
fortunes of brave men. Minstrels and troubadours thus
spread about endless and anonymous tales in praise of im-
aginary heroes who had lived long years ago. They were the
wandering expounders of legend.

The true authors of these stories and poems are, for the
most part, unknown, for the simple reason that spoken literature does not announce its sources. Manuscripts were
few, and a mere scattering of copies of doubtful accuracy are
all that have come down to us, containing variants that
crept into the text as a result of the singer's efforts to bring
his material more or less into line with the modish requirements of the day.

The *Chanson de Roland*, built round a legend that first
took shape in the sanctuaries which dotted the pilgrim route   1110
to Santiago, and usually attributed to a certain Turolde,
had all the necessary elements: an epic subject, a soldier
hero without hint of weakness, a traitor duly punished. Such
a combination could not but delight the feudal lords in
love with gallantry, and the clerks who demanded only that
war should be made upon the Saracens. Long before the
Crusades Roland was a crusading knight, and, before France
was, a Frenchman.

For listeners who preferred to hear of love there was
Tristan and Iseult or the *Roman de la Rose*; for devotees of   1150
fabulous exploits, the cycle of the Round Table, with its
complicated pattern of doughty champions and wicked en-
chanters, of Christianity and fairyland. With audiences in   1200
love with serial narration the tales of chivalry were all the
rage. There were fables, too, with a moral lesson, and so
popular did the Renard cycle become that the name of its
protagonist was widely adopted. For the educated who
valued history above fiction, Villehardouin and Joinville,

who had been witnesses of, and actors in, the events they afterward described, produced chronicles of the Crusades. For the idlers who wanted only to be beguiled with a "show," the religious fraternities rediscovered the art of dramatic presentation and set the first mystery plays and moralities upon the boards.

The language in which the philosophers conducted their disputes, proving and disproving in strict syllogistic form, was Latin. The theologians of Christendom, one and all, wasted endless hours in the vain exercise of scholastic argument. In this sterile form of mental agility the great masters —Thomas Aquinas, the Italian; Duns Scotus, the Scot—all, with the exception of Roger Bacon, expended their energies. They studied and taught in Paris, the capital of knowledge.

The various colleges that grew ever more numerous in that city, and attracted young students from all over Europe, banded together into a corporation, to which Philippe Auguste granted certain privileges. In this way did the university come into being, under the protection of popes and kings. It gave degrees to bachelors, masters, and doctors who had attained the necessary skill in arguing the points of Aristotle's teaching and in drawing nice distinctions in the canon law. Theology was the special concern of a faculty established by Saint Louis's confessor, one Robert, born at Sorbon, near Rethel. This faculty later acquired the name of Sorbonne. There were as many as twenty thousand foreign students in Paris, all working in the "greatest school in the fairest city of the world."

Other French cities too had their universities: Toulouse, Montpellier, Orléans. The Benedictines of Saint-Benoît-sur-Loire, the very spot where fifteen centuries earlier the druids had gathered from all over Gaul, attracted to their halls of learning a crowd of students and the most distinguished masters. France had become the meeting-place of civilization.

1200

1253

The Influence of France

In every field—religion, politics, and trade—the influence of France was paramount. From her the West drew light and warmth.

Who, indeed, was in a position to surpass her? After the Turks, it was the Mongols' turn to swoop on Asia. But they could build nothing to compare with the Sainte-Chapelle. Byzantium was in decline, and lived in fear of the barbarian hordes. Russia, child of the Scandinavian venturers, had only just been born. Germany, except for brief periods when one or other of the emperors ruled with a strong hand, was a prey to her feudal barons. Spain was struggling to rid herself of the Arab canker. Two nations only could claim to rival France—Italy, whose mariners and bankers were invincible (but as yet she was no more than a confused pattern of jealous cities), and England, where the dawn of civil liberties was breaking, though as yet she was poor and the barons were in open warfare with their King.

There could be no doubt of it. France had pride of numbers, and the power of her sovereign was beyond contesting. Nor were her people confined within their frontiers, but were spreading all over Europe, and beyond. They ruled in Jerusalem, in Saint-Jean-de-Acre, in Constantinople, and in Cyprus. They had a Duchy of Athens, a Principality of the Morea, a Kingdom of Armenia. Their knights were installed at Rhodes, their merchants in Egypt. After the Norman chivalry, returning from the Holy Land, had made themselves masters, first of Sicily, then of Naples, a brother of Saint Louis mounted the throne of this new Kingdom of **1285** the Two Sicilies. True, these footholds were temporary only, and at no time did any of them give to the French king anything in the nature of a genuine colony. The feudal lords were working for their own ends, and not all of them were vassals of the Crown. But the influence of France benefited, finding in these scattered places agencies and markets for trade, and an area in which the language and the ways of France could be diffused.

French was spoken in Antioch and Palermo and at the English court. *"La parlure de France est commune à toutes gens,"* said Dante's master. Marco Polo wrote in French, and what tongue, if not French, was used by that Jean, the son of a merchant of Assisi, when he preached his sermons to the birds? Certainly he used the language of France, and that was why he was called Francis. Styles as well as words became articles of export. Romanesque architecture reached Saint-Jacques and Monreale, in the south; Durham and Lincoln, in the north; Worms and Speyer, in the east; Tortosa, in the Levant. Gothic art conquered the whole of Christendom, from Toledo and Milan to Nicosia, Cologne, Uppsala, and Canterbury. In Syria and Cyprus the mountain fortresses, with their double ring of walls and their flanking towers, were copied from the strongholds of France —Margat and Krak of the Knights—and tirelessly the glaziers of the Île-de-France and Champagne were supplying painted windows to the whole of Europe.

In these Christian centuries when faith was queen,
999 France had supplanted Rome, or made of her an appanage. The scholar Gerbert became the first French Pope, under the title of Sylvester II. When the emperors of Germany
1305 threatened the Holy See, it was in France that the popes sought refuge. From the reign of Philippe le Bel onward, all the pontiffs were French, and Avignon was their place
1309 of residence. The Church now held her general councils, no longer in Rome, nor in any of the Byzantine cities, but on the banks of the Rhone, at Lyon and Vienne, and thither gathered emperors and kings. Louis IX, the crowned saint, raised French prestige so high that he was asked to arbitrate in cases of disagreement, not only between the

barons and sovereigns of Europe, but even between Moslems, on whom his virtues had shed a great light.

When the Norman Pierre Dubois was drawing up a scheme for bringing the nations into an association under the ægis of France, the French were scarcely troubled in their dreams of peace by the distant rumble of Genghis Khan and his Mongol hordes. So distant seemed the threat that they were actually regarded as newcome allies against the forces of Islam. Saint Louis sent them gifts. Philippe le Bel honored the Mongol envoy with a visit to the Sainte-Chapelle—as though the allurements of Paris were all that was needed to civilize the nomads.

Paris, the capital of the princes of the house of Capet, was the queen of cities. Philippe Auguste paved her streets, and gave her a protecting wall equipped with five hundred towers and pierced by thirteen gates. But soon the capital grew too big in its young exuberance to be thus contained. Under Philippe Auguste its inhabitants numbered 120,000, and one hundred years later, when the direct Capetian line came to an end, 250,000. It was a city of work and also, even in those days, a city of pleasure. The whole world dreamed of Paris.

All France had its share in this expansion. Its population, which had fallen to 10,000,000, doubled itself in three centuries. A tax survey of the royal domain settled the number of parishes at 23,800, with 2,470,000 separate houses. This, allowing five persons to each house, gives a total of 12,000,000 persons. But in addition there were several counties (Blois, Bar, Rethel, Nevers), a number of appanages (Artois, the Bourbonnais, Évreux, Alençon), and the four great fiefs (Brittany, Flanders, Burgundy, and Aquitaine). The kingdom as a whole must have contained 32,000 parishes, with 3,300,000 separate houses—that is to say, 16,000,000 or 17,000,000 persons. If one adds to this total

1328

the French-speaking parts of the Empire (Lorraine) and
the districts ultimately destined to be included within the
frontiers—Provence, Dauphiné, Savoy, Alsace, Navarre—the
sum total amounts to 23,000,000 or 24,000,000. The France
of this age, if account be taken of the means of production
on which it could rely, was heavily populated, and this fact
explains the ease and readiness with which it spilled over
into the whole of the Mediterranean area.

The frontiers of the kingdom had changed scarcely at all
since the Treaty of Verdun. They followed roughly the
courses of the Escaut, the Upper Meuse, the Saône, and
the Rhone. They were too close to the capital for comfort.
Paris was unpleasantly vulnerable. But the country was
prosperous. The people had emerged from long centuries of
poverty and were living well. The domain had been wid-
ened and consolidated. The central power was respected.
France had established herself as the leading nation of the
world. Such were the main items of the Capetian balance-
sheet. On the whole, the results were not bad.

CHAPTER IV

TWO ECLIPSES

(1328–1589)

England versus France

SCARCELY had the direct Capet line come to an end when a threatening thunder-cloud began to lower over the stripling kingdom. France was too rich not to arouse envy. One after another her neighbors put her into a position of the direst peril. First of all, she had to take her stand against her northern one, the island of Britain; then against Spain, in the south. On each occasion the invader found sympathizers in the French camp, and the foreign war was complicated by civil strife no less dangerous. To these two crises, in the course of which the very existence of the country was at stake, correspond two eclipses involving the monarchy and the prestige of France.

In the first of these dramas the principal part was played by England, which had grown up sufficiently to have designs upon the Continent. More than once already English and French had come to blows since the day when William the Norman had landed on the island, and the Plantagenets had later acquired the fief of Aquitaine. Occasions of conflict had not been lacking. The time for a final showdown was approaching. To all appearances, France was the stronger. In wealth, in size of population, in military strength, she outclassed her adversary. But appearances were deceptive. England made up for her initial inferiority by better organization, by superior technique, and by her alliances.

There were signs that the wealth of France was diminishing. Flanders had lost its monopoly of the textile trade to the advantage of Brabant, which belonged to the Empire. The opening of the Saint-Gothard Pass had shortened the distance from Flanders to Italy. The direct route now lay down the Rhine, via Strasbourg and Frankfurt, with the result that the fairs of Champagne were losing much of their custom. The Rhenish highway, too, was soon to be in competition with the Atlantic sea routes, along which the Genoese and Venetian galleys set sail for Bruges.

1277

The king of France lacked the monetary resources for staging a long-drawn-out conflict. The French were even then, as they always would be, bad taxpayers. Whereas England levied payments on the export of wool and hides, whereas the English House of Commons voted a tax amounting to a tenth or a fifteenth on incomes, the King of France was compelled to beg for aid, which the States granted with a niggardly hand. All who could do so claimed exemptions or reductions. No doubt in the long run the English taxpayers, too, grew tired of paying, and two of their kings went bankrupt when faced by the demands of creditors. But, in the absence of any regular or permanent fiscal system, the French king was always in a worse position than his rival for financing a war.

That was why England, though possessing only a third of the population of France (five or six million), was better able to recruit mercenaries and to purchase allies. She enrolled soldiers of the Empire at a high cost in the Low Countries. She numbered on her pay-roll contingents of Gascon adventurers—as good fighting men as she could wish for. She bought herself friends from among the German princes or the militiamen of Flanders, in the Hanseatic towns or as far afield as Aragon.

In the art of war, too, England was many generations in advance of the French, who were still bogged down in the romantic conceptions of the age of chivalry. She had instituted a form of compulsory service at a time when the French knight fought only within the contractual limits of his duty as a vassal and according to the rules of an outworn convention. The English infantry was a disciplined force, and could make a good showing against horsemen who sought out only opportunities for single combat.

Finally, the English were better armed. Against the Genoese auxiliaries of the French, who used the heavy, slow-firing crossbow, they could rely on the longbow, which was capable of putting ten or twelve arrows into the air each minute, and had a longer range (more than two hundred yards). In this way they were able to kill with impunity the chargers of the French feudal cavalry and capture their unhorsed riders. With their bombards, in which they used a powder brought from China, they made an appalling din, which was quite out of place in any battle fought according to the rules of the courtly tournament. They were common fellows who knew nothing of good manners.

Victories do not always depend on numbers. If the wars of this period brought nations face to face, the actual combats involved only a few thousand men. A hundred or so horsemen could ravage a province, and a garrison of less than ten thousand would suffice to occupy half of France. How, in the absence of any sure source of revenue, was it possible to equip, feed, and pay larger forces? Fighting took place only during the fine days of summer. In winter the combatants went home. War was still a small-scale affair, though great interests might hang upon its issue.

An Outline of French History

The Quarrels

The major point at issue, the prime motive of the quarrel, was the fief of Bordeaux, to which the English clung because it supplied them with wine, and which the French would not abandon. In the language of the south (the *langue d'oc*) it was called Aquitaine; in that of the north (the *langue d'oïl*), Guyenne. The word was the same, and so was the problem.

The Plantagenets had acquired it as a marriage portion, and Saint Louis, with simple-minded generosity, had confirmed them in their rights. But if they were masters there, it was only as vassals of the French Crown. Such an anomalous situation could not continue. London wished to be unquestioned ruler in Bordeaux, while Paris insisted on subordination to herself. The English kings tried every trick, including illness, to avoid paying homage. The French kings employed every wile, including confiscation, to impose it. England nibbled away her feudal dues: France nibbled at the territories of Aquitaine. One or the other would have to give way.

Guyenne might be one of the main sources of supply for the English market, but Flanders, another French fief, was one of its best customers. The island bred sheep and sold their wool to the Flemish weavers. The English treasury lived off the tax on the sale of wool. Thus, while the Count of Flanders was dependent on the French king, the Flemish merchants were no less dependent on the English exporters. 1337 A day came when London, in order to strike a blow at Paris, forbade the sale of wool to Flanders and sent it instead to Brabant by way of Dordrecht and Antwerp. The Flemish workers found themselves unemployed, and Bruges tottered. "Work and Liberty!" shouted the Flemish mobs, inflamed against their suzerain by English agitators. The island race

had only to reopen the wool trade to be sure of the support
of the Low Countries.

But that was not all. In addition to the quarrel about
Aquitaine and the quarrel about Flanders, there was a third
quarrel, about Brittany. Ostensibly it centered in the question of succession to the duchy, for which each of the two
monarchs had a claimant. The Breton harbors served as
ports of call for the Gascon sailors carrying wine to island
tables and salt to island fishermen. England put garrisons
into Brittany, and these secured bridgeheads for many ma-   **1341**
rauding expeditions through the lands of France.

In this way did feudal intriguers and commercial money-
grabbers play into each other's hands. War was inevitable.
All that remained now was to conclude the final alliances,
and they too brought the struggle still nearer by making
each of the antagonists feel that he was being encircled.
France had friends in Castile, and could rely on the popes
in Avignon. She supported the Scots against the English,
who reacted by building up large Continental coalitions—
the Low Countries, the Rhineland, Burgundy, Savoy, and
the Kingdom of Arles. These appeared to threaten the
whole length of the frontier.

Twenty thousand English landed at Antwerp and, their
ranks swollen by Flemish reinforcements, made Brussels   **1340**
their point of concentration. On the Dutch coast, off Sluys
(Écluse), an English fleet surprised and destroyed a French
one. For a long time the islanders were masters of the sea.
They could disembark their men where and when they
wished. War broke out. It was to last for centuries: a hundred years, according to popular belief; a hundred and sixteen, by strict chronology, if the preliminary stages be taken
into consideration; a hundred and fifty if we consider the
direct consequences; two hundred and twenty-one if we
reckon its duration to the liberation of Calais; four hundred

and seventy-eight if, from crisis to crisis, we pursue the long tale of national hatred unassuaged, and of flames constantly rekindled, until an end was reached at Waterloo.

The Valois

Had the kings of the direct Capetian line continued, Bouvines would, without a doubt, have been repeated. But with the Valois, France was fated to be unfortunate.

To pass from one branch to the other of a ruling family **1316** presents a serious problem. Already, after the death of the eldest son of Philippe le Bel, the question had arisen whether, in the absence of a male heir, the crown should descend to a granddaughter or to Philippe's second son. Except in the Empire and in the Holy See, both of which claimed to continue Rome, women could everywhere ascend the throne: in England and in Scotland, in Sicily, in Portugal, in Castile, in Navarre, in Aragon, in Poland, and in Hungary. By what right should France be administered according to the tradition of Rome? The answer to that question was quite simple: because France, too, regarded herself **1316** in duty bound to continue the Roman system. So now the crown passed, first to the second, then to the third, of **1322** Philippe's sons. The tradition was formally established. The Kingdom of France announced itself as different from, and superior to, all other kingdoms.

But when the third of three royal brothers died, the same problem arose in a different form. Women, it was agreed, could not rule, but could they transmit the right to rule? The barons of France, meeting in the Forest of Vincennes, answered the question in the negative, and chose as their King the first cousin in the direct line of the sovereigns of the house of Capet—Philippe of Valois, who mounted the throne as Philippe VI.

But Edward III of England held different views. By his

mother he was the grandson of Philippe le Bel, and nephew to the three dead brothers. Why should not he inherit? The common law, in so far as it affected successions, was on his side. Against him was merely the French dislike of treating the kingdom as though it were an ordinary family inheritance, a dislike that the lawyers dressed up in the pompous trimmings of the Salic law. He protested, at least for form's sake, against the enthronement of the new Philippe. When the Valois harassed him in his fief of Guyenne, he countered by having himself proclaimed King of England and of France. It matters little whether he believed in the   1340 soundness of this claim. All is fair in war. Anticipating a happy issue, he had a crown prepared for his coming coronation.

Thus was a dynastic squabble added to the other causes of disagreement between France and England. For the Plantagenets it may have been little more than a pretext. For the Lancastrians of the younger branch, their successors, it became the principal *casus belli*. The French were in an extremely difficult position. It was still necessary to decide where the right lay, and only victory could do that. Once the fight was won, it would be easy enough to know who had the law on his side. For the moment a certain amount of hesitation was but natural. Who was the loyalist, who the traitor? Only the victor would be in a position to describe as traitors those who had fought against him.

Had it been merely a question of a French king on one side and a foreign king on the other, there would have been little room for doubt. But the Plantagenets and the Valois were both alike descended from Saint Louis. Both spoke French and both observed French customs. How was it possible to choose between the Comte de Valois and the Duc de Guyenne? The real danger for the French was that the English King did not, seemingly, appear to be a danger at all.

The Valois, in the event, turned out to be dangerous kings, but only very rarely men with statesmanlike qualities. Fine horsemen, free-handed in giving generously of their strength and of the strength of their subjects, mighty spenders, men in love with feasts and with luxury—that summed them up. Where now were the old Capetian monarchs, avaricious, sordid, but efficient? Philippe VI was happy-go-lucky. Jean II (le Bon) was a man of daring who went through life as though it were a tournament.

Charles V was to benefit from the fact that his nickname, "the Wise," is ambiguous (the word *sage, sapiens,* means actually a man of scholarship, not sense) and from a legend that his first biographer, Christina of Pisa, built round him. The fact remains that as heir to the throne he was distinguished chiefly for cowardice and faulty judgment, and that the only reason why he managed to reign at all was that the English had most of their attention taken up by domestic troubles. This "wise" King was far fonder of gold plate than of his subjects' welfare. From sheer incapacity he lost the support of the popes when they returned to Rome, and had to set up a pope of his own in Avignon in order to offset their hostility. So stupid was he that, on his deathbed, he suppressed all direct taxation, which meant cutting off supplies from his successors and ensuring their defeat. Neither Charles VI nor the Dauphin, Charles VII, were much of an improvement. Both of them preferred the pleasures of power to its responsibilities. These Valois were, on the whole, a poor lot.

Not that their reigns were persistently sterile. The kingdom was enlarged by the addition of Montpellier, first confiscated, then bought, from the King of Majorca, and of Dauphiné, which was ceded in return for a promise that the eldest son of the sovereign should thereafter bear the title of Dauphin. Provence, too, fell to the share of the Valois kings, who, as a result, ceased to swear fealty to the Em-

1364

1369

1378

1380

1349

1381

peror. But the princes of the blood royal were granted a
number of fiefs in appanage, and this had the effect of dis-
membering the domains of the Crown—Anjou, Angoumois,
Périgord, Poitou, Berry, Maine, and several others. Burgundy, which, in the absence of an heir, came into the
King's hands, was given away to the fourth son of Jean le
Bon—a piece of generosity that involved France in a long-
drawn-out struggle with the Valois of Burgundy, who
showed themselves, from father to son, to be her worst enemies.

It was bad enough to have the Valois on the throne, but
still worse to have them off it. Good or bad, the king served
a useful purpose, even in spite of himself. With no king
on the throne, the country was at the mercy of intriguing
pretenders, a situation that resulted in every kind of evil.
Chance, which had kept regencies at bay during the Capetian centuries, produced a fine crop of *"républiques des
princes"* in the times of the Valois. Jean le Bon was for four
years a prisoner in London, whence he returned to die as
a voluntary hostage. Charles VI was a minor for another
eight years, after which he was mad for thirty. His son, the
Dauphin Charles, lived for eight years under the cloud of
presumed illegitimacy, which was dispersed only by his
coronation. Thus captivity, minority, insanity, and the suspicion of bastardy all worked together to keep France from
having a king of her own at the very time when another
King was laying claim to her throne. In consequence of
this wretched state of affairs the feudal barons once more
raised their heads, the very State, as well as the country at large, became an object of pillage, and the warring
factions tore not only each other to pieces, but France as
well.

England, under Edward III, was in the fortunate position of enjoying an uninterrupted reign of half a century,
which enabled her to pluck the fruits of victory. But a time

came when she too was involved in dynastic troubles and their inevitable accompaniment of usurpation, regency, and civil war. It was then, and then only, that, confronted by Charles VII, who, though he might be of doubtful legitimacy, did at least rule for thirty-five years, she lost the war, and with it her hopes of dominating the Continent.

The Lamentable Plight of the Realm of France

From the very outset the English had shown themselves superior. They carried the day on land no less surely than 1346   they had already done at sea. At Crécy the twelve thousand "churls" who crushed twenty thousand knights struck an unexpected blow not only at the prestige of the feudal war- 1347   rior, but at the French renown in general. Having won the battle, they laid siege to Calais and forced the citizens to surrender. For the next two hundred years the port, now "colonized" by island settlers, was an English stronghold. London turned it into a depot for the wool trade, and used it as a bridgehead for operations on the mainland.

At Poitiers a mixed force of six thousand English and 1356   Gascon troops overwhelmed King John's army of fifteen thousand men. The disaster of Agincourt was even more 1415   humiliating. On each occasion the French cavalry fell into the ambush set for them by the English and perished under the fire of their archers.

These battles, however, were more distressing than decisive. Their most serious feature was the high percentage of losses they caused in the ranks of the French nobility. Its bravest members were either killed or captured. The Count of Flanders lost his life at Crécy; Jean II was made prisoner at Poitiers, Charles of Orléans at Agincourt. As ransom for the King, the English extorted a promise of three million gold crowns, or the equivalent of more than 40,000 pounds' weight of the precious metal. Such a sum was higher than the French either could or would pay at a time when currency had become scarce.

But raids played an even larger part than pitched battles in this never ending war. The technique of these adventures consisted in the English emerging each spring from one or other of their Continental provinces, ravaging the countryside, and reaching another of their garrisoned strongholds before the onset of winter. There would be a sweep from the Cotentin Peninsula to Flanders, a descent from Guyenne on Poitou, expeditions with Calais as their base; and as objective, Champagne and La Beauce, the Île-de-France and Brittany, Morvan and Guyenne. Up and down the kingdom the English rode and ravaged. Where they encountered resistance, a battle ensued, from which they emerged victorious. When, as under Charles V, the defenders withdrew before their advancing forces, they were left free to pillage and destroy to their hearts' content.

Years passed, and the campaigns continued, interrupted occasionally by negotiations more or less protracted, periods of truce, more or less respected, and even by treaties, which the victor regarded as too soft, the vanquished as too hard. The Agreement of Brétigny, though it made no concessions in the matter of the dynastic claim, handed over to the English without qualification an enlarged Aquitaine stretching from the lower Loire to the Pyrenees, as well as Calais and a number of adjoining fiefs. The Treaty of Troyes went farther still, since it abandoned to the Lancastrian successors of the Plantagenets the whole heritage of Charles VI, thereby turning France into an English dominion.

1360

1420

Lamentable, indeed, was the plight of the realm of France! To the horrors of war were added those of an appalling scourge, the Black Death. It entered the country by way of the Mediterranean coast, brought by an infected ship from the Levant. It made its way along the old trade

1347

routes, smote the cities, and then the villages. The inhabitants fled before it as, in times past, they had fled before the Huns and the Norsemen. But it moved more swiftly than

1348   the swiftest fugitive. In a single year it carried off a third of the population (in some cities two thirds), and it spared no part of the Western World, not even England. Corpses could no longer be buried, but were left to the wolves. There were massacres of Jews and witches, whom popular ignorance held responsible for the evil. But at last the plague fell into an uneasy slumber with, now and again, a terrible period of reawakening.

Distress was universal. For want of manpower the fields lay unfarmed; heath and bog invaded lands that had formerly been won for the plow. Famine increased. Bereft of the means of life, or emptied of their inhabitants, the castles fell into ruins.

The general confusion was inevitably intensified by the collapse of the currency. The treasury, which could draw on no fixed system of taxation, had only one way of ensuring revenue. It increased the quantity of money in circulation by minting inferior alloys. Gold and silver coins were debased sixty-four times under Philippe VI, one hundred and four times under Jean II, forty-one times under Charles VI, thirty-six times under Charles VII. If Charles V took less advantage of this abuse, that was only because he preferred others—such as a forced loan, which was insufficient to make up the deficit of his budget.

The 250 different types of financial gerrymandering to

1461   which the Valois kings had recourse during the English wars did not, in the long run, reduce the value of the livre of Tours by more than 66 per cent for silver money (the metal content of which fell from 77 grams to 26), and 57 per cent for gold (from 5.63 grams to 2.42). But in the course of hostilities much debased currency passed into circulation.

1360   While Jean le Bon was a prisoner, the Dauphin Charles

(the "Wise") issued what amounted to a counterfeit coinage, because he took care to disguise its true value. The
other Dauphin Charles (the future victor) was more honest   1422
in that he made public pronouncement to the effect that
his florette, which weighed 2.04 grams, with a face value of
twenty deniers, contained only ten milligrams of silver. This
was the lowest point reached by the process of monetary debasement. But at least these issues did serve to finance the
French resistance.

In the long course of this haphazard financial jugglery
there was one bright interval of sanity, when a handsome
new coin of fine gold was issued, weighing 3.88 grams,
and worth just precisely one livre. It bore the image of a
mounted king, the emblem of the fleur-de-lis, and the superscription *"Francorum Rex."* It was known as the *franc à
cheval*, and was the ancestor of the franc.

With this mad dance of money and this shortage of
goods went a corresponding rise in prices (except for land,
which nobody wanted). But since the level of the population had fallen, workmen were hard to find, and wages rose.
The war had ruined the owners of capital, but had not much
affected the purchasing power of the humble. Other miseries were in store for them.

The Civil War

The worst scourge of all was civil war. It was more cruel
than the war against the foreigner, more constant than the
plague. It was unforgiving. Under many guises, ranging
from brigandage to feudal conflict, middle-class revolution,
and mob risings, it set Frenchmen against Frenchmen and
finally left France in an exhausted condition.

Civil disorders were, as ever, a breeding-ground for crime
and theft. Opportunities for plunder multiplied. Pillage became a lucrative profession. Even those without a natural

taste for it, or the ability to organize, found it profitable. Mercenaries at a loose end turned brigand, roaming the roads and terrorizing the countryside. Gangs of highway robbers sprang up everywhere. They were of all nationalities —English, Spanish, German, Gascon, and Breton—all seeking adventure and the chance to line their pockets. The more timid among them confined their efforts to attacking travelers and isolated farms. The more daring threatened **1366** Lyon, held the Pope at Avignon to ransom (this it was that finally determined his return to Rome), and even stood their ground against regular troops. Du Guesclin, whom Charles V made his Constable, and who has come down in history as the flower of chivalry, started his career as a highway robber more expert in surprise forays than in pitched battles. If that same Charles succeeded in temporarily freeing France from the English—who had matters of their own at home to keep them busy—it was only to abandon it to these squalid soldiers of fortune. After his death, and under Charles VII, the highwaymen revived under the name of *écorcheurs*, or "skinners," because they stripped their victims to the skin. They roamed the country, stealing, raping, torturing, killing, and burning.

These "pirates" were not seldom small fief-holders "on the make." The great barons set their aim rather higher. Profiting by the eclipse of the central power, they were now seeking to reconquer the lands and the privileges which the kings had taken from them. They were willing to sell their **1341** services to their suzerain, at a price. If that were not forthcoming, they were equally prepared to go over to the enemy. **1346** It was a Montfort, claimant to the Duchy of Brittany, who appealed to the English; a Harcourt who opened Cotentin **1355** to the invader. Charles of Navarre never ceased from intriguing against the Valois, and the dukes of Burgundy, for all they were Valois themselves, remained persistently the allies of the English.

Those barons who remained loyal were animated by mo-
tives no less selfish. The members of the house of Orléans
were at odds with those of the house of Burgundy, and mutual throat-cutting went on merrily between the two families. The Comte d'Armagnac was intent on avenging Louis
d'Orléans, who had been murdered by the bravoes of Jean
sans Peur (the Fearless). The French split into two camps,
ranging themselves behind one or other of the two champions, Armagnacs against Burgundians, between whom
there existed a relentless hatred. Each side prevailed in turn,
and each side was as pitiless as it was shameless. "To us the
spoils!" The only question was which of them should rob
the kingdom the more effectively.

In these conditions of appalling confusion the common
people could do nothing but endure. They played their part
in the general chaos. Nothing was easier for the great lords
than to work upon their passions and fling them into the
struggle. Burgesses and peasants alike had a horror of taxes
and were loud in their recrimination against the high rate
of the *fouage*, or "hearth-tax" (levied directly on each
household), against the *aides* (indirect payments on sales),
against the *gabelle* (a tax on salt, the purchase of which was
compulsory), against internal customs dues. They infinitely
preferred monetary depreciation, though it, too, was the   1355
subject of unceasing complaints. In the States-General,
where they were in a majority, they protested against excessive expenditure, decided that they themselves would vote
and levy taxes, and proclaimed a fixed value for money. The
rich Étienne Marcel, elected by the merchants as their   1358
representative, burst into the palace of the trembling Dauphin Charles, killed his officers, and forced him to put on
a cap of red and blue, the colors of the City of Paris. It was
a foretaste of the Revolutionary Convention, and the English looked on, grinning.

The States-General, it need hardly be said, changed nothing. The taxpayers behaved no better to them than they had to the King. In the long run the burgesses, thoroughly disillusioned, determined on yet another devaluation. The proud and headstrong Étienne Marcel tried in vain to enlist the support of the peasants, the barons, and even the English, whom he invited to Paris. But all his plotting and all his treachery went for nothing. The burgesses rallied to the Dauphin and put a bloody end to his ambitions.

The peasants, whom he had roused and courted, were themselves rebels—rebels against the taxes and the cruel hardships of the times. To revenge themselves on fortune they turned to burnings, outrages, and massacres. They became known as the "Jacques," after Jacques Bonhomme, the conventional type-figure of the peasant. They were anarchists from the Champagne and the country around Beauvais, the children of misery, and their actions served but to make misery worse.

Popular rising succeeded popular rising. All were modeled on the same pattern, and all closely resembled one another. During the minority of Charles VI the people of Paris sacked the arsenal and, armed with mallets, set off once again in pursuit of the tax-collectors. This outbreak was known as the "Révolte des Maillotins." Much the same thing happened in Rouen and Béziers. During the madness of Charles VI the butchers of Paris, led by Simon Caboche the "skinner," attempted to follow in the footsteps of Étienne Marcel. They laid siege to the Bastille and seized the persons of the Dauphin's favorites. The reforms they demanded in order to restore the national finances to health were in themselves legitimate. But just as Marcel had worked in the interest of Charles of Navarre and the Plantagenets, so did the "Cabochiens" compromise their cause by giving indirect help to the Duke of Burgundy and the house of Lancaster. Four hundred years before the Revolution these revolutionaries were playing the English game.

1382

1413

All these various movements ended in blood. They settled neither the social problems to which they owed their birth nor the political problem that was strangling the Valois dynasty and the realm of France.

Jeanne and Her Miracles

When Charles VI, the mad King, died, France was at the lowest ebb of her fortunes. She had been handed over to the English by the Treaty of Troyes and now had a Lancastrian on the throne. Henry VI, then a boy ten years old, had been proclaimed King of France at Saint-Denis, and his uncle Bedford was acting as his regent in Paris.

1422

To say that all France was chafing under a sense of humiliation would be untrue. Many Frenchmen seemed willing to accept the *fait accompli*. Henry VI was the child of a marriage that had united the houses of Lancaster and Valois, and was, in fact, the grandson of the mad King Charles. The Church had blessed the union, the Paris crowds had acclaimed the happy pair, and the Parlement had ratified the treaty. The burgesses were only too pleased that peace had been restored, the merchants only too delighted to think that they could once more do trade with London. Few voices were raised against the English dynasty, which after all, was as like as two pins to a French one.

Not the whole of France, however, was in Lancastrian hands. The foreigners ruled only from the Channel to the Loire and in Guyenne. Their capital cities were Paris, Rouen, and Bordeaux, and there they were prepared to take a lenient view of the competitive administration of the French government and of the partisans of Burgundy. A second section of the country recognized the suzerainty of the young Duke of Burgundy, Philippe, son of Jean sans Peur, who was still an ally of the English, though he remained autonomous in his own domain, which included Burgundy, Flanders, Artois, and Champagne. There was yet another, a third, France—Brittany, which hesitated between Armagnacs and Burgundians, or, in other words, between Valois and Lancaster, and oscillated between the two.

Central and southern France, a fourth fragment of the kingdom, had remained true to the Valois. It was by no means the smallest, for it stretched from the Loire to the Mediterranean, and comprised the rich provinces of Touraine, Poitou, and Berry, together with the district of Lyon, Langedoc, and Dauphiné. There were, too, a number of individual strongholds—Mont-Saint-Michel, for instance— which were still holding out against the English. Of this mutilated France, Orléans was the real center, though the administrative capital was Bourges, where the chancellery and the treasury were situated. The judiciary was at Poitiers, whither the Parlement had moved. All it lacked was a king. It had only a Dauphin, the tenth child of a mad King, a timid, shifty young man who was commonly supposed to be a bastard. He himself was far from certain of his legitimacy. Was he really an issue of the blood royal and the true heir to the throne? His mother had disowned him, and he had been disinherited by his father. The lords and functionaries around him sniggered. The unhappy Kingdom of Bourges was unsurely founded on indiscipline and intrigue.

The Dauphin's one piece of luck was that he symbolized resistance to the foreigner. An occupying power is never popular. The French might accept the Lancastrian King, but they found it hard to put up with English garrisons, even though most of them had been reduced to skeleton proportions. They grumbled at the English taxes and the English requisitions. The peasants refused to collaborate. Islands of resistance were formed in Normandy, in the Île-de-France, in Champagne. Legitimate or not, the Dauphin was in opposition to the invader. A whisper began to travel

from mouth to mouth that a virgin would come and drive
the English out.

And lo, the hoped-for savior came! She appeared at the
crucial moment when Orléans, the key to the kingdom, was
on the very point of falling into the hands of the besieging
English. Her name was Jeanne d'Arc. Legend has it that
she was a shepherdess of Lorraine. In strict fact she was the
daughter of a landowner in easy circumstances, whose family hailed originally from Champagne. "Voices," she said—
and among them that of "Monsieur Saint-Michel," the
archangel of the hilltop now in such dire peril from the
English—had told her to go seek the Dauphin. In her parish
church she had been taught how Saint Remy, patron saint
of Domremy, had at Reims made Clovis King of France.
An avenging Amazon, she raised the siege of Orléans and   **1429**
had Charles VII crowned at Reims. With dramatic sudden-
ness the whole situation was transformed. If the "great
trek" came to a bad end, with Jeanne captured, condemned,   **1431**
and burned as a witch at Rouen, her mission had been fulfilled, and France once more had got a king. His anointing
had removed all doubt of his legitimacy, and he was now a   **1431**
monarch sanctified. In vain did the English try to stage a
counterblow by arranging, in Paris, at Notre-Dame, a coronation for the young Henry VI. It was at Reims, and with
oil from the sacred ampulla, that kings were made. From
now on, the Lancastrians were no better than usurpers.

Fortune changed sides. The Duke of Burgundy, in return
for the recognition of his autonomy, rallied to the French   **1436**
King. Paris, reconquered after sixteen years of occupation,
resumed its position as capital. One by one the English were **1450**
forced to relinquish the last of their Continental provinces.
As the result of a crushing defeat at Formigny they lost Nor- **1453**
mandy; beaten at Castillon, they lost Guyenne. They were
"driven from the whole of France" except Calais. The Lilies
were victorious.

This miracle was due, first and foremost, to Jeanne d'Arc, for she it was who had pointed the eyes of Frenchmen to their King. But credit too must go to Charles VII. Faced by the little King of London, he had taken cognizance of his rights and his duties. He set about reorganizing the States. A realist King had stepped into the shoes of an indolent Dauphin. He unified the realm without coming into colli-

1443 sion with local privileges. He reformed the finances by establishing a single, annual budget and by setting up a permanent system of taxation (a *taille*, or direct levy, and a number of *aides*, or indirect taxes). In this way did the central power free itself from the tutelage of the States-

1445 General. It no longer had to ask their consent. Assured of regular resources, it could consolidate the currency, wage a struggle against the still dangerous barons, maintain a permanent army equipped with an efficient body of artillery. These innovations were cause of rejoicing neither to the taxpayers, whose opinion was no longer asked, nor to the princes, who at long last could be brought to heel. But with money and an army the monarchy at last had a weapon that could be relied on to bring it victory.

It would be rash to assert that the French had emerged from their hundred years of turmoil with a firm sense of national solidarity. But at least they stood loyally behind their King, who was himself trustee for a heritage he had no right to alienate. Rome had been a city and a legal system. France, under the Capets, had been a domain with its overlord. The new France, fresh from its ordeal, was a kingdom built round a family.

Missed Opportunities

To say that the war was over would be untrue. England had signed no peace. For a long time to come the English sovereigns would keep their coins with the emblem of the fleur-

de-lis, and the empty title of King of France. The day would   1475
come when an English army would again be seen concentrated on Calais, another army preparing a landing in Guy-   1487
enne, contingents overrunning Brittany. But, to meet those   1489
threats, France had, in Louis XI, the son of Charles VII,
an unequaled master of maneuver.

In him, Valois though he was, the blood of the Capets
flowed again. He built a system of government out of lies
and dissimulation. Against the English, against the leagued
forces of the barons, against the Duke of Burgundy in par-   1465
ticular—that Charles le Téméraire (the Bold), who was
bold indeed to beard him—he employed all the resources of
his political genius. He yielded, the better to deceive. He
violated treaties that he had signed. He took back fiefs that
he had granted. He bribed the friends of his enemies. He
sacrificed his allies. He married off his daughters so as to
round out his territories. He gave a pension to an English
King to keep him quiet. He bargained, corrupted, impris-   1467
oned, beheaded, confiscated. Charles le Téméraire, who,
with the support of the Medici of Florence, dreamed of re-
constituting to his own advantage that kingdom of Lothaire
which had stretched from the North Sea to Switzerland,
found a master in this mulish, stingy man who hoarded territories as a miser hoards his gold. Louis XI recovered Burgundy and Picardy, Maine and Anjou, Roussillon and Cer-
dagne. Provence was his by inheritance. With the overthrow   1477
of the house of Burgundy there vanished the last trace of
the buffer state born of the Treaty of Verdun.

The Kingdom of France had now the Empire for a neighbor, that elective Empire so long dissolved in anarchy,
which now the Habsburgs were to make their own for cen-   1478
turies. Scarcely had the English danger been removed when
a new danger threatened, this time on the Continent itself.
The Habsburgs had grown rich by exploiting the silver
mines of Styria. Of the Burgundian heritage, they took from

Louis XI Franche-Comté, Artois, Flanders, and the Low Countries. Between the two assaults, the English and the Imperial, France had scarcely time to draw breath.

Safe she might be, but healthy she was not. The English war, the war against the barons, and civil strife had exhausted the national economy. Many villages were reduced to a few houses. Much of the agricultural land had been abandoned. Famine was frequent. Without money, without cannon, the barons had lost the major part of their resources. If they could still defy the King, it was no longer from the shelter of their castles and their provinces, but in Paris itself. Often their land had been taken over by men of the middle class, who kept a sharper eye than they had ever done on the expenses of their estates. The taxes were heavy, and, though they might assure the revival of the monarchy, they checked the process of private reconstruction.

France had lost too many of her people, too much of her wealth, to be able now to play a leading part in the world. She was far removed from the new trade routes, and her activities languished, bogged down in the controlled routine of the guilds. In spite of the efforts of the citizens of Lyon, where the earliest silk factories had been established, the great fairs had migrated to Geneva and the Rhine Valley. In spite of a few new rich, of whom Jacques Cœur was an outstanding example, it was the Italians and Germans who were now the real bankers of Europe and the champions of a mercantile capitalism. When England began to spin and weave, Flanders and Artois lost their monopoly of the wool trade, and Bruges entered on the period of its long-drawn-out decline. In any case, these provinces were no longer part of the kingdom.

The French had lost their predominance in the Levant. At about the same time as the English were driven from France, the Turks took Constantinople. Distant though it

1467

1453

might be, the irruption of the Ottomans caused grave dis-
quiet in the West. The last of the Crusades mustered the
last of the knights for unproductive enterprises on the Danube and the Bosporus. France had too much to do, to do
over again, to spare her forces in an attempt to stem the
advance of the conquerors.

Because of the Turks the Mediterranean became a blind
alley. The future lay on the Atlantic. A few Norman sea-   **1368**
farers had been far-sighted—the men of Dieppe, for instance, who had set up trading-stations on the coast of   **1402**
Senegal and Guinea, or Jean de Béthencourt, who had
founded an ephemeral kingdom in the Canaries. But the
great overseas adventures and the discoveries were the work
of foreigners. The Portuguese and the Spaniards, better
situated, better informed, and less absorbed in other matters, outdistanced the French on the ocean highways and in
the New World. It was a period of missed opportunities.

Nor was it in France that the new technical methods and
inventions made their appearance. Movable type was used   **1445**
to produce the first Bible—but on the banks of the Rhine,
a good twenty years before a printing-house was set up at the **1469**
Sorbonne.

Even in the arts France was fast losing her predominance.
She had certainly not abandoned the building of fortified
castles—Charles V at Vincennes, the popes at Avignon—
but she had interrupted or slowed down the construction of
cathedrals, the uncompleted skeletons of which bore witness to hopes unfulfilled. The new rich were raising luxurious houses for themselves, but these were in the already
outmoded style of flamboyant Gothic at a time when
Brunelleschi had already built the Duomo at Florence.
Exquisite painters—Jean Fouquet, for instance—were frequently reduced to employing their talents in the minor
task of illuminating. The century was hard on poets,
whether princes or ragamuffins. Charles of Orléans was for

twenty years a prisoner in England; François Villon lived a life of penury, and escaped the gallows only to go to jail. How was it possible that such troublous times should be productive?

The Bright Interval of the Renaissance

The four kings who followed Louis XI were true sons of the house of Valois, men of knightly courage, brilliant exponents in every field of sport, whether war or love, passionate worshippers of luxury and the arts. But not all of them forgot the lessons of Louis XI. They knew, on occasion, how to dupe their friends, betray their promises, and break their treaties—when it was in the interest of France to do so.

For them the Renaissance was primarily political. The French were being brought up in the religion of monarchy: "one faith, one law, one king." Like the Emperor in Rome, the king had now become the "living embodiment of the law." Right was concentrated in his ordinances. There was no need for him to justify them—"for such is our will and pleasure." Abandoning religious emblems—the Cross or the Lamb—coinage diffused throughout the country the fleur-de-lis and the royal effigy. Thus it was that the teston, or "tester" (from the word *tête*, "head"), became a means of publicizing royalty.

Evidence that the monarchy was firmly established may be found in the fact that periods of regency, and the transference of power from one branch to another, now proceeded smoothly. The minority of Charles VIII, the shift of authority from the direct Valois line (which had only female heirs) to their Orléans and Angoulême cousins, the captivity of François I, produced no convulsions.

1483
1498
1525

In the provinces the king was represented by governors and lieutenants-general. Justice, like the administration, was unified. François I established the pre-eminence of the

1539

king's judges, and at the same time replaced Latin in the
courts by French, the language derived from the *langue
d'oïl*. He further made the registration of civil status obligatory.

The economic Renaissance was dazzling only by contrast with the appalling distresses of the previous reigns.
Once the kingdom was at peace it could once more spread
its wings. The birth-rate began to rise, and the forests to recede before the onset of the plow. New crops were imported
from Italy—the artichoke, the asparagus, and the melon.
New forms of animal life were bred—for instance, the silkworm. Taught by the Italians, and employing their work-
people, their looms, and their secrets, Lyon took to producing velvets. Silk stockings were woven at Dourdan, silken
textiles at Orléans, Fontainebleau made tapestries, Nîmes
serges. Saint-Germain-en-Laye excelled at glasswork. The
younger industries prospered—printing and papermaking,
cannon-founding. France was doing a big trade in the export of salt, grain, wine, iron, timber, and woven stuffs.
Already alive to the dangers of a debit trade balance, she
protected herself against foreign competition either by pro- **1548**
hibition of imports or by a tariff charge of two crowns per
quintal, or four per cent ad valorem.

Roads and waterways were restored. At the same time an
attempt was made to bring life back to the port of Montpellier. Special facilities were accorded to Marseille. The
Atlantic harbors, though they could not hope to rival Lisbon or Antwerp, recovered a considerable amount of local
traffic. Next door to Harfleur, now silted up, François I **1520**
founded the future Le Havre. On the high seas the French
had fallen behind in the race, and never succeeded in
making up their loss. The New World had been discovered
without their participation. But, at least, the people of **1524**
Lyon did finance the voyage of the Florentine Verrazano,
who took possession of Newfoundland and reached the

estuary of the Hudson. The brothers Ango, of Dieppe, competed with the Portuguese on the coasts of Brazil and Su-

1535 matra. Jacques Cartier, of Saint-Malo, penetrated into the
St. Lawrence, which he took to be quite close to Tartary,
and brought back with him a number of redskins, who
spoke much of their *"canada."* This word, which means a
Huron village, was later to become a proper name. It was
on a map issued by a Lorraine printing-house that the word
America appeared for the first time.

These colonial enterprises were far from being disinter-
ested experiments in adventure. Those who found the
money for them expected in return spices or precious
metals, those two forms of treasure which the Crusaders
had found in the East, but now, because the Turks had set
up an unbreakable barrier between Europe and the Orient,
must be procured by westward expansion. Spices, the chief
commodity of large-scale trading, could be bought cheap
and sold dear. They enriched those who dealt in them. Precious metals offered a still higher prize. They were the very
sign and symbol of wealth. The world was hungry for them.
Their shortage was no new sickness. Rome, in her day, had
known what it meant to be ill-supplied with the means of
payment. The relief brought by the Crusades had been no
more than temporary. Fresh needs and new industries demanded more money than was available, and the alchemists
had so far failed to discover the philosophers' stone.

Would the discovery of America, and, following hard

1545 upon it, of the Peruvian silver mines, heal the monetary ail-
ment? In a single century the Spanish galleons multiplied
by ten the quantity of the precious metals available for the
requirements of Europe. France came in for a large share
of this windfall, receiving it as money paid for what she was
in a position to sell to her neighbor—grain, textiles, paper,
books, dyed fabrics—and as wages too, earned by her workers from Auvergne and Limousin, who found employment

beyond the Pyrenees. Nor were her privateers idle, but attacked returning galleons on the high seas and took many a valuable prize.

The flow of precious metals into Europe increased the general quantity of money in circulation, stimulated economic enterprise, and forced prices up—set in motion, in fact, all the normal processes of inflation. From the beginning to the end of the sixteenth century the price of grain increased four times, eggs trebled, meat doubled. The upward movement of wages and rents was at a slower pace, with the result that the position of workers and landed proprietors deteriorated. But the peasants grew more and more prosperous, because their incomings were higher and their outgoings less. The merchants too were reaping a golden harvest, and it was they who were buying up the estates of the impoverished aristocracy.

1524

The cost of living was certainly high, but there was no longer much extreme poverty. Even with prices soaring, more meat and wine was being consumed, even in working-class homes, than they were ever to be again in the history of France.

Encirclement

All the same, this age of the Renaissance was not wholly tranquil. The English danger had passed, but that of the Habsburgs had taken its place. By alternately attacking and remaining on the defensive France managed to keep it at bay, though it could not end it for good and all. The fight for Continental supremacy had once again become a life-and-death struggle. The Austro-Spanish monster was threatening to strangle the life out of France.

The Habsburgs had a genius for making profitable marriages, and their strategy was primarily a matrimonial one. By means of the provinces that they received as dowries or by inheritance, they succeeded in drawing a circle round the

Valois kingdom. Maximilian of Austria had the German
Empire at his command and, in addition, through Marie
de Bourgogne, daughter of Charles le Téméraire, held
Franche-Comté, Flanders, Artois, and the Low Countries.
Left a widower, he contracted a secret union with the
Duchess Anne of Brittany. There was a grave risk of France
1491   finding herself caught between two fires. As a result of pres-
1499   sure, the marriage was annulled. Charles VIII took both
Duchess and duchy, and Louis XII, by confirming this
double wedding, gave Brittany to France.

Maximilian countered by taking to wife a member of the
1493   house of Sforza, thereby gaining access to Milan. France
was now menaced from the Italian side, and the danger
was the greater since both Naples and Sicily had recently
passed from the house of Anjou into the hands of two
Spanish princes. It was in Italy that the stranglehold must
be broken.

But the political marriages of the Habsburgs were not yet
1496   ended. Maximilian's son, by taking to wife the Queen of
Castile, brought Austria into close association with Spain—
a Spain now freed from the Moors, unified at last, and
on the point of carving for herself from the New World
an empire of unprecedented magnificence. This vast ag-
glomeration of claims and legacies descended to Don
Carlos, Maximilian's grandson: Madrid, Mexico, Lima, Pa-
1519   lermo, Naples, Vienna, Lille, Besançon, Antwerp, and Amsterdam. In Spain he reigned as Charles I. Should he be
elected, as were all the Habsburgs, he would be Charles V
of Germany, and it is as the Emperor Charles V, in fact,
that he is known to history.

It was against this accumulating growth of dangers that
France had now to fight. In its beginnings the war may well
have seemed a gay adventure, since nothing could be more
attractive than a trip to Italy. There was intoxication in the
very thought of Tuscan cypresses, Roman ruins, and Nea-

politan sunshine. But the expedition turned out badly. The
French had bitten off more than they could chew. To meet
them the Habsburgs had collected a doughty coalition:
England, the Pope, Venice, and the Swiss—those hardy
mountaineers who were prepared to sell their services to the
highest bidder. Seven times, in four separate reigns, Lombardy was won and lost. One of the greatest of the feudal
barons, the Duc de Bourbon, went over to the enemy. Useless victories (Ravenna, Melegnano) alternated with bitter
defeats (Novara, Pavia). The treaties settled nothing, ex-   **1515**
cept one that, after Melegnano, solemnly proclaimed be-
tween France and Switzerland a pact of "perpetual peace,"
and—miracle of miracles—it was respected! At Pavia, Fran-   **1525**
çois I was taken prisoner, as Jean le Bon had been at Poitiers,
and his liberation cost the country dear. On all sides France
was the sufferer. In the south she had to give up Roussillon.
Provence was invaded and Marseille besieged. In the north
fighting broke out in Picardy and Champagne.

In order to defeat the coalition, the Valois contracted
alliances with Scotland and the Scandinavian countries. By   **1532**
ranging themselves behind the German princes against the
Emperor, by assuming the role of protector of the German
liberties, they gave proof of an intention to maintain Ger-   **1534**
many in a condition of profitable confusion. By allying
themselves with the Turks (who handed over to them the
defense of the Holy Places) they showed themselves as
proved traitors to the spirit of the first Crusades and incurred the opprobrium of all Christendom. Nevertheless,
they scored a point.

The struggle ended with each side agreeing to abide by
the *status quo*. France lost Italy, but gained Toul, Metz,   **1559**
and Verdun—which she had taken from the Imperial
forces—and recovered Calais as the result of a surprise attack by the Duc de Guise. The Spanish Habsburgs retained
control of Italy, while those of Austria were confirmed in

their possession of the Low Countries. But after Charles V the two branches separated, and the threat of encirclement grew less.

The main reason for the conclusion of peace was financial. Both sides were in imminent danger of bankruptcy. The French had been able to put forth so great an effort only because they possessed a regular system of taxation that enabled the Valois to amass a fighting fund in one of the towers of the Louvre. Even so, they were compelled to have recourse to a number of extraordinary expedients— sales of lands, sales of crown jewels, rent charges on the clergy, lotteries. The kings also began the system of creating a number of public offices that were offered for sale. But their most important innovation was the issuing of a loan.

The Italian bankers in Lyon had the handling of the funds earmarked for the financing of the war. Lyon was the exchange center of Europe, and it was there that the Valois tried to raise capital, by offering as security the proceeds of the national taxes for several years to come. They undertook to pay interest at the rate of ten per cent, sixteen per cent, twenty per cent. On the other side it was the German banking-houses, the Fuggers and the Welsers, who provided the necessary financial backing for the Habsburgs, because they needed the trade outlet afforded by Antwerp.

The great money battle centered on the election of the **1519** Emperor. François I took a chance against Don Carlos, the Austro-Spanish champion. It was a question who could bid the highest for the support of the electors. François I, the richer of the two, offered money down. Charles's bankers were more shrewd, and issued bills of exchange payable after the election. The result represented a victory of credit over cash, of negotiable bonds over hard coin. The Empire went to Charles V.

Forty years later the Habsburgs had still not paid off their **1559** debt, the sum total of which had been swollen by later ac-

cretions. The Valois owed forty million livres. A peace of
exhaustion was signed under the threat of bankruptcy. But
the double inflation had shaken Europe to its foundations.
Lyon, Antwerp, and Augsburg were left tottering. The
event constituted the financial crash of the Renaissance.

The Lesson of Italy

Tragic though they were, these wars did not really put an
excessive strain on the French nation. Such invasion as
there had been in the course of them had neither stuck deep
nor lasted long. At no time had more than thirty thousand
men been called up for service with the armies. The policy
of loans had resulted in a wide diffusion of a new form of
wealth. The circulation of a multiplicity of currencies had
brought ease, if not opulence, and in this way a climate had
been formed which favored the flowering of literature and
the arts.

Simultaneously the Italian campaigns had revealed to the
French a universe of marvels. True, they brought back from
Genoa and Naples that sickness which other countries
labeled "French," but they acquired other things as well. In
Florence they learned the secrets of banking and cookery,
and the use of forks. Milan and Turin offered them new
styles in silks. At Faenza they were initiated into the mys-
teries of faïence; from Viterbo they gained a knowledge of
card games. Wherever they went, they found a new form
of art to be learned, and in Rome they came on the dazzling
revelation of the antique world.

The new art of Italy looked backward to the beauties of
the pagan centuries. It repudiated the soaring ecstasies of
the Gothic and revived the Roman column and the rounded
arch. Conquered by their own conquests, the French, in
their turn, adopted the Italian formula. Away with massive ·
walls! More air and more light! Feudal keeps and manor   **1508**

houses must make way for palaces. The Breton calvaries, the new clock-tower at Chartres, the Hôtel de Sens in Paris, the Palais de Justice at Rouen—these were the final flowering of the despised Gothic. But even in them a mingling of the two styles was already evident. Italian masters were invited to France—Boccador and da Vinci, Primaticcio and Benvenuto Cellini. Louis XII, himself the son of a poet, employed Fra Giocondo as his architect. François I brought back from Italy Leonardo's *La Gioconda* (*Mona Lisa*), Raphael's *Holy Family*, and Michelangelo's *Two Slaves*. Italians were set to work at Amboise and at Blois. French craftsmen, marrying the new technique of Italy to their own national tradition, adapting the Roman line to the

1546   contours of the valleys of the Loire and the Seine, built Chambord, Azay, and Fontainebleau. In Paris, Pierre Lescot refashioned the Louvre, where the kings, after a long flirtation with the country of the Loire, had finally taken up their residence. Philibert Delorme made a start with the Tuileries. In the service of the young school of architects a young

1547   school of sculptors offered the products of a style that derived more from Paris than from Greece. Jean Goujon modeled the *Fontaine des Innocents*, Germain Pilon a somewhat tousled *Three Graces*. On canvas, Clouet, true child of the old illuminators, was still painting fine portraits in an earlier manner. In wood that was seldom ebony the *ébénistes* were fashioning furniture on a new model. Tables were ousting trestles, and presses competing with chests. Chairs "with arms" were rivaling the backless stools of a former age. Italy was spreading a taste for marquetry and for inlaid work of every description.

French humanism, too, bore the stamp of Italy, which every writer visited. Nor was it only Italy that they discovered, but Rome and Athens which, in and out of season, the new men set themselves to imitate, with heady delight, on printed paper. As often happens with the young practitioners of art, the new school was frequently guilty of exaggeration. In revolt against the Gothic, it went to antiquity for inspiration, drawing from it both form and content, metaphors no less than ideas. Enthusiasm turned to idolatry. The charming Ronsard, with his stage dryads, sometimes foundered in the quicksands of involuntary pastiche. Fortunately the French writers who without artifice retained a mastery of the French tongue were less inclined to borrow. Du Bellay preferred his village in Anjou to the Palatine Hill; Marot was more interested in the young women of Paris than in the goddesses of Olympus; and when Rabelais wrote his farcical lives of Gargantua and Pantagruel, it never occurred to him to plagiarize Virgil.

The passion for antiquity was productive of other excesses, some of them innocent, others the reverse. There was a fashion for Greek and Roman names—Alexandre and Hercule, Horace and Phébus, Hélène and Diane. Many Italian terms were taken over and incorporated in the French vocabulary: from banking, *agio* (premium) and *crédit*; from the art of war, *soldat* and *arquebuse*; from diplomacy, *brigue* (cabal) and *intrigue*; from fashion, *escarpin* (low-heeled shoe), *parfum, pommade*. All were free to remake their native tongue. Men began to notice that popular speech had begun to distort the roots of words. An attempt was made to substitute *apothicaire* for *boutiquier, avocat* for *avoué*. Words were remodeled according to their etymology, no matter whether true or false. Much learned effort went into the reform of spelling.

But the assaults delivered by a few pedants beat in vain against the solid good sense of the mass of Frenchmen, who remained as faithful to their traditional names (Colin, Guillaume, Martin, Margot) as to the language of their daily lives. The lessons learned from Italy were passed

through the strainer of French reason. But enough remained to pave the way to the desiccated morrows of the
classic age.

The Reformation

Clear sky of the Renaissance, sunshine and shadow of the
Reformation—the two are inseparable. By resuming old contacts with antiquity, and by discovering new worlds, men
were enlarging their horizons. Minds began to stir and
ferment. For this the printing-press was primarily responsible, because it spread a knowledge of the sacred books. In
the churches it was no longer only the Roman priests who
read them and commented on what they read. As though
to make reading easier, the architects were turning their
backs on the mysterious glimmer of stained glass, were
banishing darkness, spreading light everywhere. On all sides
the critics, Gospel in hand, were beginning to make themselves heard.

The Catholic Church was far from being beyond reproach. From the schism of Avignon the Papacy had
emerged with its stature by no means increased. After their
return to Rome the pontiffs had more than once yielded to
the temptations of luxury and warmaking. The traffic in in-
dulgences had moved men to indignation. In France, Rome
and the kings had found many causes of disagreement—
taxes and ecclesiastical appointments among them. They
1516   had ended by concluding a concordat which, though it cut
the Gordian knot of their essential difficulties, settled none
of them. Outside France apostles had been springing up
everywhere for a long time past, demanding basic reforms—
a whole Reformation: Wyclif in England, John Huss in
Bohemia, then Luther in Germany, Zwingli in Switzerland.
Persecution had served only to strengthen their cause. Finally came John Calvin of Picardy, with his mouth full of
protests. The "Reformers" and the "Protestants" preached

freedom of conscience against the authority of Rome—and
all that Rome could do to save the unity of Christendom   **1545**
was to hold a council, which dragged on for eighteen years.

The new doctrine was propagated under many forms.
Sometimes it offered the delights of revolutionary projects,
as when it demanded the community of goods and the recognition of polygamy. Those who call for reform find it
very difficult to hold a middle course. But much of what
was being proposed echoed the voice of public opinion. The
whole of northern Europe caught the infection—Germany
and Switzerland, England, the Low Countries, Scandinavia.
The Mediterranean world, over which Rome could more
easily maintain her hold, stayed "Papist."

France caught fire at a comparatively late stage. She had
only recently emerged from civil strife and a foreign war.
She had no taste for new embroilments. Until the reign of
Henri II the Valois had no great difficulty in keeping the
trouble within bounds. Although in Germany and England
the sects were up in arms, they managed to hold their kingdom in the bonds of unity.

But with the death of Henri II everything fell apart. It
needed no more than an ill-fated splinter of wood in the   **1559**
royal eye during a tournament to reveal how fragile was the
Valois power. Three sons of Henri II came in succession to
the throne, and these three brothers sufficed to turn a living
branch into a dead one. Already, with three brothers, the
direct Capetian line had ended, and in another two centuries and a half the house of Bourbon would pass forever
from the scene.

At once problems began to thicken, appetites to revive.
The three brothers were young and sickly. There was a general feeling that they would die without issue. François II
began to reign when he was seventeen and died two years   **1560**
later. Charles IX came to the throne as a minor, and inevitably there was a regency. When he died, at twenty-four,   **1574**

his brother Henri III was in Poland, of which country he had been elected King. He returned to France at leisure, and without enthusiasm. Three reigns, all fragile, all overcast. To whom, now, would the crown revert? To the Bourbon princes, who ruled in Navarre and had been converted to Protestantism. Was Catholic France, then, to fall a prey to the Reformers? No sooner did royal authority show signs of weakening than the country became convulsed. Feebleness in high places, disorder in low. Suddenly the King ceased to be of any account. The French, caught up in the prevailing turmoil, forgot all about him. They were neither for nor against. They were Catholics or Protestants, Papists or Huguenots.

Huguenots was the name popularly given to the Calvinist "confederates" (*Eidgenossen*). Who were they? Nobles, landowners, wage-earners—in other words, those who, more than other Frenchmen, had suffered from inflation and rising prices. Living on fixed incomes, they constituted the "new poor." Discontent led them straight into the ranks of the Reformers. Those on the other hand whose incomes varied remained Papist—those who had benefited from inflation, the peasants and the merchants. The country people were still predominantly Roman, and in Paris there was always a Catholic majority.

Behind both Huguenots and Papists the heirs of the old feudal estates were hard at work attempting to stage a revenge against the monarchy. Routed from their strongholds, stripped of their fiefs, they seized this heaven-sent chance to play a great role. On one side or the other they plotted and betrayed with frank delight. Among the Reformers the families of Coligny and Condé led the dance. Among the Catholics the Guises played at being dictators—François, the liberator of Calais, whose victory had made him a popular figure, and then his son Henri, whose ambitions knew no bounds. All these men were concerned less with purifying or defending the faith than with gaining power. The Wars of Religion were religious only for the mob. For their leaders they were primarily political.

The Realm in Fragments

To trace these opposed rancors in all their hateful details would be useless. Civil wars are much the same all the world over. More productive of plots, murders, and massacres than of pitched battles, the struggle took on a peculiar bitterness because it sundered villages and families. The rapes and slaughters of the Catholic bands under Montluc were paralleled by similar horrors committed by the Protestant forces of the Baron des Adrets. The Parlement was divided, one chamber condemning the Romans, the other the Reformers. At Carcassonne the upper city was Papist, the lower Huguenot. In the ensuing terror it was a question which could be the more fanatical, the more intolerant. Lyon fell into the hands of the Calvinists, and heard no Mass for a whole year. In Paris the Catholic populace applauded with frenzied enthusiasm the Protestant executions. The great lords among the Reformers forcibly converted the dwellers on their estates. The Catholic cities compelled the Reformers to abjure their errors—always under the threat of summary justice.

Both sides sought foreign aid. The worthier Protestants emigrated to the New World, where they tried in vain to establish small colonies, first at Rio de Janeiro, later in Florida. The others called in their coreligionists of the Low Countries, who were in revolt against the Spaniards, of Germany and England. Coligny and Condé agreed to hand over Le Havre and Calais to Elizabeth. Coligny, a hardened traitor, invited the English to La Rochelle.   1555   1562

On the other side the Catholic party entered into an alliance with Spain, though everything pointed to the fact that

she was the most dangerous of France's enemies. For the
Spain of Philip II, having absorbed Portugal, was now mistress of two empires and held sway from Madrid to Mexico,
from Lisbon to the Philippines. In her the Roman Church
1571 had found a champion. She defeated the Turks at Lepanto,
and also, by means of the Inquisition and the Society of
Jesus, was putting up a strong resistance to the Reformation.
She was only too glad to make the Huguenots an excuse for
swallowing France whole—a proceeding in which the Cath-
1576 olic League, organized by Henri of Guise, was prepared to
assist her. Philip II subsidized the League to the tune of
fifty thousand crowns a month, and, with its help, quartered
his troops in Paris and in the provinces. France had been
bought by Spanish pistoles.

Treachery to the country was tantamount to treachery to
the King. Protestants and Catholics alike, by entering into
1560 agreements with the foreigner, were necessarily taking sides
against the dynasty. Condé, at Amboise, was planning to
seize the government. François de Guise laid hands on
the person of the King at Fontainebleau, and Coligny attempted a similar stroke at Meaux. The Guises were fully
prepared to supersede him. They asserted, quite seriously,
that they were descended from Charlemagne, and that the
1589 Capetian and Valois monarchs had been no better than
usurpers. The League passed from words to acts. Paris was
already occupied by foreign troops, who proclaimed a
1590 wretched Cardinal de Bourbon king as Charles X and issued
money bearing his effigy. But his kingship was purely titular,
and he died far from Paris without having made even the
gesture of reigning. With him out of the way, the candi-
dates for the throne showed their hands. There was the
Duc de Savoie, the Duc de Lorraine, the Duc de Mayenne,
and, worst of all, there was the terrible Philip II, who
claimed France for the Infanta Isabella, who had been born
of his marriage with one of the daughters of Henri II.

There was one other possibility. Why not a republic instead of a change of dynasty? The Renaissance had awakened memories of the Roman Republic and the Greek democracies. Had not the diminutive Low Countries, after shaking off the Spanish yoke, formed themselves into a republican federation? The idea of a republic certainly reflected the general feeling of the Reformation. Coligny almost certainly let his mind move in that direction. So did the Catholics, for fear of seeing a Huguenot on the throne. They set up in Saint-Malo a republic, which lasted for six years. The League organized Days of Revolution, with barricades and the suppression of taxes, rents, and private incomes. It clamped down on Paris the dictatorship of a Council of Sixteen, and subjected France to the rule of a Council General, until such time as it could sell the country to Spain.

1588

In the general mess and confusion who was there capable of preserving order and independence? No doubt there were plenty of Frenchmen uncommitted to either of the two parties, either of the two religions, but they were too often mere dilettantes like Michel de Montaigne, who valued personal comfort above responsibility. "What do I really know?"—that cautious question he asked of everything under the sun. "I can make up my mind about nothing. I remain in a state of doubt." But at least he made up his mind not to remain at the Mairie of Bordeaux, from which he fled at the first threat of pestilence. "Time and time again," he wrote, "I have gone to bed convinced that I should be murdered during the night." That was how many people were feeling who were honest but not courageous. It was no use depending on them to rebuild France.

1580

The Kingdom Saved

The preservation of French unity was due to the three weaklings who followed one another upon the throne. They had neither the vigor of François I nor the shrewdness of Louis XI. The last representatives of the house of Valois had terrible defects, which the lampoons of Protestants and Catholics alike—on which later history was based—represented as vices. They were effeminate in the Italian fashion. They had the brutality that goes with timidity. They were guilty of faults, some of which amounted to crimes. But under the able direction of their mother, Catherine de Médicis, they did, at least, remain true to their kingly function. They alone, in the general laxity and confusion, had some feeling for the general good. It was their own heritage that they were defending, and in saving their crown they saved France.

Their foreign policy varied but slightly. Since the greatest danger came from Spain, it was better that France should seek alliance with the Protestants. When François I entered into an agreement with the Turks, he initiated a venturesome diplomacy. Learning from his example, François II collaborated with the Lutheran princes of Germany, and Charles IX sent subsidies to the Protestants of the Low Countries, who were in revolt against Philip II. At the same time he made an approach to Elizabeth, even though she was holding Mary Stuart, the widow of François II, prisoner.

In internal affairs the royal tactics were no less astute. Instinctively the Valois were inclined to make a show of tolerance toward the Reformers, though Catherine de Médicis leaned to the Papist side. The immense majority of Frenchmen had, in fact, remained loyal to the Catholic faith. In thirty-five thousand parishes it would have been impossible at any time to find more than two or three thou-

sand Protestant places of worship. Out of a population of
fifteen million, there were never more than two million
Huguenots. The kings, therefore, had no choice. They must
remain Catholic. But they were determined to do so without yielding to a public opinion that was ever eager for
massacres and violent suppression. Only when the situation became desperate did they have recourse to extreme
measures, when the pressure put upon them was too strong
or when one or other of the parties became too powerful.
Thus they acquiesced in the murder of Coligny and his   **1572**
Protestants on the night of St. Bartholomew, and had the
Guises, father and son, assassinated at an interval of twenty-   **1588**
five years. They espoused wholeheartedly neither the lessons of Machiavelli nor the solution of Shakespeare's
dramas, but found safety in a well-placed dagger stroke.

They preferred, normally, to rule by other methods. How
easy conciliation and reconciliation would have been if only
the country had consented to listen to them! They were   **1560**
prepared to grant the Protestants freedom of worship, and
even to hand over a few strongholds in appeasement of
their claims. Charles IX began his reign by granting an am-
nesty. Later, as a pledge of union, he gave his sister Mar-
guerite to Henri de Navarre—and this first mixed marriage   **1572**
was a great cause of scandal. Henri III surrounded himself with Calvinist advisers. When the League drove him
from Paris, he joined his brother-in-law, who was legal heir
to the throne. He had a feeling for Capetian continuity and
was anxious that the first of the Bourbons should succeed
the last of the Valois.

Together they laid siege to Paris, which was defended
by Catholics and Spaniards. Under the walls of the city a   **1589**
monk's dagger put finis to the Valois family. But Henri IV
was there to carry on the work of Henri III in spite of feudal
claimants and foreign enemies.

The end was near, because France was weary. The Bour-

1593   bon Huguenot knew beyond a doubt that a Catholic king
         was the only solution. Was not Paris worth a Mass? After
1594   giving the League a good thrashing he abjured his faith at
         Saint-Denis, and was crowned at Chartres (since he could
         not get to Reims). He was prepared to forget all and to
         tolerate all. In the end Paris opened its gates, and the Span-
         iards evacuated France. The French asked nothing better
         than to rally round the white plume of Navarre.

Among the Ruins

All that remained was to take stock of the ruins that had
accumulated during the third of a century given over to civil
strife. Stones were eloquent, and would long remain so. In
their fanatical eagerness to purge France of idolatry the
Protestants had everywhere set about destroying images
of the Virgin and the saints. They mutilated the statues
in many of the cathedrals—Nîmes, Montpellier, Vienne,
1568   Tours, Cléry, and Vendôme. They "cleansed" the porches
of Bourges, the church fronts of Lyon and Auxerre. They
blew up the Cathedral of Orléans with gunpowder. They
dispersed the treasures contained in the library of the Abbey of Cluny. Needless to say, the Catholics took their revenge on the Protestant places of worship.

Men suffered no less than monuments. Brigandage had
grown throughout the troubled years, adding its toll to massacre and pillage. It is hard to say whether the bandits who
scoured the countryside, looting and holding for ransom,
were Catholics or Protestants, thieves or soldiers. At their
approach the villagers had fled, the cities had closed their
gates. They burned the castles and carried off the livestock.
The misery of the times gave rise to feelings of class hatred.
In Périgord there was a peasant rising. The plague returned
to take a hand, and swept across the south.

Once again the fields were abandoned. A third part of Languedoc relapsed into heathland. There was a shortage of bread. In one year the grapes hung on the vines un-gathered. The roads were left unrepaired. Industry collapsed. Four times less textiles were produced than in the years before the civil war, six times less dyestuffs. The workers were unemployed. Though customs dues were raised, foreign goods carried all before them—wool, woven materials, hats, and shoes. Prices continued to rise at lightning speed. A plan was devised for taxing wages and prices (except grain, rents, and luxury articles). But, as usual, nothing could stop the rot.

The purchasing power of the wage-earners fell to a very low level. The humblest class of manual workers earned no more now per year than the equivalent of slightly more than twenty-seven bushels of wheat, or four times less than in the early years of the Renaissance. In the general confusion of inflation great fortunes were built up. The rich were called *milsoudiers* because they could afford to spend a thousand sous a day.

Money, thanks to the flow of precious metals from America, increased in quantity, and was not much debased. When the Valois line ended, the livre still represented 11.70 **1589** grams of silver (as compared with 25 at the beginning of the reign of Louis XI), and 1.08 grams of gold (as compared with 2.42). In other words, it had lost only sixty per cent of its content value in the course of a century. The Huguenots and the leaders of the League had issued a **1575** species of currency, but it was left for Henri III to mint a silver franc worth twenty sous as well as to issue for the first time small change in copper.

But if the treasury abstained from financial jugglery, it was forced to borrow here, there, and everywhere. The taxes were badly in arrears and frequently were levied by

the warring parties to their own advantage. It was found
necessary to put public offices up for sale. The national debt
rose from forty million livres to close on three hundred.

But in the general disintegration the State still made a
show of surviving. When things were at their worst, the
Valois insisted on initiating grandiose schemes of civil and
administrative reform. It was Charles IX, with the assistance of de l'Hôpital, the Chancellor, who made an attempt
to unify the seventy-two different local systems of weights
and measures to which the provinces and the various dis-

1564   tricts clung tenaciously. It was he too, in face of opposition
from the Parlement, who ordained that the year should
begin on the 1st of January instead of, as previously, at
Easter. Henri III, acting on instructions from Rome, suppressed ten days in 1582 so as to adjust the calendar to the
movement of the sun. Furthermore, he completed the sys-

1576   tem of post-stages established by Louis XI for the exclusive
use of the royal couriers, and organized the first service by
which letters, goods, and travelers could be carried from
Paris regularly to a certain select number of provincial cen-

1579   ters. With considerable courage he did his best to reform
the administration, to cut down the number of officials,
and to bring about economies, but his efforts in this direction failed, as did all the other expedients aimed at encour-

1577   aging deflation. He decided to merge money of account and
cash currency by issuing a golden crown worth three livres
as the standard unit, and boycotting all foreign currency.

1602   But the golden crown disobeyed his instructions by rising
above the three livres maximum, foreign money continued
to circulate, and Henri IV had to revert to the old system of
accounting in livres, sous, and deniers.

The climate of these tormented years was unfavorable to
artists and inventors. Of the sciences, only surgery benefits
from wars. Ambroise Paré introduced the use of ligatures in
cases of amputation as an improvement of the old custom

of cauterizing with red-hot irons. Jean Nicot brought back   **1561**
from Portugal, whither it had found its way from America,
a new herb, which he presented to Catherine de Médicis—
the "Queen's herb," later called tobacco, of sovereign use in
treating wounds and ulcers.

But what herb could cure the wounds received by the
Kingdom of France? A social crisis followed hard upon the
religious and economic troubles. The guilds were in a bad
way. The Renaissance, by exalting the art of letters, had
brought discredit on the manual crafts. An impecunious
treasury tried hard to sell for cash the letters patent of the
masters, who formed the highest class in the professional
hierarchy, and they, in their turn, strove to establish a monopoly in the various trades. Journeymen and apprentices,
finding the road to advancement thus barred, banded together against the capitalists. In this way an industrial proletariat came into existence, which was ready at all times to   **1539**
react to unemployment by rioting. Serious trouble broke
out in the printing-house at Lyon, spread to Paris, and   **1572**
lasted for more than thirty years, causing much embarrassment to eight hundred business concerns in the capital. A
settlement was finally reached by the terms of which the
workers were granted fixed wages and a limitation in the
number of apprentices. Henri III went so far as to suggest
the setting up of an inclusive workers' statute. But it is
doubtful whether that would have proved an effective way
of curing the evil. The guilds had far too many rules and
regulations as it was.

The heritage of the Valois was no easy one. They left to
the Bourbons a battered and exhausted France. Nevertheless, even after her two eclipses, the country was still a living entity. After a testing-time which had lasted for two and
a half centuries she might have ceased to exist or have
broken into a mosaic of fragments. She had seen the English in Paris, and, after them, the Spaniards. On two sepa-

rate occasions her kings had fallen into the hands of the
enemy. The throne had been occupied by an English
Henry VI and a Charles X. She had been the prey of feudal
barons and religious factions. Yet, caught between Armagnacs and Burgundians, Catholics and Huguenots, she had
managed to identify herself with none of them. The Valois,
for all their lack of prudence, for all their follies, had stood
firm. They had driven the foreigner from their frontiers,
had saved the unity of France, had enlarged the boundaries
of their realm. It was still possible to build upon the ruins.

CHAPTER V

THE SUN IN HIS GLORY

(1589–1789)

The Bourbons

I T is best to let figures and dates speak for themselves. Between the rise of the Bourbons and their fall—that is to say, between 1589 and 1789—precisely two centuries elapsed. In those two centuries there were only five kings: Henri IV and four Louis. Two of these kings—the first and the last—had their reigns cut short, one by a Catholic dagger, the other by the people's guillotine. The two longest reigns, those of Louis XIV and Louis XV, accounted between them for one hundred and thirty years. With them the house of Capet recovered the secret of continuity.

These five kings followed one another without a break. But the continuity was of time, not of character. All of them had the same nose, but by no means the same brain. Henri IV was jovial; a hail-fellow-well-met sort of king, clever without being cunning, fond of life, of his kingdom, and of his subjects—men and women alike, but especially women. Louis XIII was too timid to be a king, too scrupulous not to be. Louis XIV was a king born, completely sure of himself, and reveling in his job. Louis XV was too intelligent not to realize where his duty lay, but too indolent to do it consecutively. By no stretch of the imagination could Louis XVI be called any sort of king. He was a fat, middle-class citizen who, alone of all the five, seemed to be completely lost upon the throne.

The misfortunes of the dynasty were due, not to the men
1610 who wore the crown, but to the regencies. When Henri IV
died, Louis XIII was only nine. The Queen Mother became
1643 Regent, and she was an Italian. When Louis XIII died,
Louis XIV was five. Again the Queen Mother became Re-
1715 gent, and she was a Spaniard. When Louis XIV died, his
grandson, Louis XV, was also only five. This time there
was no queen mother, and it was a prince of the house of
Orléans, a cousin of the younger branch, who administered
the regency. Advantageous though these interregnums
might be to the representatives of the great feudal families,
they broke the royal continuity and unsettled the kingdom.

Now, it is almost without exception on the evidence of
these same feudal representatives that later historians have
based their views of the monarchy. The memoirs left by
the great lords—whether eaten up by vanity, like Retz, or
saturated with venom, like Saint-Simon—are all of them
monuments to bitterness and rancor. Taken in conjunction
with the many pamphlets from the hands of France's
enemies, both domestic and foreign, they have set history
moving on the wrong tack. How is it possible to strain so
much gall away and come upon the residue of truth?

What makes it still more difficult to do so is that the
average Frenchman, following in this the example of the
aristocracy, set his personal interest above the common good
and would never admit that he was satisfied with his government, whatever its nature, for the simple reason that it *was*
his government, to which he had to pay taxes. If there is
any master key to the history of France, it is that: the
Frenchman in perpetual revolt against any kind of fiscal
constraint. With the best will in the world, he cannot refrain from calling down curses on any regime that inflicts
such constraint upon him. He complains endlessly and, in
the hope of getting rid of government, will have recourse to
Fronde and Revolution.

It is only by looking beyond these aristocratic grumblings, these fiscal grievances, by surveying the Europe of that period, that one can get a true idea of what France really was. Long before Europe was French, France was European. In that fact lay her self-assured supremacy. Nationalism was an invention of the Revolution, and with nationalism came the isolationist attitude born of frontiers. The Frenchmen of the seventeenth and eighteenth centuries found nothing strange in having as ministers Concini, who was a Florentine; Mazarin, who came from Sicily; the Scotsman Law; or the Genevese Necker. They found it quite natural, as soldiers, to serve under the English Berwick, who was a Marshal of France, or Maurice de Saxe. The Swiss Guard and the regiment of the Royal-Suédois were part and parcel of the French Army. Where lay the danger, seeing that the country was incarnate in the person of the monarch?

The two great centuries of the French kings were more wholly European than any centuries to come would ever be. Guilty of many errors the Bourbons may have been, and of some crimes, but these things did not seriously affect their policy. By opening France to the world, they also opened the world to France, and established her as the greatest of all the great powers. They made the French people the most prosperous in all the world—though the French people might not always be conscious of the fact.

Religious Unity

The first task was to establish religious unity. The sixteenth and seventeenth centuries found it hard to realize that a state could tolerate a multiplicity of faiths. England was persecuting the Catholics, Spain the Protestants. No more than her neighbors could France achieve the miracle of conciliation. The majority of her people was Catholic and

1598　would not have toleration at any price. When Henri IV granted the Huguenots possession of more than a hundred walled towns, he was making a concession that seriously endangered French unity. Under Louis XIII those of the

1628　reformed faith were a state within a State, having the English as their allies and La Rochelle as their citadel. After a long siege they were forced to capitulate. Their strong places were taken from them, though they were allowed liberty of conscience. But public opinion was intolerant and wanted more than that—wanted, in fact, no less than a general conversion, whether as the result of persuasion or of force. There were still a million Protestants in the country, with more than six hundred churches, and they were suspected of still conspiring with the English. Louis XIV stripped them of such small liberties, one by one, as yet remained to them. Terrorized into compliance,

1685　the Huguenots accepted mass conversion, and the King could persuade himself that they had rallied round him to a man. He won popular applause by revoking the edict that had been granted to them, and forbidding them to hold their services. Much to his surprise, he found that a number of recalcitrants remained. Some of them, in the Cévennes and in Dauphiné, ventured on armed revolt. Others emigrated. Nobody blamed the King. Madame de Sévigné waxed indignant over the resistance of "these demons." La Bruyère rejoiced in the "extinction of heresy." It was not until much later that the full extent of the royal error became evident. Its effect at the time was not realized. It was morally blameworthy in that it involved the persecution of decent people; it was politically stupid because the emigration of between three hundred and four hundred thousand citizens did grave damage to the national economy. But there was some consolation to be derived from the thought that this exodus had the effect of diffusing the French language and the French way of life throughout the world, brought relief to an overpopulated country, and strengthened its cohesion and security.

One of the most definite, but quite unforeseeable, results was that France lost its chance of becoming a musical nation. The only part of the Roman liturgy retained by the Protestant church was its singing, and as a result of the break France remained cut off from choral education. Lutheran Germany developed a strong musical sense. Roman France never learned the art of singing.

It is true that, once the storm had passed, the Protestants did manage to make for themselves a small corner within the confines of France. It is even doubtful whether   1684
Louis XIV's hostility went deep or far. After the death of his Queen, Marie-Thérèse, he married Madame de Maintenon, who, as the granddaughter of a militant Huguenot, had been born in prison and educated in the Calvinist faith. He abolished the Inquisition in Roussillon, and was   1744
careful not to disturb the Protestants of Alsace. Halfway through the reign of Louis XV the existence of more than 250 Reformed churches was still tolerated in the provinces, especially in Languedoc, Dauphiné, Poitou, and Nor-   1787
mandy. Louis XVI restored full civil rights to the Protestants.

If the kings treated the Protestants with brutality, they were scarcely more gentle to the Catholics. They distrusted   1610
both sides, Rome no less than Geneva. A Papist had assassinated Henri IV, and it is far from certain that it was not a Jesuit who staged an attempt on the life of Louis XV which came to nothing. Meanwhile it was the royal policy to counter the machinations of all sects and sectaries, irrespective of their faith. Louis XIII, it is true, in dedicating France to the Virgin, was prompted by a desire to remove forever any suspicion that might still be felt about the son of a Huguenot. Louis XIV, on the other hand,   1682
fought a long battle with the Papacy. He aspired to free the

French clergy from the tutelage of Rome, and at one moment actually occupied Avignon, which was the property of the Holy See.

For a whole century a quarrel raged between the Jansenists, who represented Puritanism within the Roman Church, and the Jesuits, who championed a more easygoing and more worldly Catholicism. The kings frowned, turn and turn about, on each. They closed and later pulled
1732 down Port-Royal, the rallying-place of all true Jansenists,
1764 and when the latter countered by claiming a number of
1768 extravagant miracles, the police had to be called in to restore order. The Jesuits, though supported by Rome, were
1773 finally expelled from the kingdom. Louis XV, by once again occupying Avignon, brought pressure to bear on the Pope, who resigned himself to the necessity of dissolving the Society of Jesus.

These reverberating thunders had little effect upon the ordinary folk of France. They were Catholic, and meant to remain so, without giving overmuch thought to interpreting the dogma of the Fall or bothering about the teachings of Saint Augustine. They admired the active piety of such men as Monsieur Vincent, the chaplain of the galley slaves, and of the many orders whose members were busy opening hospitals and schools for the poor. But for the kings the matter was one of public policy. They saw not much difference between Protestants, Jansenists, Jesuits, and the witches or sorcerers whose punishment was the stake. All alike were disturbers of the peace and must be curbed. They knew what miseries the quarrels of religion had already brought to France, and they were merciless in suppressing them.

In every department of the national life they made their intentions perfectly clear. Wherever possible they sacrificed equity to policy, the individual to the community, sentiment to reasons of state.

The Reconstructors

It is time to resume the sequence of our narrative, and to
see how the kings tackled their task. What the first Bourbons had to do was nothing less than to reconstruct a
France that had been ruined as a result of the Wars of
Religion. Henri IV brought pacification, Louis XIII built.
With the names of these two kings are inseparably linked
those of two ministers: Sully and Richelieu.

Henri IV and Sully were bearded and likable. They were
fortunate because—though in their lifetime they suffered
from a good deal of unpopularity, since they were both of
them Huguenots who had more or less sincerely accepted
conversion—legend has been kind to them. The average
Frenchman has always tended to see himself in the gay and
mettlesome monarch and his parsimonious Minister. He
has forgotten the crushing taxation and remembered only
the facile slogans: the Sunday chicken in every pot; and
plow and pasture figuring as the life-giving breasts of the
French land. He likes to think, with an indulgent smile, of
the honest, domestic virtues of the pair. He remembers that
they brought back peace.

Louis XIII and Richelieu (bearded too, but more dis-
creetly) form no less—and in spite of ill-natured gossip—a
closely welded couple. It was some time before the King   1624
discovered his Minister, but once he had got him, he never
let him go. When it came to keeping Richelieu, the weak
prince was strong. To schemers he turned a deaf ear, and
he even banished his own mother. Of his own free will he
had chosen Richelieu, and in him he acknowledged a
master. So wholly did he make of him his second self that
he could not survive him.

The novelists have turned Richelieu into a police chief
of popular melodrama, nor is this view of him entirely
wrong. It is true that the Cardinal did make of the police

one of the chief instruments of his dictatorship, though before he could establish it on a firm foundation he had to
give and take many heavy blows. "The only enemies I have
ever had," he said, "have been the enemies of the State."
That is true, but it is no less true that the State reborn was
never short of enemies. Against them Richelieu set himself
to act with tireless zeal, keeping an eye (and a hand) on
everything, less from natural inclination than necessity.
He was a Prince of the Church. He was a sick man who
was never wholly free from pain. Nevertheless, he wore
the sword and breastplate of a soldier. He was at once general and admiral, engineer and diplomat. He directed commerce and stimulated colonial enterprise. Cleverer at spending than at saving, he was forced to adopt many financial
expedients. He prided himself on his literary gifts. He
scribbled verses and contributed to Renaudot's *Gazette*.
He was chancellor of the Sorbonne, and procured for it
1635 many privileges. He established a literary tribunal and,
when it became the Académie Française, gave it his patronage. There was no field of activity that did not come within
his empire.

He had a line of conduct from which he never departed.
It was his intention to build France anew, even at the expense of the French. He it was who mastered the rebel
Protestants; he it was who dared to attack the feudal families, even the greatest, and brought them to heel.

The religious troubles had bred in the nobles a belief
that the time had come for them to take revenge upon the
people and the monarchy. They appropriated the hunting-
rights of their estates and, to their own advantage, deprived
the peasants of their rights to wood and pasturage. They
did their best to reassert their feudal privileges. In their
attitude to the King they were turbulent and arrogant. The
brother of Louis XIII, Gaston of Orléans, became involved in princely conspiracies. It was a question of who

among the great ones of the land could most successfully
flout the central power and so make it clear to everyone
that they were above the law. Duels were forbidden—therefore they indulged in dueling. Spain was a standing threat
to France—therefore they negotiated with Spain. It was
Richelieu's fixed intention to restore discipline and impose
the royal authority. The nobles raised their heads—he cut
them off. Henri IV had executed Biron, and now Chalais,
Montmorency, Cinq-Mars followed one another to the
block. No longer, as under the Valois, was it a question of
ambushes or street-corner murders. The Cardinal's justice
passed sentence, the King's headsman carried it out. Everything was done according to the rule of law. By making an
example of the most illustrious families of France, by pulling down their strong castles, and founding a reign of le-
gality, Richelieu built up the sovereign State.

Unfortunately, the nobles were cowed only for a time.
They realized that in Richelieu they had too tough a nut
to crack. But no sooner had the Cardinal passed from the 1643
scene than they seized the opportunity with both hands.
Louis XIII was dead. Louis XIV was a small boy. The
Regent, Anne, was inexperienced. The small and insignificant Mazarin, whom Richelieu had recommended as his
successor, seemed scarcely of a stature to resist. The time
had come to finish, once and for all, with those Capetians,
who for six centuries had oppressed the barons. Now was
the moment to take a chance with revolution.

The Fronde, or the Revolution that Failed

Revolution was in the air. In Catalonia, in Portugal, in
England, monarchy was on the defensive. Nothing is more
infectious than revolt. In France the nobles did not lack
for allies. They had, as always, on their side the grudging
taxpayers. The middle classes had been touched in their

material interests by a decision that had the effect of strip-
ping them of one quarter of their incomes. They waxed indignant over the threat of new taxes (levied to pay for the
war against Spain—taxes on certain types of building, on
the rich, on looms, and on foodstuffs). That they would
not stand! The Parlement of Paris supported them the
more readily because it feared that it might be one of the
sufferers. Was there not a scheme afoot to reduce the payment of its members? Though only a court of law, it was
ambitious to play a political role, like its namesake of
London, which had taken the liberty of tumbling a king
from his throne. It demanded the dismissal of Mazarin.
It could rely, in the streets, on all the friends of trouble
and indiscipline, on the young men who, in open dis-
obedience to the King's archers, shot stones from slings
1648 (*frondes*). There were pamphlets, there were songs, and
there were barricades. "Frondeurs" versus Mazarin. This
was no simple rowdyism, but organized disturbance, perhaps something even better still. There were those who
talked of pulling down the Bastille, and recalled to men's
memories that the French monarchy was, in its origins,
elective. The word *Republic* was uttered. More than one
mazarinade held a hint of the carmagnole to come.

The monarchy might have been overthrown one hundred and forty years in advance of the time-table arranged
by destiny had it not been that Jules Mazarin, the man
whom everybody despised and mocked, was superlatively
clever. Foreigner though he was, he had in his bones the
very feel of French continuity. Hated alike by low and
high, he had managed to charm the Queen Mother, who
loved him passionately. Richelieu had ruled through a
police force; Mazarin ruled through spies. Instead of ex-
ecuting his enemies, he bought them. In his largess he did
not forget himself; both greedy and stingy, he succeeded
in amassing a personal fortune. Still, if he looked after him-

self, it can at least be said that he looked after France as
well.

The Fronde lasted for four years, with intermissions and
resumptions. Blood flowed in Paris and Bordeaux, in Normandy and in Auvergne. Twice the Regent and the young
King were forced to flee from the insurgent capital. The
aristocratic leaders were shameless in their treacheries.
Condé handed over fortified cities to the Spaniards. The
republicans of Bordeaux treated with the English. The
duchesses took a hand—Chevreuse, Longueville, and the
Grande Mademoiselle, daughter of Gaston of Orléans. But
what was afoot was full-dress civil war, and no game for
women. The Bastille fell into the hands of the Frondeurs,
and the Hôtel de Ville was fired.   **1652**

Alone against a world of enemies, the subtle Mazarin
bent, but never broke. Alone? Not entirely, since he had
the Queen on his side. Against a world of enemies? Almost, since he had against him a coalition of princes and
magistrates, of middle-class militiamen and aristocrats
holding high office in the Church. He made concessions;
he maneuvered. He suppressed some taxes, reduced others.
He went into exile; he waited. When the middle-class revolutionaries began to realize that the uprising was not going
to improve their chances of getting their money, Mazarin   **1653**
felt that Paris was ripe for his return. The French were
tired, disillusioned, and, once again, ruined. The monarchy
had won the game.

Who was the real beneficiary of the Fronde? Louis XIV.
The French now wanted nothing so ardently as civil order.
But they would no longer put up with the dictatorship of
a minister. The way was open for the King to rule in his
own person. When Mazarin died, Louis, who was then
twenty-three, declared to his ministers: "Gentlemen, from   **1661**
now on, I myself shall govern"—which was precisely what
his subjects wanted.

As a result of the revolutionary days of the Fronde the young King entertained a strong distrust of Paris. He preferred the terraces of Saint-Germain, the fountains of Marly, the marbles of Versailles.

An even more important consequence of the Fronde was that the nobles had to get down from their high horses. They crept back into a semi-obscurity with their tails between their legs. The families of Condé and Turenne made the *amende honorable*. La Rochefoucauld, in an embittered mood, turned to the writing of his *Maximes*. The great men of the kingdom were now no more than courtiers, than the King's servants. The whole complicated ceremonial of Versailles was a carefully contrived means of humiliating them.

The last of the rebels was Fouquet, the Superintendent of Finances, who had stolen the public money and fortified Belle-Île to serve his personal ends. Richelieu would have had his head. Louis XIV merely sent him to the Bastille— where, no doubt, he did a good deal of thinking to the effect that this was a king with whom it was wise not to play fast and loose.

Nobility of birth was not alone in having to foot the bill. The nobility of the gown had its share to settle. The Parlement had been made to feel the curb and was now confined within its legal function. If it so much as dared to voice a remonstrance when asked to ratify the royal edicts, Louis XIV grew angry. The legislative as well as the executive power was henceforward vested in the King and his councils.

Everything seemed to point to a future of unquestioned absolutism. The historians, in all good faith, have laid it down as an axiom that France stood on the threshold of a period during which kingship would be omnipotent. But they are wrong. The monarchy of the Bourbons was not absolute. In many respects it was no more than relative.

Monarchy Absolute . . . and Relative

About the theory there can be no doubt. The act of coronation set the king above his subjects. "It is your duty to obey me," the good Henri IV had said to the Parlement, "since God has chosen me." The king must needs rule by Divine Right if he were to stand up to the pope, if he were to override all feudal privileges. "In my person alone resides the sovereign authority," insisted Louis XV, and public opinion was only too ready to echo his words. "All is well under a monarchy," wrote La Bruyère, "in which the interests of the State are one with those of the prince."

1766

The king was the legislator (through his ordinances), the supreme head of the law, the master of the finances of the realm, the chief of the army, and the man on whom lay the sole responsibility for order inside and outside the kingdom. He had, indeed, to help him with his task a number of councils, a number of ministers (from three to five), whom he seldom changed. He was represented in the provinces by intendants. In general, and except in the matter of collecting the taxes, the total of officials was small. The administrative machine was simple and strongly made.

It was essentially a middle-class machine. The King was too mistrustful of his nobles to use them in high employments—a fact that enraged Saint-Simon (who denounced "this vile regime of the middle class"), and Argenson (who complained of "this satrapy of commoners"), and other men like them. Mazarin was the son of a groom, Colbert of a dry-goods merchant. Louvois came of a family of merchants. Fleury traced his descent from a tax-collector. Cardinal Dubois's father was an apothecary. Daguessau, Machault, Maupeou, had the law as background.

But there is nothing to prevent a middle-class monarchy from being despotic. That of the Bourbons did, in fact, ignore even the most elementary forms of liberty, begin-

ning with the liberty of the individual. The King could
commit any of his subjects to prison merely by issuing an
order in one of those sealed documents which were known
as *lettres de cachet*. But this arbitrary method was employed mainly when it was a question of removing criminals from the normal processes of the law, or of satisfying the requests put forward by families worried by the
profligacy of one of their members. The *lettre de cachet*
was more often an instrument of indulgence than of despotism, a favor rather than a punishment, and the Bastille,
where its victims were confined, was a luxurious place of
detention.

The monarchy knew nothing of, and did not recognize,
any other of the great human freedoms—freedom of
thought, freedom of speech, freedom to write, freedom to
publish. Except in matters of religion, no one bothered
about such things. The question did not even arise. Where
cases of intolerance occurred, they could be imputed as a
rule to the aristocracy, to the sects, or to the Parlement.
Louis XIV found it admirable that Molière should mock
at certain types of pious persons, and that La Bruyère
should voice his criticism of the great. It caused him no
concern that La Fontaine should poke fun at the lion (see
Les Animaux malades de la peste) or that Bourdaloue
should preach sermons denouncing royal immorality and
lust. Later, it is true, Voltaire was shut up from time to
time in the Bastille, but he was always released and sent to
live in some safe place, and eventually the court smothered
him with bouquets. Rousseau was the pampered darling
of Versailles. The *Encyclopædia* was encouraged. The
plays of Beaumarchais could be performed without let or
hindrance. Did such laxity come of a failure to realize what
was happening, or was it a form of intellectual masochism?

If the France of those days knew nothing of abstract and
individual liberties, she was bristling with concrete and col-

lective ones in many clearly defined and important fields. These could be invoked by innumerable Frenchmen. Above the Bourbons there was nothing to keep their power in check, but side by side with them and all around them there existed a tangled network of customs and freedoms and privileges by which they were bound hand and foot and reduced to a condition of paralysis. Had they wanted to play the game of tyrant they could have done so only within the walls of their palaces. Once across the threshold, they would at once have found the way blocked by centuries-old charters or by agreements of more recent date. In Provence they could not levy grants-in-aid, nor in the fiscal district of Auch a tax on gold- or silver-work. In Bayonne they could not draw revenue from tobacco, nor at Gex from the sale of foodstuffs, nor at Lille from the traffic in stamped paper. They could not impose the poll tax at Nancy nor draw a revenue from mortgages in Roussillon. Mountebanks were exempted from paying toll at the Petit Châtelet in Paris, and the citizens of the capital had the right to bring poultry, lambs, and wood from their country estates into the city without the payment of any dues. The villagers of Montargis-le-France were liable for neither the *ban* nor the *arrière-ban*—in other words, for military service in time of war. The King had no power to set up a tariff wall between Alsace and the Empire, to suppress the Academy of Besançon, to impose statute labor on the metalworkers of Champagne, or in any part of France to make seizure of horses and oxen used in plowing. It was impossible for him to expropriate anyone without paying heavy compensation, even for the purpose of building fortifications.

But what, it may be asked, could guarantee the observance of these many liberties, some of which were legitimate, though others were absurd and out of date? In the first place, the force of tradition; in the second, the passion-

FRANCE;
The Pre-Revolutionary Provinces
and Provincial Capitals

ate love felt by all Frenchmen for inequalities, exemptions, and "something for nothing" (provided they are the gainers). The lawyers had laid it down that certain laws styled "fundamental laws of the realm" must be obeyed by the sovereign. It was incumbent upon him to govern in accordance with the dictates of justice, to oppress nobody, to protect the good and punish the evildoer, to refrain from alienating any part of the kingdom, and not to modify the order of succession to the throne. Had it been merely a matter of the lawyers, the King might have ignored these injunctions, but the privileges of private citizens were otherwise protected. A vast number of public employments could be bought for money, and the State had no power whatever over their holders. The judges, for instance, had no promotion to look for, no dismissal to fear, and were completely independent. Adjudication in the courts was their function, but not their duty, and the same held good of various hereditary offices. Against them the King was powerless.

He was only a little less so in his dealings with the assemblies. It is true that between the reigns of Louis XIII and Louis XVI the States-General, in which the taxpayers made the law, were not summoned, but there were always the Parlements to be considered, and the local councils (there were seventeen of them scattered throughout the country). These, after Louis XIV, recovered their right of remonstrance, refused to ratify taxes, no matter how just or necessary, and carried on a relentless struggle for their privileges. There were also the assemblies of the annexed provinces—the states of Brittany, of Burgundy, of Languedoc, of Provence, of Artois, of the district centering on Cambrai, of Flanders, and of Hainault—which levied their own taxes and distributed them as they thought fit, organized their own work programs, and floated their own loans. These assemblies were often under the thumb of the local aristocracy, sometimes of the bishops (as in Languedoc), sometimes of the rich middle class (as in Provence). Beneath these states again were the district assemblies—of the Albigensians and the Vivarais—and the municipal bodies: *échevins* (or magistrates) in the north, *consuls* in the south, *jurats* (or aldermen) in Bordeaux, *capitouls* in Toulouse. Finally, there were the general communal bodies of citizens who had to give leave for the sending of deputations.

Irremovable magistrates, sovereign bodies. Very little freedom of action was left to the central power. On one occasion, when Louis XV ordered the arrest of a Breton noble whose drunkenness had created a public scandal, his lieutenant-general found it necessary to present his excuses —and do nothing. The competence of the State was strictly limited. It could rarely take action on a national scale. It controlled neither the judges, the army (the regiments belonged to their colonels), nor the educational authorities (the schools were all in private hands). The "public domain" lay within very narrow limits. Although Louis XIV almost certainly did not say *"l'État, c'est moi,"* he might have held that view without being guilty of arrogance. The King and the State were, indeed, one, but the State in the seventeenth and eighteenth centuries was, to all intents and purposes, nothing.

A Partitioned Economy

Just as the monarchy was incapable of asserting itself absolutely, so too was the State unable to conduct the economic affairs of the country in any real sense. Historians have not always grasped this fact, because there were economic controls at every turn. But it was the corporations and the provinces that made the regulations, though never on a national scale.

In Paris there were 124 organized trades, ranging from
the tailors and cobblers to the leather-gilders and scale-
makers. There were six merchant-artisan guilds, known as
the *six-corps,* heading the hierarchy of trade corporations—
drapers, glovers, mercers, furriers, hatmakers, and goldsmiths. Each guild was jealous of its prerogatives. It controlled its own statutes, and abused its power to prevent
journeymen from becoming masters. It also did its best to
eliminate all competition. Some of the rules and regulations benefited the workers (night work was forbidden, and
strict observance of Sundays and of the numerous feast-
days of the Church was imposed). Many of them, however, put a brake on initiative and barred the way to progress. For instance, the shape, style, width, and quality of
textiles was strictly laid down, as was the length of time
that beer must be allowed to ferment. Removal of plant
was forbidden, and no silk-mill, however small, could be
opened without due authority. The guilds claimed to be
protecting the consumer; in fact they were doing him an
ill service.

But behind the façade of regulations there was, in practice, a good deal of liberty. The various industries dealing
in objects of art were independent of corporative discipline. So were the big-business organizations, the capital-
issuing concerns, the banks, the Stock Exchange, and
wholesale trade in general, all the more recent trades (the
glaziers, the lacemakers, the stocking-weavers and tin-
workers), the suppliers, under warrant, to the king, and
all the newly established royal manufactories (the Gobe-
lins, which had absorbed all the tapestry enterprises, and
were turning out better work than the Flemings; the
Savonnerie, where efforts were being made to produce
carpets more exquisite than those of Persia and Turkey;
Vincennes and, later, Sèvres, where the finest porcelain was
made). Guild regulations were unknown in the villages, in

some of the cities (Bordeaux, Lyon), in certain quarters of Paris (the faubourg Saint-Antoine, the Palais-Royal, and the parish of Notre-Dame), and in some of the provinces (Burgundy, Champagne, and Poitou). Controls could be circumvented without much difficulty. If a closed shop was declared, the worker was granted a master's certificate. If advertisement was forbidden, show-windows were devised which gave rise to a rivalry between shops. If workers' collectives and strikes were banned, clandestine unions managed to elude the prohibition. From time to time class conflict flared up. The edicts issued by Colbert in an effort to unify trade organizations and workers' conditions had but a middling success. In all fields diversity triumphed over uniformity, inventiveness over rigorous control. A system that, grudgingly or not, permitted so many exceptions to the general rule can scarcely have been very oppressive.

Internal trade, too, erred from an excess of independence so far as the central power was concerned. In vain did Paris try to simplify and standardize. Local peculiarities won the day. Each province, each fragment of a province, clung to its own system of weights and measures, as to the very sign and symbol of freedom. The foot might be anything between ten and thirteen inches, the yard anything between five and eight feet, the perch anything between nine and twenty-eight. The league varied from two thousand to three thousand yards. The Paris arpent differed from that of the Gâtinais. The Normans insisted on using the acre as a unit of surface measurement. The demi-queue of Orléans was the only one to contain 240 "pintes." Only the Bordeaux cask was reckoned at the equivalent of one thousand bottles. Such differences were the breath of life to the French people. Edicts and ordinances strove to bring some kind of order into this chaos, to establish a common measure for the contents of a carafe, to impose an official system of weights, or merely to lay down accurately the proportion between local and Paris measures. But all these efforts broke against the obstinacy of the regions and the villages. Each was determined to go its own way. The provinces were no less mulish in clinging to their traditions. Up to the time of the fall of the Bourbons there were sixty-five versions of customary law, with three hundred local variants. "In France," said Voltaire in one of his sallies, "a traveler changes his laws as often as he changes his horses." Colbert more or less succeeded in unifying procedure, but the monarchy was compelled to respect the varying forms of private law.

Similarly, customs barriers not infrequently separated the provinces one from another. Nor was it merely a matter of paying toll. The fear of famine sometimes led local intendants to stop the movement of grain at the risk of letting people in the next province die of hunger. Each time Paris tried to organize a free circulation of cereals the countryfolk were up in arms at once against so flagrant an abuse of power. All attempts at centralization had to yield to local selfishness.

Was this criminal obstinacy wholly without excuse? To understand it we have only to think of distances in terms of days rather than of miles. It was by time that space was measured. In spite of improved methods of transport, it still took eleven days to travel from Paris into Languedoc. The provinces felt themselves to be very far removed from the capital. This was a reason the more why the northern parts of the kingdom were without any sense of community with the west or the south. Thus it came about that, in spite of a mass of regulations, vocational as well as local, France was a pattern of hermetically sealed compartments. If she had a directed economy, it was as a result of private interests rather than of state action. Absolute monarchy that could impose neither a standard unit of measurement nor a common system of law on its subjects was curiously misnamed.

The Wealth of France

While the State accepted or submitted to a diversified economy within its own frontiers, it did its best to establish a policy of commercialism in its relations with the outside world. The basic argument was simple. France must export as much, import as little, as possible. Only so could a trade balance in her favor be assured, only so could the national ownership of precious metals be increased.

The hunger for gold and silver had not been appeased by the flow of these metals from America. A growth in population and an increase in production had intensified the need for money. The only way to get it was by selling a great deal and buying very little. Long before Colbert public opinion had reached this conclusion. Richelieu had banned the import of certain articles (printed textiles among them). He had given to French vessels a monopoly **1667** of the carrying trade. Colbert defined this "mercantilist" strategy more precisely. If national production was to be protected, the export of raw materials and the import of manufactured articles must be checked, the export of finished goods and the import of raw materials encouraged. In order to produce an expanding commerce an ordinance was issued permitting nobles to engage in sea-borne trade without loss of status. Recourse was had to protective tariffs, state subsidies, and boycotts. In France, as elsewhere, economic nationalism was not slow to discover its proper weapons.

A policy must be judged by its results. In this case they were staggering. In spite of wars, in spite of the Barbary pirates, French commerce took a prodigious leap forward. When Louis XIV died, annual exports exceeded imports

by one third. From that time until the fall of the Bourbons trade increased five times—from 216 to 1,159 million.
Necker observed that the France of his day was enriching
itself each year by as much as the whole of the rest of Europe put together. Bordeaux, Nantes, La Rochelle, were
the capitals of big business.

France was selling because she was producing. The progress of her commerce reflected the progress of her agriculture and her factories. In the countryside waste land was
continuously diminishing. Under Sully's administration
marshland had been drained (Sologne and Flanders), heavy
soil irrigated (in the valleys of the Rhone and Durance),
forests cleared (Bondy), and common land plowed.

The development on a large scale of Beauce and Brie
started in the seventeenth century. In general, however,
France was still divided up into small holdings owned by
innumerable peasant proprietors. In the eighteenth century the whole country was swept by a fever of agricultural
activity. Florian's tales and the doctrines of the physiocrats
made the "return to the land" fashionable. Farming im-
plements, once of wood, were strengthened with iron as
soon as that metal became less costly—spades, plows,
wheelbarrows.

The vine retreated from Normandy and all the northern
provinces, where the yield was poor, and became established in those parts of the country which enjoyed more
sun. The international market for French wines was growing. Flanders had a special liking for the growths of Fron-
tignan and the Roussillon, England for clarets, the Baltic
States for the vintages of the Loire, and the Scandinavian
countries for the wines of Alsace. The first sparkling cham-   **1695**
pagne was produced in the cellars of the Benedictine Dom
Pérignon.

Rotation sowing superseded the old system of leaving
land fallow. This method of alternation, as well as the

introduction of artificial manures for grassland, brought
about a revolution in agriculture. The quality of livestock
was improved by the importation of horned cattle from
Holland. Rambouillet introduced the merino sheep. The
example of England led to the breeding of thoroughbred
horses and the institution of horse-racing. Two veterinary
1761 colleges—the first of their kind—were opened. In a Normandy village Marie Harel invented the Camembert
cheese. In Strasbourg a cook named Closé perfected a recipe
for truffled *pâté de foie gras.*

Cereals were no longer the only crops. Flax was beginning to be grown in Brittany. In the south there was a
newcomer, the mulberry tree, and this was quickly followed
by the madderwort, which yielded the secret of red dye
(jealously guarded hitherto by the Turks). Elsewhere many
new plants made their appearance—corn, used for fattening pigs and poultry, green peas, cauliflowers, and, finally,
beets and potatoes. It soon became evident that such small-
seeming innovations were destined to change the whole
basic problem of economics and society.

In the eighteenth century the annual value of agricultural production topped the two-and-a-half billion mark,
and that of manufactures, hitherto negligible, the billion.
How had this miracle been achieved? The monarchy had
systematically set about turning France into an industrial
power with the object of making a mercantilist program
possible. It offered inducements to foreign workers to settle
in the country. It reduced taxation on manufactured articles. It offered industrialists every kind of privilege and
monopoly. As a result of this policy many enterprises were
in a thriving condition—silk-weaving, papermaking, textile-
printing, glass-blowing, and the earliest efforts of Saint-
Gobain. Languedoc sold cloth to the Levant, Normandy
linen to South America, Rouen cotton goods to the Antilles, Picardy woolen goods to Spain. The first systematic

extraction of coal took place in Brioude, the mines of
which were worked before those of Forez and the Limou-
sin, of Aniche and Anzin. As a fuel it had hitherto been   **1742**
neglected, but now it was beginning to oust wood all over
the world. The first blast furnaces began to make their appearance, the first steel-mills. The great age of Creusot was   **1768**
beginning. Deposits of china clay were found in the Limousin, and the porcelain industry of Limoges achieved its
earliest successes. The great industrial families began to
play a part in the national life—the Wendels (heavy industry), Dollfus and Oberkampf (textiles). Machinery
now began to be used on a grand scale, and steam as a motive power was in process of development. Already the lines
of the future Industrial Revolution were being laid down.

There was certainly no unemployment in the building
trade. From the days of Henri IV to those of Louis XVI,
in the provinces no less than in Paris, architects and masons
were changing the face of France. It was not only a question of the domed churches, which were Rome's answer
to the uncompromising bareness of the Protestant places
of worship, but of town-planning on a large scale—as at
Nancy and Bordeaux—of monumental compositions—as in
the Place Royale and the Place Vendôme. Thousands of
town mansions, dwelling-houses, small country-houses, and
farms were going up everywhere, making staring white
patches in city streets and country views. During the last
thirty years of the monarchy ten thousand houses were
built in Paris alone, houses that for years to come were to
seem perfection itself to solid, respectable folk.

To give new life to this spreading world of industry,
transport was speeded up. Sully, Colbert, and Trudaine
saw to the upkeep of the roads, and not seldom had them
paved. No finer thoroughfares had been seen since the
great days of Rome. The institution of the *corvée royale*
(or obligatory state labor), which mobilized all peasants

for five to twelve days in each year, made it possible to construct a network with a total mileage of 120,000 leagues,
which was the wonder of the world. There were systems of
public conveyance. Cities were linked by coach and dili-
gence. The carriers of merchandise covered no more than
seven leagues a day, but passenger vehicles could do from
three to four leagues an hour. The waterways were still the
natural arteries of the kingdom. On the Loire, the most
important of them all, whole flotillas of vessels were based
on Orléans and Tours. The intending traveler from Paris
to Provence would take boat at Orléans and go direct to
Roanne, whence he would continue by way of Lyon to
Avignon. On her journeys from Paris to Nantes, Madame
de Sévigné regularly made use of the Loire from Orléans.
Timber was floated from the forests of Burgundy and
Morvan to Paris. River valleys were connected with the
1681   sea by numerous canals—those of Briare and Orléans, the
Canal du Nord, the Canal du Midi, the latter constructed
by the engineer Riquet—a triumph of French technical
achievement. In the matter of waterways as of roads, France
led the world.

Poverty or Easy Living?

If France was rich, were her people poor? There are
grounds for believing that they were. They complained.
They made a display of poverty. A celebrated outburst
from La Bruyère and the lachrymose reports of the intendants seem to confirm the impression that the French were
in dire distress.

But let us look a little closer. As always, the French refused to pay their taxes, adopting any shift to get out of doing so. Since they were assessed on the basis of the figure
they cut in the world, they did all they could to make that
figure eloquent of distress. They put on as plausible a show

of indigence as possible. The intendants, who were responsible for the incidence of taxation, left no stone unturned
to spare their provinces, and in their reports were only too
pleased to paint a gloomy picture.

These documents have long misled historians. We must
go behind them if we are to get at the true facts about day-
to-day realities in this period of easy living. Not that poverty did not exist. Far from it. There were plenty of "poor
woodcutters"—those favorite figures of the fairy-tales. There
were times of famine too, when the great mass of Frenchmen lived no better than the "wild animals" of whom La
Bruyère speaks. The winter of 1708–9 was particularly severe, with the rivers frozen, ice in the Channel and the
Mediterranean, olive trees blighted, chestnuts destroyed,
wine congealing in the casks, all hope of a good crop
ruined, the people reduced to eating grass and roots (in
other words, cabbages, turnips, and carrots), Madame de
Maintenon and everybody else at court compelled to make
do with oatcake, dysentery spreading through the country,
the hospitals full, deaths amounting to one or two million,
and the distant rumblings of revolt. In 1720 at Marseille
the spectacle of plague was far from cheering. But such
things were no more than terrible accidents. Normal, every-
day life was a great deal less tragic.

What was the usual diet of the ordinary run of the
French people? In the poorest classes it primarily consisted
of farinaceous foods (peas, beans, and lentils). Meat,
which was expensive, was eaten only on feast-days, at harvest, on occasions of weddings and funerals. But fish, both
fresh and salted, was easy to come by. An average menu
would consist of herring or cod, cabbage, turnip, and
cheese. The peasants still ate off earthenware platters. The
middle classes, copying Louis XIV, had adopted china.
They had learned to drink coffee, which came from Mocha,
in Arabia, by way of Suez and Marseille.

Lighting was no longer confined to smoky tallow dips,
resinous torches, or oil lamps. Wax candles made it possible to sit up longer and to go to bed later. The hours of
mealtimes were changing. *Déjeuner,* which used to be
taken on rising, tended now to be delayed until noon.
Dinner, instead of supper, became the evening meal.

Prices varied greatly from province to province, from season to season, and according to whether shortage or abundance was the rule. Making due allowance for such ups
and downs, they were at their lowest under Louis XIV and
during the first third of the eighteenth century (because
1734   there was a lack of the means of payment), at their highest during the remaining years of the century (because supplies of silver from Mexico increased the general flow of
money, because credit had begun to come to the help of
hard currency, and because consumer needs were increasing).

Taking one thing with another, the purchasing power of
the average Frenchman remained fairly high. The un-
skilled manual worker earned (all food found) a daily
equivalent of 3.80 liters of grain during the Fronde, 6.10
liters under Louis XV, 5.70 under Louis XVI. Between
1689 and 1789 prices and rents doubled, but wages increased three times. The only people to suffer the extremes
of poverty were the agricultural laborers and the unemployed. But their plight was not forgotten. It was forbidden
to let animals into the stubble until the poor had gleaned
the bruised or broken ears, or to enclose the fields, because
after the harvesting of the first crops they had to remain
accessible to all the droves of the parish. In this way the
claims of collective ownership were not allowed to suffer
from the rights of private property.

The peasants lived well. Their presses were bursting with
linen, and not seldom their drawers with silverware. La
Fontaine wrote of the "rich farmer." These rich farmers,

who never tired of buying land, owned more than one half
of the acreage of France. "There is no country in the
world," declared Voltaire, "where the farmer is better off."
Nor were the workers in the towns to be pitied. It is well
to remember the words put by La Fontaine into the mouth
of his "jolly cobbler": "Each day brings its meed of bread."
Everywhere men were singing *Auprès de ma blonde*, playing ball, and learning how to eat ices at the café or the con-
fectioner's shop.

That the middle classes were opulent is almost too obvious to need saying. They ruled the roost in the cities, and
quite often at court. Just as no unbridgeable gap separated
the humbler people from the shopkeepers, or the shopkeepers from the wholesale merchants, so too the middle
classes were drawing nearer and nearer to the aristocracy.
A noble lost caste and became a commoner if he engaged
in certain trades. A commoner could become ennobled
without difficulty, by attaining to senior rank in the fiscal
administration, by purchasing certain public offices, by
rendering some outstanding service (Louis XIII granted
a title to the builder of a ship of three hundred tons), or
by acquiring letters of nobility (which would cost him
three thousand livres at the end of the seventeenth century). Many rich citizens assumed the *particle* of their own
accord. With or without it they climbed to the top of the
ladder and occupied positions of power. Not only might
they become ministers, but princes of the Church as well.
Bossuet was the son of a magistrate, Fléchier of a grocer,
Bourdaloue of a notary. Actors were generally held in con-
tempt, but not servants. Does not the Knave [1] come next
after the King and Queen in the pack of playing-cards? No
one considered it derogatory to hold the post of page or
chamberlain. It needed the Revolution (and *Ruy Blas*) to
discredit domestics. Under the monarchy it caused no sur-

---

[1] The Knave, or Jack, is called by the French *Valet*.

prise that a lackey should become prime minister. Cardinal Dubois is a case in point.

It was even possible to rise from humble circumstances **1684** to the steps of the throne. In the person of Madame de Maintenon, whose first husband was called Scarron, **1745** Louis XIV married a middle-class woman of spirit. Jeanne Poisson, whose father was a shop clerk, was made Marquise **1768** de Pompadour by Louis XV, and Jeanne Bécu, of unknown parentage, Comtesse Du Barry. Both these women became near-queens and incurred the hatred of the genuine aristocracy. It is one of the ironies of history that the "people" should have banded themselves together against favorites who had emerged from their own ranks.

Certainly a daughter of the middle class or a prostitute might become the King's mistress without the condition of the country at large being improved. But there is plenty of less exceptional evidence to show that well-being was widespread. We have only to consider the solidity of the houses, the quantities of expensive furniture, to see that. It needed a great many rich men to pay for so many pier-glasses, commodes, and chests of drawers. Only a general condition of well-being can account for the presence of so large a quantity of vast wardrobes, even in the depths of the country.

It was a period of large families, a time when the population, as a result of security, was increasing rapidly. The total moved from 19,000,000 under the Fronde to more than 27,000,000 at the fall of the monarchy. No doubt death was a constant threat, but there was more longevity among the peasants and the city workers than there was at court, perhaps because these classes lived more soberly, and because they did not fall into the clutches of the doctors and were not debilitated by drugs, purges, and bleedings.

Cradles were multiplying at a quicker rate than graves. Under Louis XVI between 900,000 and 1,000,000 French

babies were born each year, and each year the total number
of inhabitants increased by about 120,000. From the time
of Louis XIV onward Paris contained 500,000 persons. A
century later Lyon accounted for 160,000, Marseille for
100,000. Certain villages in the Cambrai district saw their
population treble in the course of the last two reigns, simply as the result of a rising birth-rate. No nation of Europe,
not even Austria, not even Russia, was so densely peopled.
Such a degree of human density, when one takes into account the quantities of food available and the state of production, cannot but have raised grave problems of over-
population. France was bursting, if not with happiness, at
least with health.

The Poverty of the State

It was in the poverty of the State that the real drama was
to be found. Frenchmen were rich, but the State had an
empty purse. Why was this? Again, as always, because the
taxpayers refused to do their fiscal duty. The Bourbon
monarchy suffered from a lack, not of taxes, but of those
who paid them. A great variety was devised—income tax,
capitation tax, a temporary ten per cent, a permanent five
per cent. Recourse was had to indirect levies, all more or
less oppressive, on luxuries and necessities alike. The worst
was the old gabelle, exacted on the sale of salt, the purchase
of which was compulsory. The collection of all these
amounts was farmed out, thus guaranteeing to the treasury
at least a minimum total of receipts. But nothing was of
any use: the French would not pay. They invoked out-
of-date privileges, traditional immunities—or compounded
once and for all at a cheap rate. Any stick was good enough
to use for beating the administration. A tax that hit one's
neighbor was fair enough, but when it came nearer home
it was quite a different matter. When the State tried to lay

it down that tax liability must be shared equally, a cry of
"Robbery!" was raised. There were threats of revolt, and
the State capitulated.

Direct taxation did not touch either nobility or clergy.
The revenue attempted to make up for this by exacting a
fee for the registration of armorial bearings and for the
franking of letters. The State's intention was that the capi-
1710   tation tax should spare nobody except the very poor. "Monstrous exaction!" declared Saint-Simon. When the tithe
system was instituted, everyone did his best to get out of
1749   it by compounding or by making installment payments.
When it was replaced by a twenty-per-cent levy without exceptions, the clergy rose as one man against such a flagrant
violation of prerogative, while the Parlement took a similar
stand on the ground of magisterial immunity. There was
the same inequality in the matter of sales tax. The gabelle,
for instance, was imposed only in those provinces which
had formed part of the old royal domain. It was unknown
in Brittany, Artois, and Béarn. Limousin, Guyenne, and
Poitou had compounded out. Dealers in contraband salt
did their best to get round this manifest injustice: constraint
was met with fraud.

The privileged felt that their complaints were justified.
"It is we who have to meet the cost of religious services, of
poor-relief, and the hospitals," said the clergy. "We pay for
the safety of the country with our blood, we pay for our
regiments and are responsible for their upkeep; when we
go abroad as ambassadors, the cost falls on us," said the
nobles. "We ought to be completely independent, even of
taxes," said the Parlement. One and all, including the free
cities, the compounding provinces, and the exempted guilds,
based their claim of privilege on promises and contracts, on
services rendered in the past or to be rendered in the future.
Against such an outcry, such a universally negative attitude,
the "all-powerful" monarchy was helpless.

In the long run, weary of struggling, it fell back on other expedients, many of them pitifully inadequate—such as lotteries and the sale of patents of nobility. The one most frequently used was the traffic in public offices. Why should the State refrain from so obvious a way of making money when it could amass cash and at the same time gratify the French liking for official status and official titles? Anyone who was willing to pay for the privilege could become notary to the Châtelet, superintendent of bridges in Paris, stevedore at Nantes, royal scrivener in the Dauphiné. Anyone, for a price, could be inspector of tanneries or assessor of coal mines. Every office, and every grade within that office, were for sale: barber, colonel, public trustee, controller of woods and forests, gauger of casks, caretaker at the Central Markets, beer-taster, inspector of wine, town crier, tollkeeper, registrar of births. Such purchasable appointments could become hereditary in return for an annual payment. It all helped to feather the treasury's nest, The middle classes and the Parlement were delighted. These honors gave them their heart's desire and enabled them to make a fortune.

Drawing what money it could from these strange and precarious expedients, the State had to face ever increasing costs. Wars were becoming more and more expensive, what with improved equipment, and armies growing constantly larger. Great nobles had to be rendered innocuous, faithful servants to be rewarded, by the grant of honors and pensions. In satisfying their exhibitionist passion for building, the kings spent public money wildly. Not content with constructing châteaux and parks for their own use, they set to work beautifying the cities. Henri IV presented Paris with a Pont-Neuf, which could boast the first known pavement. To the existing 510 streets of the capital Louis XIV added a further 120. All were lighted at the public expense, and for this purpose five thousand lanterns were necessary.

Louis XIV laid out what was to be the Place de la Concorde and planned the Champs-Élysées and the Étoile. All
this, like Versailles, was town-planning for posterity. When
the kings built, they built in a big way. For themselves, the
Louvre and its Colonnade; for disabled soldiers, or *invalides*,
a palace; for the astronomers, a palace too; for the Military
College, yet another palace. There must be no skimping.
The siting of these great buildings was superb, only—the bill
had to be paid.

Progressively, from the days of Henri IV to those of
Louis XVI, the annual expenditure of the State rose from
fifty to six hundred million livres. In the same period the
national income increased from thirty to five hundred million. A deficit was the rule; rarely was the budget balanced—
and then only accidentally—by Sully, Colbert, and Fleury.
There were plenty of spiteful tongues to accuse the ministers of avarice and to maintain that the King was squander-
ing the public money on his mistresses.

In order to cover the deficit, the King borrowed from
anyone who was prepared to lend. The national debt, now
swollen by fresh issues, now contracted as the result of re-
payments, reduction of interest, and bankruptcy, rose from
some three hundred million livres under Henri IV to more
than three billion under Louis XIV, and close on four billion under Louis XVI.

From Sully to Necker, those responsible for the country's finances brought to their task many varied and sometimes contradictory talents. Sully saved money like a careful householder; Richelieu borrowed with the nonchalance
of a great noble; Colbert had the gifts of a good accountant;
Noailles economized; Law gambled; Fleury put by. But all
of them were faced by the same recalcitrance on the part of
the taxpayers, the same restiveness of the privileged. No
matter what they did, the State remained poor, the country
rich.

Paper Money

In the course of the previous centuries the State had financed its wars by debasing the currency. When the Bourbons first came to power the "livre of Tours" contained
seven times less silver than under Saint Louis (11.70 grams
instead of 80.84) and eight times less gold (1.08 grams instead of 8.27). The Bourbons had recourse to the same expedient, but they applied it timidly. In the two centuries
of their rule the livre declined to 4.50 grams of silver and
290 milligrams of gold (which was to be the basic equivalent of the future franc). In the first forty-six years of
Louis XIV's reign and in the last sixty-three years of the
monarchy, the stability of the currency was exemplary—
nothing like it had been seen since the days of Rome. The
two handsome coins struck at that time in the palace constructed on the banks of the Seine to house the Mint acquired a lasting prestige: the silver crown (*écu*), and the
golden louis.

There was, all the same, a continuing shortage of the
precious metals. The yield of the American mines, even   1734
when Mexico became a great silver-producing country, was
not sufficient to meet growing needs. The general total of
currency increased more slowly than the economic activity
of a mounting population. All efforts to improve relations
with Spain—through which bullion reached France—were
vain: preferential treatment in matters of trade, the sending   1680
of sixty thousand French masons, carpenters, and saddlers
to settle beyond the Pyrenees. Vain, too, was the effort
made by Louis XIV to ease the situation by melting down
the royal plate. The circulation of metal coinage was no
more than doubled during the last century of the monarchy—that is to say, that although in terms of the livre of
Tours it rose from 500 million (in 1683, under Colbert) to
1200 million (in 1730), and 2200 million (in 1780, under

Necker), yet in weight of silver the comparable figures are: 4,340 tons in 1683, 5,400 in 1730, 9,900 in 1780. Though this progress proves and confirms the fact that Frenchmen were growing richer, it was too little for the needs of an expanding economy. Might not paper be called in to redress the insufficiency of metal? In the ancient world Persia and China had been no strangers to the idea. Venice and the northern countries had already been making experiments, and both the Bank of England and the Bank of Scotland had issued notes. But such innovations were mistrusted by the average Frenchman. Only by chance were their possibilities revealed to him. When, in 1701, an extensive re-coining operation took place, the Mint issued to depositors a written promise to pay them in currency as soon as the new issue should be ready. These undertakings went into circulation under the name of "treasury notes" to a total of 187 million livres. In this way the first step to a fiduciary system was taken.

1715   The second step went a great deal farther. When Louis XIV died, the Regent Philippe was anxious to make himself popular, and knew that he could not do so by re-ducing expenditure. An inventive Scot, John Law, sub-mitted a wonderful scheme by which paper money would solve the whole problem. Law was by no means a mere shrewd adventurer. He had a presentiment of the part that credit would be called upon to play in financial affairs. Unfortunately, he came on the scene too soon, he moved too quickly, and he went too far. Precursor of genius he may have been, but of evil genius.

1716   The French responded with avidity to the notes issued by Law's Bank and given the legal standing of currency, as well as to the stock in the Mississippi Company (granting
1719   a monopoly of overseas trade), which the venturesome Scot persuaded the bank to handle. The stock was snapped up, and went from 500 livres to 20,000. The quantity of bank-

notes in circulation rose to three billion. But this frantic
speculation was succeeded by a mood of doubt, and the
system collapsed. Law attempted to obtain by compulsion
what he could not get from public confidence. He planned
to prohibit payments in specie, and even tried to confiscate
metal coinage. The only result was to precipitate disaster.
Paper values melted away, the stock dropped to fifty livres,   1720
bank-notes gave up the ghost. Law, threatened with popular
violence, fled.

In the course of this their first lesson in inflation the
French had made acquaintance with a glittering Cloud-
Cuckoo-Land. They were to learn that credit must be built
on something tangible, that though it has advantages, it has
also certain limitations. Law's system had certainly created
wealth, but, more important still, it had shifted the incidence of wealth. Its failure discredited not only the idea
of paper money, for generations, but the monarchy as well.

For all his failure, Law had at least set capital moving. In
the rue Quincampoix, in the heart of the financial district,
the word *millionnaire* was born. The Paris Stock Exchange,
which was just beginning to get into its stride, soon became
a dangerous rival to the older Stock Exchange of Lyon.   1724
There was a big increase in the number of insurance companies. Joint-stock concerns marked the opening phase in
a period of collective capitalism.

In these ways French economy did, in fact, benefit from
the drama of inflation. The State, which had hoped to find
in it a solution of all its difficulties, was, in the long run, its
only victim. Such help as paper money had at first seemed
likely to afford had vanished, and no real answer had been
found to any of its financial problems.

War in Lace Ruffles

Although wars laid a heavy burden on the budget in the course of these two centuries, they did not play any very large part in the life of the average Frenchman. They were numerous, and they were long-drawn-out, but they were fought, for the most part, by professionals—that is to say, by aristocrats and mercenaries. Since, too, the troops were active only—except in very exceptional circumstances—during the summer months, and even then as a rule either on the frontiers or in foreign countries, the great mass of the people was not greatly affected. The mysterious "beast" that ravaged the district of Gévaudan in 1765 was productive of far greater consternation and aroused considerably more interest than did distant battles or the fact that French armies might be advancing or retreating around Danzig or Prague. Even defeats did not cause widespread alarm. After Malplaquet, Marlborough, the victor, became the hero of a popular song, as did Soubise, the vanquished, after Rosbach. It seems doubtful whether the wars were taken seriously at all. At the very height of the struggle with Spain, when the hegemony of Europe was at stake, Corneille produced his *Cid*, a play in which Castilian heroism was extolled. It was usual for travelers, even when fighting was in progress, to move freely through hostile territory. Fortunate age when men did not much bother their heads about whether or no their compatriots were guilty of "dealings with the enemy"!

War in lace ruffles? With or without lace, death was still death. When the Imperial forces laid Burgundy waste, or when the French devastated the Palatinate with the object of transforming it into a defensive no-man's land, they were not playing at war. But, at least, in these centuries of ordered government good manners still ruled, even on the battlefield: *"Messieurs les Anglais! Tirez les premiers."* National hatreds were rarely invoked, as is shown by the ease with which men changed sides. Condé, for instance, gave the Spaniards a thorough beating at Rocroi and then, ten years later, captured the same Rocroi in the service of Spain.

Though the army was a permanent institution, it was never very large. In peace-time Henri IV had 10,000 men under arms, Louis XIV 15,000. On active service the total number of effectives might be as high as 150,000, but never more. Recruiting was carried out by free enlistment. The soldier "La Tulipe" was a volunteer attracted by the prospect of glory, money, and wine.[2]

Companies and regiments were the property of their captains and colonels, men of noble birth who were delighted to have the opportunity of carrying on the tradition of their feudal ancestors. But the King, always suspicious, made them subordinate to brigadiers, *maréchaux de camp*, lieutenants-general or marshals of France, who might be great lords, like Condé, or, equally well, members

---

[2] *Fanfan la Tulipe* was a popular song. Its hero was Fanfan, the French equivalent of GI Joe. It circulated as a barrack-room ditty about 1819, and was set to the tune of a much older song. *Fanfan la Tulipe* inspired a number of plays written round this popular figure. The first two verses of the song are as follows:

> Comme l'mari d'notre mère
> Doit toujours s'app'ler papa,
> Je vous dirai que mon père
> Un certain jour me happa.
> Puis me m'nant jusqu'au bas de la rampe
> M'dit ces mots qui m'mirent tout sens d'ssus d'ssous.

> J'te dirai ma foi,
> Qu'il n'y a plus pour toi
> Rien chez nous
> V'la cinq sous, et décampe.
> En avant Fanfan la Tulipe,
> Oui, mill'noms d'un pipe,
> En avant!

This information comes to me from M. René Ledésert, to whom my thanks are due. (Translator.)

of the lesser nobility, like Turenne or Vauban, or commoners, like Fabert or Catinat.

Who was the enemy? The official reason for a war almost always had to do with succession—War of the Spanish Succession, of the Polish Succession, of the Austrian
Succession—but the deep, underlying causes were the same.
Nor did the nature of the antagonists change. Two powers,
and two powers only, were in a position to dispute with
France the hegemony of Europe: Spain and England. The
word *Spain*, in this connection, must be understood as covering all the Habsburgs—those of Vienna, who were the
rulers of Germany; those of Madrid, who reigned as well
in Brussels. France had to wage a long struggle before she
could break the circle and drive the Austro-Spanish enemy
1648   from positions in which he could threaten Paris. The peril
from the east was finally liquidated by the Treaty of Westphalia, which, by breaking up Germany into 343 sovereign
states with 2,000 enclaves, organized the long-existing anarchy beyond the Rhine under French protection, to the
complete satisfaction of the Germans. The danger from the
1700   south was dissipated when Louis XIV set one of his grandsons on the throne of the Habsburgs and kept him there.
Spain under a Bourbon king was no longer an enemy, and
Austria without Spain, even though enlarged by the addition of Belgium and northern Italy, ceased to be dangerous.
It was the great merit of Louis XIV, and of Louis XV after
him, that they understood this and set themselves to bring
about an Austrian alliance, though French public opinion
remained firmly bogged down in a now completely out-of-
date hostility. Both these kings saw clearly enough that
Prussia was growing in strength and aiming to make the
German heritage her own. From now on, *that* was the
danger against which protection must be sought.

England was harder to tackle, because, being an island,
she was inaccessible. English diplomacy consisted in oppos-

ing whatever power on the Continent might for the moment be strongest by a European league built round the Dutch, the Imperialists, or the Prussians. From the moment that France assumed a position of dominance, war became endemic. It was at once a struggle for political leadership and for markets, the end of which was not yet in sight.

Who were France's allies? All those countries in a position to take the enemy in the rear: Portugal, Turkey, Sweden, Poland—but Russia and Prussia intervened, at the expense of France's friends in the East.

By a series of battles (Rocroi, Lens, Denain, Fontenoy) and of treaties (Westphalia, the Pyrenees, Nijmegen, Rijswijk, Utrecht, Vienna, Aix-la-Chapelle, and Paris) the kings achieved their object, and France assumed her final pattern. The "bounded field," dear to Richelieu and Vauban, began to take shape. Henri IV had welded Navarre into the kingdom. Louis XIII occupied Alsace. Louis XIV began by recovering the Roussillon, and went on to annex Flanders and Franche-Comté. Without firing a shot, he incorporated Strasbourg in the realm and purchased Dunkerque for five million. Louis XV garnered Lorraine from his father-in-law, Stanislas, and Corsica from the Genoese (though in the event it would be truer to say that Corsica dominated France rather than France Corsica). Were these conquests carried through for the sake of prestige? Some of them. But more often it was security that made them necessary. Those responsible for French policy were concerned to push the enemy as far as possible from her vital centers, to simplify the line of her frontiers, to hold and fortify the most suitable operational bases. They worked more as geographers and engineers than as soldiers. Vauban made the decisions; the necessities of peace had the last word.

The only credit that the balance-sheet of all these wars

1607

1766

1681   could show for France was—peace. *Clausa Germanis Gallia* was the superscription on a medal struck after the annexation of Strasbourg. But in truth it was to all her enemies that France now was closed. Except along the northeastern fringes, where surprise attack was always possible, the provinces lived in a state of tranquillity till then unknown. Not once did Paris experience the humiliations and sufferings of enemy occupation. Her old fortifications were turned into elegant promenades—the *grands boulevards* of the future, and a symbol of fair weather.

France Overseas

On the seas, and beyond them, France and England came into head-on conflict, and each scored in turn. The English were more favorably situated. From being a peasant nation they had become a race of merchants and sailors, destined for a great colonial future. Not only were the French distracted by their European problems, and held in check by the necessity of providing for their security on the Continent; they preferred tangible investments to distant speculations, and put their available capital into land or honorable state employments more readily than into commercial undertakings. The colonies, to them, were in the nature of a freakish luxury.

It was only because of the initiative of a few statesmen, of a few heads of commercial enterprises, that France built up a navy and founded an empire. It needed a Richelieu, that "master of navigation and trade," a Colbert, who put new life into the dockyards, a Choiseul, who reorganized the arsenals, to increase the number of ships of war and merchant vessels, without which any colonial effort would have been in vain. But ships and sailors cannot be improvised, and one unsuccessful battle may easily spell ruin for a fleet and breed discouragement. More than once, as a result of the sheer lack of the necessary squadrons, France had to confine her activities to isolated actions. It happened that the bravest of her admirals—Duquesne and Tourville, Jean Bart and Duguay-Trouin—were reduced to adopting the methods of corsairs. But not by privateering can a country establish, maintain, or protect a system of colonies.

Nevertheless, the French were anxious to play a part in the great world, not because they were hungry for territory or eager for domination, but because an expanding nation needs air and space. Even after the Spanish and Portuguese conquests there remained plenty of spots on the earth's surface for such Frenchmen as were resolved to seek out new lands, to carry Christianity to the heathens, or to trade in gold and spices.

They took a chance on three continents: in Africa, in Asia, and in the New World. Neither disappointments nor checks served to deflect them from their purpose. Such setbacks as they met were due not so much to any fault of their adventurers as to the failure of the French at home to understand them.

In the Dark Continent they set up trading agencies. Senegal produced a small quantity of gold and a large quantity of Negroes for the slave trade. L'île Dauphin, later rechristened Madagascar, supplied them with tobacco. Far away, in the Indian Ocean, two marvelous small islands became French, Bourbon (the future Réunion) and Mauritius, which took the name of île-de-France. Both became a paradise of sugar-cane and coffee.   **1642** **1721**

Asia was less accessible, because it was already peopled by the heirs of an old civilization. But the lure of spices was hard to resist. For centuries the very name of the Indies had set the West dreaming. The Compagnie des Indes, to which Colbert gave special privileges, set up its factories, first at Chandernagor, then at Pondichéry. One   **1676** of its directors, the self-willed Dupleix, encouraged the rivalry of nabobs and rajas, risked the whole of his personal fortune, and, with a handful of men, in the very teeth of London, which fought him, and of Paris, which left him unsupported, succeeded in carving out an empire of thirty million subjects. But the timid Compagnie des Indes, which was concerned with commerce rather than conquest, washed its hands of him, and had him recalled.

1608   In America the achievements of France were no less astonishing, and no less fragile. Under Henri IV, Champlain founded Quebec and reached the Great Lakes. Colonized by French peasants, "New France" extended its boundaries. It gained the friendship of the Algonquins and the Hurons, but incurred the hostility of the Iroquois. Here and there forts and trading-stations took root, and from them arose cities with French names (Montreal, Detroit).

1673   Colbert, mistrustful of such scattered successes, handed over the infant Canada to the Compagnie des Indes Occidentales. Jolliet and Père Marquette discovered the Mississippi. Cavelier de La Salle sailed down the river as far as

1682   the delta and took possession of its course in the King's name. He called this new possession Louisiana. Law, who

1717   made it the center of his speculations, provided a number of colonists and a capital—New Orleans. In this way, along the arc of a circle measuring 1,817 miles, the French pioneers traced the general lines of an immense province. But it threatened the English possessions with envelopment, and London grew restive.

If these precarious establishments, manned by a few tens of thousands of Frenchmen (alongside a million English), were to be maintained, public opinion would have to be roused. But public opinion was disappointed. Gold had been found neither in Canada nor in Louisiana. Grain— well, there was nothing very out of the ordinary about grain; furs—they were not particularly exciting. Law, with his fine promises, had given a bad name to the American venture. The *philosophes* laughed it out of court: "an icy waste," they said, "inhabited by barbarians, bears, and beavers," "acres of snow." "I could wish," said Voltaire, "that Canada were at the bottom of the sea." Diderot and Rousseau condemned all colonies without exception. "Men should stay where they have been put," wrote Montesquieu. The Parlement went on strike against taxation in the very year that the English captured Quebec. What could Louis XV do in the teeth of public opinion? The reinforcements that he sent to Canada and the Indies were nothing like sufficient in view of English numerical superiority. France was compelled to renounce her two empires, as well as Senegal. Choiseul, the friend of the *philosophes*, rubbed his hands.

1763

France did, it is true, retain what, with hand on heart, she could consider as essential—five trading-stations in the Indies and, more important than all else, the brilliant coronet of islands in the Antilles. They, at least, were worth their weight in gold! In the Caribbean Sea, under Louis XIII, French privateers had conducted a profitable trade in brigandage. Colbert had acquired a whole archipelago for less than a million. He had sent settlers to Cayenne, and aided the freebooters of Santo Domingo. The islands had become prosperous. They produced not only indigo, coffee, cocoa, cotton, and tobacco, but sugar, which was sent home to be refined in Rouen, and later in Bordeaux. Holland and the Hanseatic cities bought it for redistribution throughout Europe. In return they got from Nantes a supply of "black ivory"—in other words, Negro slaves from Guinea. Men and money flowed to these islands, in comparison with which Canada seemed poor and empty. Even the *philosophes*, greedy, perhaps, for exotic foods and fat dividends, excepted them from their general condemnation. With Santo Domingo and Guadeloupe

1664

from which to draw, France became one of the largest sugar-importers in the world, and Bordeaux the rich capital of the refining trade. By the end of the monarchy, thanks to sugar and coffee, which accounted for one third of the exports of the islands (ranking ahead of wines and spirits), French foreign trade was the largest to be found anywhere. It was greatly superior to the English. The Americas produced twenty-four per cent of all French overseas commerce, as compared with a mere twelve per cent at the death of Louis XIV; and the Americas meant, first and foremost, the Antilles.

There was to be some consolation for the loss of Canada and the Indies when France took her revenge at the outbreak of the American Revolution. When the English colonists of the Atlantic coast rose in rebellion, first Lafayette, then Rochambeau, went to their assistance. Louis XVI may have taken very little interest in the business of kingship, but he had a passion for geography and for everything to do with the sea. In the reconstituted fleet Suffren and de Grasse won fame. The war cost two billion and dug the financial pit into which the regime collapsed. It resulted in more than the independence of the young United States. It meant for France the recovery of Senegal and the possibility of building an African empire. Resplendent in her newly gained prestige, she got a footing 1768 in Annam, and took the first steps toward developing a new empire in the East. Bougainville in the antipodes had 1786 reached Tahiti. La Pérouse had been killed in Polynesia. At the very moment when in France the monarchy was throwing in its hand, the nation was pursuing an active policy on the high seas.

The Classic Age

True glory is won by the conquests, not of sword or count-
ing-house, but of the human spirit. It is true, however, that
the three go together and give one another mutual support. A reign is great, or a century, only in so far as it can
bind into a single whole the political, economic, and intellectual achievements of a people. This happened in the
France of the seventeenth and eighteenth centuries. In
every department of activity she radiated light to the world.

At the heart of this glowing pulsation was the King, the
"Roi Soleil." He quickened and inspired and protected, he
paid and he pensioned. Before his time Henri IV had made
Malherbe a gentleman of the chamber; Richelieu had given
Corneille a pension. After it Louis XV could call friend
that Quesnay who had renewed the art of political economy. All the Bourbons gave employment to poets, painters, musicians, scholars; offered them positions at court,
and loaded them with gifts that amounted to fortunes. On
their behalf they multiplied the number of academies the
members of which drew fees for their attendance. Thus
subsidized, genius and talent had air to breathe and elbow-
room in which to expand.

The zenith of the classic age coincided, quite naturally,
with that of Louis XIV. It had been foreshadowed by Corneille, Pascal, and Poussin, all three of them questing
spirits in search of a discipline. The way had been made
plain for it by Descartes, the teacher of method. Order had
been imposed upon it by Boileau, Lebrun, Mansart, and
Lulli, dictators in their several fields of poetry, painting,
architecture, and the violin. It reached its moment of triumph in Racine and Molière, in La Bruyère and La Fontaine, in Le Sueur and Claude Lorraine, in Puget and
Coysevox, Perrault and Le Nôtre. All these men deliber-

ately set themselves to observe and give practical form to
the same general theory of art, a theory at once sober and
grandiloquent—whether it found expression in designing
the grouped and clipped groves of gardens *à la française,*
in the wearing of great built-up wigs, in the writing of
dramas on the rigid framework of five acts and with due
respect to the unities of action, time, and place, or in the
construction of palaces with long and regular façades. The
park at Versailles, the colonnade of the Louvre, *Andro-*
maque, a funeral oration by Bossuet, an opera by Lulli—in
these and other fields the same sense of form was consciously applied.

It would be a mistake to regard these masters of the classic style as cold and academic high priests of the arts. On
the contrary, in the eyes of the *précieux* and the *baroques,*
deep drinkers of the philter of disorder, they figured as
young revolutionaries. Before their coming, popular approval had been given to Voiture and Scudéry, to Quinault,
and the Jesuit style, to the obscure and the pedantic. To
all such gaudy excesses of language and design the classicists sought to oppose their love of reticence. They valued
reason above passion (though without ignoring or excluding the latter), order above disorder. They preferred the
horizontal line to the soaring lacework of fretted stone, the
straight avenue to virgin nature. To be classic meant to say
less than one thought, to simplify, to dissect. It meant
working within a frame, though not to be loaded with
chains. Even the classicists at times, when the fancy took
them, escaped from the constriction—La Fontaine always,
Molière frequently, and Madame de Sévigné, who wrote as
though she were chatting with a friend.

Later generations drew profit from the lesson, adapting
it to the changing taste of future years. Less pomposity and
more elegance. Country houses, armchairs, and wigs grew
smaller. Style began to show a new purity, whether in an

author's written pages or an architect's elevations. Who could write better than Voltaire or build more admirably than Gabriel? Both could imitate their predecessors, Voltaire when he thought he was copying Racine, Gabriel when he rebuilt the Cathedral of Orléans. But they knew still better how to be themselves and scale the heights of French perfection with *Candide* and the Petit Trianon.

Sometimes, however, in its easy movement from the showy to the charming this art did drop into insipidity. The fall is sharp from Montesquieu to Florian and the Abbé Prévost, from Watteau to Fragonard and Boucher, from Rameau to Philidor. But the new houses were more comfortable to live in. The formal gallery gave way to the boudoir, and the furniture was more practical—sofas, chests of drawers, desks, commodes, writing-tables, dressing-tables, card-tables.

All through these two centuries France was the arbiter of elegance for all the countries of the world. To Versailles came Bernini and Mozart. All the courts of Europe strove to imitate Versailles. Its mirrors of glass and its mirrors of water were widely copied, its gardens and its fountains, its manners and its modes. Every king wished to live like Louis XIV. Every queen wanted to wear clothes like Marie-Thérèse, or Marie-Antoinette's headdresses. Schönbrunn and Potsdam, Dresden and Bayreuth, St. Petersburg and Stockholm were but extensions of Versailles.

It was an age in which all Europe thought and spoke in French. The *Mercure de France* had the biggest circulation of any periodical in the world—7,000 copies. The *Journal des Savants* was a source of inspiration to London, Leipzig, and Amsterdam. Ten years before the end of the monarchy, twenty-seven Paris newspapers were supplying, both inside France and beyond the frontiers, the material of information and discussion. The language of Racine was taking the place of Latin in diplomatic treaties and in the academies of the world. It had become the universal tongue of princes and scholars, of drawing-rooms and kitchens.

Science on the March

Nor were the sciences lagging behind letters and the arts. Gone were the days when they had fumbled uncertainly in the dark night of doubt. They were advancing now into what they took to be the bright light of certainty. In the seventeenth century Descartes had simplified algebra, founded analytic geometry, and discovered the law of the refraction of light. Even his mistakes were fruitful, as when he reduced the human body to the status of a machine or declared that the universe was a system of vortices. Fermat created the calculus of probabilities, and laid the foundation of the infinitesimal calculus. Pascal demonstrated atmospheric pressure. Mariotte studied the movement of liquids and the physical bulk of gas. Denis Papin pored over his boiling pot, invented the piston, and built the first steamboat. Foreigners too were swarming to Paris, lured by the golden prospect of pensions; Cassini, from Nice, who was put in charge of the Observatory; Huyghens, the Dutchman, who fitted clocks with pendulums; Roemer, from Denmark, who measured the speed of light.

Only the doctors, in spite of the King's Garden (later a museum), still clung to their old methods, their robes, their beards. With their enemas and bleedings, their drops and herbs and tinctures, they would, had their numbers been greater and their fees lower, have been responsible for a great many deaths. Fortunately there were few of them, and they charged high prices for their services.

The eighteenth century, curious about everything under the sun, and intoxicated by the idea of progress, had its men of science in good measure. It had, also, its fair share of mountebanks. Posterity, no doubt, has preserved the

memory only of the former—of mathematicians like Le-
gendre, Lagrange, and Condorcet; of physicists like Ré-
amur or Monge; of naturalists like Buffon, who explained
the mineral and animal worlds, and of Jussieu, who classified the vegetable families; of chemists like Lavoisier, who
discovered the composition of air and water. The earliest 1770
conquests of steam were registered when Cugnot utilized
it to move a carriage, and Jouffroy launched a steamboat 1776
on the Doubs. The reign of electricity began when Romas, 1752
at the same time as Franklin, captured it with a lightning-
conductor. New forms of illumination were making their
appearance—Quinquet's oil lamp, Lebon's gas. As a final
triumph, to delight the gaping crowds, men actually succeeded in rising into the air. Montgolfier invented his hot- 1783
air balloon, and Blanchard and Jeffries flew from Dover to 1785
Calais.

The closing years of the monarchy were made glorious
by these marvels. The happenings of one single year may
serve as an example, the year that was marked by the independence of America and the return of Senegal to
France: Rivarol published his *Discours sur l'universalité de
la langue française*, which was crowned by the Academy of
Berlin; Lamarck composed his botanical encyclopedia;
Cassini, the grandson of the astronomer, issued his *Description géométrique de la France*, the first map of the kingdom constructed on the meridian of Paris; Lavoisier separated hydrogen and oxygen from water; and at Passy, Pilâtre
de Rozier was the first man to ascend into the air. There
was enough in all this to go to the heads of the mob.

But it was the charlatans, even more than the men of science, who enjoyed popular success. The belief in progress
went hand in hand with a wild passion for the sort of child-
ishness which, under the mask of science, revived the ancient practices of magic and sorcery. Adulation was showered on a Portuguese who called himself the Comte de

Saint-Germain, melted diamonds, and was widely believed
to be a contemporary of Jesus. Crowds gathered round the
Sicilian Cagliostro, who made gold and could foretell the
future, and the German Mesmer, who achieved cures by
means of a magnetic tub. The century of enlightenment
was also the century of superstition.

Not that these weaknesses were wholly nonsensical. They
did at least bear witness to the fact that men find it difficult to follow blindly the rhythm of science, that they
crave the supernatural. Were those who exploited this simplicity merely adventurers? History may one day uncover
the secret of their occult activities. So far it has done little
more than guess, concluding that these men, whether
Masons or spies, were working on behalf of foreign powers
or the sects of the Illuminati, to pave the way for the overthrow of the monarchy. In this task they had everything in
their favor. The French *philosophes* had already undermined that institution of a thousand years.

Ideas on the March

The first intellectual offensive was opened by the great
feudal nobles. Tamed after the Fronde, they had enjoyed
only a temporary revenge under the Regency. Their ambitions could find no real satisfaction at Versailles. They
dreamed of an aristocratic regime in which they would
shine as kings. The Duc de Saint-Simon did all he could
to blacken a system that failed to give him the degree of
precedence to which he thought himself to be entitled.
Fénelon, who took enormous pride in the fact that he was
descended from one of the noblest families of France (in-
termarried with the Talleyrands, the Montmorencys, and
the La Trémoilles), threw himself heart and soul into the
work of bringing about a feudal reaction. The intriguing
Archbishop of Cambrai took his revenge for his failure to

make a mark in politics, by setting cloudy policies in motion. The Baron de Montesquieu was eager, too, to set up between King and people an "intermediate body" in which the nobles of the realm should take their place.

Embittered aristocrats and liberal-minded *philosophes* united in criticism of the existing regime. Did not scientific and technical progress justify a belief in some similar progress in human and social relationships? In condemning the *status quo* were they not merely criticizing an outworn system of government? But in this the attitude of the two groups showed itself to be equivocal, for while the nobles damned the monarchy on the ground that it had sapped their privileges, the *philosophes* blamed it for being powerless to abolish them. Nevertheless, they waged the struggle in common.

Foreign influences played the midwife to philosophical theories, first and foremost the influence of England. Montesquieu was an admirer of Locke. Voltaire found in London the model of political and civil liberties. The simpler-minded were seduced by Prussia, thinking to find in Frederick II the champion of an enlightened despotism. They did not realize that he was just a despot and nothing more. Since the monarchy was in favor of an Austrian alliance, its enemies rallied to Prussia. Later the American example raised them to the seventh heaven. Across the Atlantic, citizens had shown how men might liberate themselves, how a republic could be born. Franklin, the man who never wore a wig, was acclaimed. The discontented looked to him for guidance.

When foreign experiments were insufficient, the necessary evidence was invented. Montesquieu created a Persian who was disconcerted by what he found in Paris. The sparkling Voltaire set down an artless Huron or a common-sensical inhabitant of Sirius among the absurdities of French civilization. The lachrymose Rousseau went farther still. For him truth could be found only in the noble savage—and long live the return to nature!

Nature, indeed, was coming back into fashion. English parks were superseding French gardens; solitudes and labyrinths, lovers' isles, thatched cottages, stage ruins, hermits' grottoes—a world of nature for the oversophisticated. Monsieur de Condé had a chasm, Monsieur de Lauraguais a volcano, the Queen a rustic hamlet. Louis XVI, catching the infection, plowed a furrow. Marie-Antoinette played at tending sheep.

But in politics nature surely meant the absence of organized government? There, beyond any doubt, lay the purity of human infancy, equality in its most perfect form. No laws, no king, no taxes. That way lay anarchy. But the *philosophes* lacked the courage to tread the road to its end. They stopped halfway. Voltaire, for whom "the great mass of mankind has ever been, and long will be, stupid and idiotic," remained an aristocrat. Rousseau's democracy could exist only in small states, something on the scale of the Swiss cantons.

In default of political liberty, which seemed to them to be beyond attainment, the *philosophes* claimed at least the human freedoms—freedom of authorship, though it might lead at times to license (the French reputation for obscene literature dates from this period); economic freedom ("Let matters adjust themselves"—"*Laissez faire, laissez passer*," was what Voltaire preached long before the physiocrats); religious freedom, in the name of which the Catholic faith was mocked and attacked in Bayle's *Dictionary*, Diderot's *Encyclopedia*, and a host of those lesser compendia which were the favorite reading of the eighteenth century. Stress was laid on the errors of the Bible, on the greed of the Jesuits, on the fiscal immunity of the clergy. These were the chosen subjects on which philosophical irony was expended.

In this campaign those who were free to think and the freethinkers, served by a limpid language and a mordant wit, found their audience in the cafés, and very soon in the drawing-rooms too. They conquered the Academy, they annexed the court, they seduced the ministers. Bernis, Choiseul, Malesherbes, and Turgot were their friends and defenders, taking pride in their own philosophical leanings. The Pompadour was their protector, who housed and pensioned them. It was she who made of Voltaire—the favorite's favorite—an official historian, a gentleman of the chamber. She helped d'Alembert and Rousseau. The aristocrats lauded Beaumarchais to the skies, and his *Mariage de Figaro*. Far from being the victims of power, the *philosophes* were its masters and used it for their own ends. They forgot that they were fighting intolerance and became in their turn intolerant. They had unfriendly newspapers suspended and hostile books suppressed.

Their victory would have been complete had public opinion rallied to them. But the majority of Frenchmen knew nothing of them. Their influence was confined to an élite of letters, the members of which, for the most part, were more interested in the *Henriade* than in the *Essai sur les mœurs*, in the *Nouvelle Héloïse* than in the *Contrat social*. In the *Encyclopedia* they turned more frequently to the article on gardening than to the article on God.

The *philosophes* had a hold only on the thinking minority, but it was the thinking minority that held all the positions of power.

Abortive Reforms

Louis XV saw clearly where the danger to the dynasty lay, and the way too in which it might be countered. The opposition assumed an active form in the parlements. These judicial bodies aimed at becoming political—not only from a taste for power, but in order to defend their own status and their own privileges. They blocked the way to all reform and deliberately obstructed the machinery of taxa-

1771 tion. In a moment of energy Louis XV, assisted by the Chancellor, Maupéou, deprived the magistrates of their functions and dissolved the parlements, in spite of an indignant outcry raised by the princes of the blood. The alliance between nobles by birth and nobles of the robe did not disturb the King. He decided that the judges should be irremovable civil servants, and that justice should be free. The

1774 way was clear now for the correction of abuses, for the suppression of exemptions, for the restoration of the finances of the kingdom.

With Louis XVI everything collapsed. He was no king, but a kindly, flabby man with a weakness for overeating. He had plenty of good intentions, but no *intention*—no will. He was called a tyrant because two centuries of authority had worn away the power to think. In fact, the wretched Louis XVI was the very reverse of a tyrant. Brought up in the mental climate of the *philosophes,* and himself a Freemason, he was the friend of his enemies, ripe for Utopias, ready for surrender.

His first mistake explains all his later failures. He recalled the parlements, the members of which reassembled in embittered mood and were more than ever hostile to anyone who might seek to end abuses. From that moment Louis XVI and his ministers were fated to be the prisoners of the parlements. Their best intentions remained sterile. Because they had failed to set political reforms on a firm basis, every other reform was bound to be abortive.

Economic Reform. On two occasions, once under Turgot (a successful intendant) and once under Calonne (a shrewd magistrate), free trade in grain was proclaimed, which meant the suppression of all internal customs dues and all taxes on the marketing of wheat. Each time the Parlement and the interested parties were loud in protest. The provinces, fearing a food shortage, wished to keep a tight hold on their stores of flour. The people dreaded a period of dear bread. Each time Necker re-established crop-control.

Social Reform. Turgot suppressed the power of the masters, threw open every trade, proclaimed the right to work, **1776** and submitted quarrels between employers and employed to state arbitration. The guilds rebelled against so daring a departure and, with the support of the Parlement, insisted on the restoration of their disciplinary powers.

Administrative Reform. In the old provinces of the kingdom, assemblies were created to oversee the distribution of **1787** taxes, in the same way as the states did in the more recent ones. The Parlement, jealous of an infringement of its powers, refused to recognize them.

Financial Reform. What could be done to put an end to the privileges, factual as well as legal, which, by reducing the revenue, led to an unbalanced budget? The American war had added enormously to the state deficit. Calonne, with great courage, proposed to abolish all fiscal immunities, and to impose, in place of the "twentieth," a "territorial subsidy" payable by all landed proprietors irrespective of their social position. Only by some such innovation could the country be saved. But nobles, members of the Parlement, and prelates were, all of them, large landowners. In the Assembly of the Notables, convened for the purpose of dealing with the situation, they formed a coalition to oppose the **1787** project. Why did Louis XVI yield? This attempt at fiscal reform failed as all other reforms had failed. The banker Necker resumed his niggling manipulations, in which loans played the leading part. They made him popular, but solved nothing.

In 1789 the revenue reached a total of 475 million, expenditure 600 million, half of which was accounted for by interest payments on loans. How was the balance to be found? The privileged would not hear of any economy or any tax that might fall on them. The King, no doubt, could have raised all the money he needed by a variety of financial expedients—either by issuing notes, as Law had done—and the treasury, too, after 1777, though on a very small scale (80 millions' worth were in circulation in June 1789)—or by devaluing the livre, after the manner of so many of his predecessors. But Louis XVI was too honest. French currency was stable, and it never occurred to him to manipulate it and so make everything come right as though by magic. What did

1789 occur to him was an expedient of a quite different kind, now fallen into disuse, which was far worse than devaluation. He would convoke the States-General—in other words, would ask the taxpayers to give their consent to sacrifices.

And so it came about that on the one and only occasion when Louis XVI made a decision, that decision amounted to a surrender. It sounded the death-knell of the "relative" monarchy, and the prelude to the absolute republic.

Let us, before turning the page, take one last backward look at the regime now on its deathbed. Inability to reform itself had condemned it. It died of weakness at the very moment when it was being accused of despotism.

Squalid scandals, cleverly exploited by its enemies, had
1785 spattered it with mud. The Affair of the Diamond Necklace —dirty water in which Cagliostro fished—had involved the Queen. She was not beloved. Her crimes were that she was Austrian, and that she was proud—even though she had made a pilgrimage to Rousseau's grave. The King was still popular, though his subjects would have liked it better if he had been less stout, more martial, and not quite so preoccupied by the problem of getting the taxes paid.

A vague desire was at work among the people of France, a desire to change something, though what it was they were to change, and how, they did not know. They grumbled, but did not take account of the fact that France, by reason of her agricultural production and her trade, was now the fore-most country of the world. She led, too, because of her re-constituted armed forces (Gribeauval's artillery and Sar-tine's navy). Everything was poised for future victories. But these collective advantages were not sufficient to make up for empty coffers.

The fact of the matter was that the face of France, with or without revolution, was about to change. The fear of fam-ine was becoming a thing of the past, and that for two rea-sons—the introduction of rotation farming, which had increased the productive area of the country, and the culti-vation of the potato as a substitute for cereals in times of bad harvest. Other human miseries too were on the point of be-ing alleviated. The Abbé de l'Epée had conceived a method for helping deaf-mutes, and Valentin Haüy was working out a system for aiding the blind. The Industrial Revolution was on the way. Vaucanson, the magician of the machine, had already invented a mechanical loom, and new sources of mo-tive power—coal, steam, gas—were there for the using. The whole of the material side of life was in the process of being transformed at the very moment when, because of the pres-ence on the throne of a king who did not know his job, the monarchy was bogged down in the slough of habit.

The age of the Bourbons was coming to an end, and with it the long tradition of the Capetians. The dynasty had lasted for nine hundred years. At the cost of much unhappi-ness, in spite of foreign enemies without and recalcitrant no-bles within, it had built France into a unity. In its early days the sovereign had been to all intents and purposes a king without a kingdom. From now on, France was to be a king-dom without a king.

CHAPTER VI

THE GREAT STORM

(1789–1815)

Why?

FRANCE had suffered from no
lack of revolutions. There had been Étienne Marcel, there
had been the League, there had been the Fronde. Once already the mob had compelled Charles V, while still the
Dauphin, to wear the liberty cap, and it was to do the same
to Louis XVI. Henri III and Louis XIV, as a child, had fled
from the capital, as Louis XVI was to try to do. The League
had lasted for ten years—precisely the same length of time
as that of the greater Revolution yet to come. The Fronde
had paved the way for an authoritarian monarchy: the Revolution was to spawn the dictatorship of Napoleon. But this
new Revolution was the one that counted. The shock of its
impact was to bring new life to France and to overturn the
world.

That there was need in monarchic France for new life is
proved by the fact that she was incapable of producing it.
Is that by itself enough to account for the metamorphosis
that overcame her? To bring it about, an exceptional combination of circumstances was necessary—economic, financial,
and political.

Let us take a brief glance at the total picture. In the economic field the discovery of the silver mines of Potosí had
increased the flow of currency and forced prices up by fifty
per cent. The rather half-hearted success of the notes is-

sued by the Caisse d'Escompte, in Paris, had had the same
effect, with the result that prices had jumped ahead of
wages. The purchasing power of the mass of Frenchmen had
fallen, and the country was in a mood of sullen discontent.

At the same time the supply of foodstuffs had diminished
in consequence of a series of unusually bad harvests. Anything from two to three million Frenchmen were dependent for their living on the cultivation of the vine. Exception-
ally good years (and falling wine prices) had recently been
alternating with bad. In 1787 floods and bitter cold had
brought about a catastrophic grape harvest. The same freakish weather had done terrible damage to the crops. The   **1788**
summer of '88 had been too dry, with frequent hail. On
July 13 (a year and a day before another July date that was
to assume historical importance) a terrible storm had devastated the north of France, leaving the south, with its vineyards, untouched. The peasants' reaction to the threat of
famine had been to hide what remained of their cereals. In
the spring of '89 the price of corn was higher than it had
been for eighty years, while that of wine had rarely, if ever,
been lower. Too little bread, too much drink. The cities
grumbled and soaked. Their inhabitants had less than
enough to satisfy their hunger, and a great deal too much
with which to quench their thirst. There could be no better
soil in which to sow the seed of revolution.

Urban discontent was increased by unemployment.
France was overpeopled, and not infrequently there were
too many workers for the work available. True, the commercial treaty concluded with England by the liberals in 1786
had opened the English market to French wines, but it had
also reduced by ten per cent the customs duty on manufactured articles from across the Channel, where the cost of
production was low. Textiles and hardware poured into the
country. There was a wave of bankruptcies. The volume of
protest grew. The unemployed crowded into Paris.

Financially speaking, the distress of the treasury was, of all the problems, the most difficult to deal with. The American war had increased the national debt. The bankers supported Necker and his policy of loans, which was profitable to them. The bondholders began to fear that they would not be paid. There was a general unwillingness to produce the taxes. It was less a question of men insisting on their right to vote the taxes than of their determination not to pay them.

Politically the dynasty was at the end of its tether. Louis XVI had all the qualities that go to make a good workman, none of the qualities needed by a king. In 1789 the Dauphin died and the royal family went into mourning. In the same year the compilation of the *cahiers*, or lists, of complaints and the summoning of the States-General gave to all the adversaries of the monarchy a chance not to be missed. They lost no time in turning it to account. There was little need to batter down the gates of power. The King threw them wide open.

But it is impossible fully to understand this business of revolution unless we realize the nature of the intellectual climate in which it started. This, unexpectedly enough, was the climate of Rome. The new discoveries at Herculaneum and Pompeii had brought pagan antiquity into fashion. Furniture began to lose its curves. The modish had their beds made with architraves, their chairs with legs designed as columns. Jacob turned for inspiration to Etruscan models. Artists traveling to Rome brought back with them a passion for the pure simplicity of the antique line. Houdon draped Voltaire in a toga. David, in rebellion against the insipid elegance of painters on silk, depicted heroism on a grand scale. He preferred grandiloquence to grace, and, because he had a knack, anticipated the temper of the times or at least kept abreast of it. His *Oath of the Horatii*, which had a tremendous success, not only exalted love of country, but popular-

ized an attitude. Naturally enough, the middle-class deputies who assembled in the Tennis Court posed for his pencil
almost as consciously as they posed for posterity. Just a year
before the Revolution, David entranced the mob by his *Bru-*   1788
tus, the republican. Brutus had put an end to monarchy in
Rome. A day was to come when David would register his
vote for the King's death. Triumph attended his efforts.
After *Brutus* there was no quelling the rage for all things
Roman. Women gave up wearing stays and high-heeled
shoes (the change was their Declaration of Independence).
Men laid aside their powdered wigs. David was making
ready to become the scene-painter and costumer of the Revolution.

Those were the days when the young Talma played tragedy no longer dressed in the clothes of the period, but in a
Roman toga; when the poets (from Bernis to Chénier) were
busy translating Virgil and mobilizing the forces of Olympus; when cultured circles were going into raptures over
Livy, Tacitus, and even Plutarch. Montesquieu had
preached the "grandeur of the Romans," and the idea took
root that nothing in the world was more natural than for a
plebeian republic to take the place of the primitive institution of royalty. After the Tarquins, the Catos. After slaves,
citizens. The very word *republic* hailed from Rome, as the
whole political vocabulary of the Revolution was to do, with
its "tribunes" and its "triumvirs." Newspapers and speeches
were filled with references to the "rages of Sulla," to the
"beguiling accents of Plutus," to "Nero's fetters." Mirabeau
invoked the Tarpeian Rock and the Capitol. Marat denounced the heirs of Tiberius and Caligula. Children were
christened Scævola and Gracchus. Grown men, instead of
continuing to go by such names as Pierre or Jean-Baptiste,
chose instead Anaxagoras (like Chaumette) or Anacharsis
(like Clootz). The Republic, when it came, took for its
badge the lictors' *fasces,* and for emblem a cock—by virtue

of a pun on the two words *gallus* and *Gallia*. All France was
soon to copy Rome. Nor was it just amusing make-believe.
Neither chance nor artlessness led men to exalt Brutus.
They talked about him so much that in the long run they
found themselves following in his footsteps. It was a Roman wind that blew upon the economic, financial, and political clouds and rent them, and this Roman blast let loose
a storm in France.

Who?

And now to bring the characters upon the stage. The popular picture of the Revolution shows a man of the people cutting off the head of an aristocrat. It is just as well that we
should take a look at another version, which is that of an
aristocrat cutting off the head of a poor tradesman.

In the coalition of interests which sapped the monarchy
it was the representatives of the old feudal nobility who occupied the foremost places. Stripped of their ancient fiefs,
they longed to be the star performers. In the *cahiers* of '89
it was they alone who demanded the destruction of the Bastille, which was the prison of the privileged. In the States-
1789 General many of them were ardent adherents of the new
theories—either from natural generosity of mind or from a
liking for subversive activities. The Duc de la Rochefoucauld was among the first to demand the suppression of the
religious orders and the nationalization of Church property.
The Vicomte de Noailles (perhaps merely to irritate his
cousin, the Duke) clamored for the doing away with all titles of nobility. Others, like Clermont-Tonnerre and de
Broglie, fell into step with him. Talleyrand, a descendant of
the Chalais whom Richelieu had executed, had a bone to
pick with kings. The mere presence among them of Rohan,
who had insulted the Queen, was a challenge to the throne.

Did these great names disappear when the first wave of
the assault had passed? Mirabeau and Lafayette, a count

and a marquis, were the bright particular stars of the developing drama. The Marquis de Condorcet kept the game going by demanding that the death penalty should be restored in political trials. In the worst days of the Terror, Clootz von Gnadenthal, a millionaire baron and the son of one of Frederick of Prussia's councilors, raged and roared among the loudest. Maximilien de Robespierre (whose family had belonged to the *noblesse de la robe* since the fifteenth century) and Hérault de Séchelles (one of the Queen's intimates) saw to it that the guillotine never went hungry. The Duc de Biron (whose ancestor had been executed at the order of Henri IV) commanded the "Blues" in La Vendée against the "Whites," led by the gamekeeper Stofflet. La Tour d'Auvergne, descended from Turenne, was one of the earliest of the Republic's grenadiers. Saint-Simon, a near relation of the famous Duke, quite happily trafficked in national property and became the possessor of the roof of Notre-Dame. After Thermidor the supply continued with the Comte de Boissy d'Anglas, the Vicomte de Barras ("as noble as a Barras" was an old Provençal saying), and other patricians.

Bishops, too, as well as obscure priests, Benedictines, and Capuchins figured among the dramatis personæ. In addition to Talleyrand, Bishop of Autun, already mentioned, there was the Abbé Sieyès, the regicide; Bishop Grégoire, who was one of the signatories of the decree setting up the Republic; Fouché, the Oratorian, "butcher" of Lyon; Chabot, the Vicar-General, who wished to see all whose hands were not "horny" proscribed; and the communist curé Jacques Roux, who was the leader of the *"Enragés."*

In the assemblies nobles and priests rivaled the middle classes in revolutionary ardor—former members of the Parlement, like Le Pelletier de Saint-Fargeau; lawyers and advocates by the hundred, like Pétion de Villeneuve, Danton, and Vergniaud—all of them famous spouters, great makers

of phrases, "latter-day Ciceros," ready in and out of season
to denounce the "modern Verres." Where could the true
proletarians be found? Out of the 749 members of the Convention, only one was a workingman.

The men of the people were absent, if not from the Revolution, at least from the ranks of its leaders and executants.
They were scarcely, if ever, consulted. The *cahiers* of the
States-General were the work of a handful of intellectuals
stuffed with the catchwords of "philosophy." Those from
the country districts were filled with Latinisms. The deputies were elected, in the first instance, by no more than
2,500,000 voters (scarcely one in ten of the population),
1791 and, in the second, by 25,000. For the Legislative Assembly
there were two ballots, each on a property basis. The members of the Convention were chosen by universal suffrage,
but care was taken to frighten away all suspect voters. Out
1792 of the 7,000,000 enfranchised citizens, only 700,000 registered their choice. In many Departments results were decided, just to make sure, by a show of hands. Since the Revolution began, the public had grown sick of elections. They
had been called upon to vote about everything under the
sun (ten times a year or more)—for the appointment of
judges, civil servants, administrators; for the calling up of
soldiers and the promotion of noncommissioned officers.
Pétion was elected Mayor of Paris by 13,000 voters out of a
voting-list of 15,000. To the uneducated crowd this new passion for voting was a mystery, and on the whole they took
very little part in it. Under the Directory the ordinary
man was prevented altogether from expressing his views.
The "plebiscite" that established the new Constitution
1797 amounted to no more than 208,000 votes, and on two occasions the government quite frankly invalidated such ele-
1798 ments as they felt might be an embarrassment—Royalists in
the first, anarchists in the second.

Would it be true to say that the "people" made up for

their inadequacy at the polls by rioting? In strict truth, the "Revolutionary days" never succeeded in mobilizing more than very small bodies of men drilled and controlled by professional agitators. In Paris, with its 500,000 inhabitants, 10,000 at the most could be got into the streets. It was a minority that resorted to violence, as it was a minority that voted. And even this minority was manipulated by yet another minority. Of what did it consist? At no time was the Revolution anything like a spontaneous movement. Paris, said Michelet, was "at the mercy of three hundred Jacobin agents." It would be more accurate to say that France as a whole was at the mercy of the clubs. It was they who made public opinion, they who theorized, decided, and acted. They had been born under the monarchy in the innumerable provincial academies, which officially were concerned with matters having to do with literature and agriculture. All of them were more or less Masonic. Their activities were continued in the Club of Thirty, which had a whole network of satellite organizations. These it was that established the standard of the *cahiers*, financed the first electoral campaigns, and distributed tracts. The Breton Club grew out of the meetings of the deputies from Brittany. It met in what had once been a monastic building, and as a consequence became known as the Jacobin Club. It very soon had 1,900 associated branches, controlling 21,500 Revolutionary committees—from which it can be seen that the network covered the whole country. Other clubs, founded by dissidents or rivals, spread their slogans everywhere.

1794

Does all this mean that there really was, somewhere or other, that "invisible hand" of which mention is to be found in certain contemporary reports? It seems probable that at the outset Philippe, Duc d'Orléans, desired, organized, and financed the revolutionary uprising. He was a Masonic Grand Master, a born plotter, and a pure-blooded feudal aristocrat. He hated the King, and still more the Queen.

He was greedy for popularity and power. In 1787 he had
called for the demolition of the Bastille and urged the Parlement to resist the royal will. In '88 he got himself elected
contrary to the King's wish. In '89 he joined the Third Estate, and coined the name "National Assembly." His bust
was paraded through the streets of Paris. It was from the
1789 Palais-Royal, where he lived and in which the headquarters
of civil disturbance were established, that the offensive
against the Bastille was launched. The Gardes-Françaises,
to whom the weakly defended fortress surrendered, were in
his pay. Posters were publicly displayed proclaiming that
the throne was vacant and calling upon him to assume the
regency. The attempt miscarried. He poured out money like
water. In October, from a booth in the Champs-Élysées, he
directed the march on Versailles. He was banished. Under
1792 the name of Philippe-Égalité he was elected to the Convention as a member of the extreme Left. He had Danton and
many others on his pay-roll. He voted for the death of his
cousin Louis XVI. But his efforts all went for nothing. The
Revolution got out of control. It had no use for a substitute
king. The *deus ex machina* was no longer master of the machine he had set in motion. He, too, lost his head.

Beneath the same blade perished many less high-born
victims. Three quarters of all those guillotined were peasants, artisans, and small shopkeepers.

How?

So much for the cast. Let us see now how the play developed. Was it drama or was it farce? Something of everything is to be found in it, of the worst as of the best—sub-
limity and burlesque, masquerade and epic.

It was in the provinces that the first troubles flared up—
in Béarn, Brittany, Dauphiné, and Provence. The King gave
1788 way. Contrary to expectation, the elections for the Estates-

General passed off peacefully. The *cahiers* breathed not a word against the regime, nor against the person of the sovereign. They were at one only in their hostility to taxation. The States met at Versailles. Almost at once they forgot that they had been summoned to resolve a purely financial problem. Instead they discussed politics, and turned themselves into a Constituent Assembly. The King gave way.

1789

Feelings in Paris were at boiling-point. Already in April dear bread and low wages had led to the looting of papermills in the faubourg Saint-Antoine. By mid-July the fever had grown more acute. Gangs of rioters seized weapons from the Invalides, besieged the Bastille, released four forgers, two madmen, and a sadist, and massacred the governor of the ancient fortress as well as the controller of the markets. In the space of a few hours a heroic legend was born. The King gave way. He withdrew the numerically insufficient troops at his disposal (they were, in any case, completely under the thumb of their *philosophe* officers and self-appointed soldiers' councils), ratified the people's victory, and raised the tricolor cockade, which combined the colors of the monarch with those of the City of Paris—or at least of the Orléans livery.

Not Paris alone but all France was on fire. That is no figure of speech. There were burnings, there was destruction, there was looting. All over the country there were acts of vengeance for old grudges, and a general settling of accounts. Genuine brigands took advantage of the state of anarchy. The citizens armed themselves in self-protection, and very soon men were hard put to it to be sure who was attacking, who defending, law and order. This was what came to be known as the *"grande peur."* But the taxpayers, at least, did not lose their heads. They destroyed the registers and official lists, set fire to the tax offices, and harried the collectors. The Revolution was well under way.

Until that moment it had been entirely negative, concerned only to wipe the slate clean. To what goal, if any, was it working? The people had no program, nor had the King. Only a few of the leaders, declared or hidden, knew what they were after. But they were not all of them after the same thing. Those drawn from the ranks of the Parlement dreamed of a weak monarchy with all real power in the hands of its magistrates; the nobles hoped for an aristocratic system, with themselves lording it as kings; the disciples of the *philosophes* had in mind a government of enlightened thinkers; a score or more of individuals in the clubs were working to lay the foundations of a republic.

One thing these various groups had in common: a conviction that the King was an embarrassment. He must be brought from Versailles to Paris and held there as a hostage. A skillfully planned operation, in which Lafayette flattered himself that he played the leading part, produced the hoped-for results. The King gave way. He had the regiment charged with the duty of acting as his personal bodyguard disarmed. Now that he was in the hands of the Revolutionaries what should the next step be? The Royalists still formed an immense majority in the country at large and in the Assembly. They drew up a Constitution, embodying the noblest sentiments and preceded by a high-minded Declaration of the Rights of Man. Its failure was a foregone conclusion. By handing over the legislative power to a "sovereign" Assembly, while leaving only the shadow of executive power in the hands of a ministry responsible to that same "sovereign," it did nothing to resolve the conflicts that would inevitably arise between the two powers concerned.

All true authority in the State lay with the elected municipalities and the elected officials. It was exercised no longer from above, but from below. No matter how many the oaths of loyalty to this bastard Constitution, it was foredoomed to failure. Furthermore, the clubs did not want it, and it was in the clubs that the Revolution was developing, not in the official assemblies. The clubs proposed, and disposed too. They had their machinery for bringing pressure to bear—the sections, the communes, the tribunes, petitions and newspapers. If the King or the Assembly resisted their will, they staged a "day." The instruments of their will carried pikes and wore red caps, short jackets called *carmagnoles*, and trousers held up by shoulder-straps, of which they were so proud that they called themselves *sans-culottes*.

The more powerless did the King become, the better did his mind work. He called on Mirabeau for help—but too late. He decided on flight—but too late. He was forcibly detained, and knew that he was lost. Weak in the discharge of his kingly duties, he stood firm as a rock in adversity. Insults left him unmoved, and he faced imprisonment without a murmur. When he was brought to trial and condemned to death, he showed no fear. His behavior on the scaffold was that of a king. He was born to be a victim.

1791

1792

1793

With the King gone and the Republic proclaimed, it was necessary to draw up another Constitution. A new Assembly, the third in four years, undertook the task. It was called the Convention. But there were urgent matters to occupy it: war (in other words, the life of the nation), finance (in other words, the life of the State), its own survival, and that, too, of each of its members, who lived under the constant menace of a rising tide of danger.

1792

For in the meantime the faubourgs had begun to move, and the clubs were hard at work. It was not enough to have got rid of the King and his family. The fainthearted, the halfhearted, the cowards, must be eliminated. They were accused of being counterrevolutionaries. They were declared suspect. Moderation was now a crime, and those guilty of it were ripe for stringing-up. Thus pressed, the Girondins went one farther than the Feuillants, the Cordeliers one farther than the Girondins, the Mountain one farther than the Cordeliers, the Enragés one farther than the Mountain.

1792 Danton-the-Bought ordered, or allowed, the massacre of those confined in the prisons. Marat-the-Fanatic demanded two hundred thousand heads. Robespierre-the-Incorruptible kept the headsman working overtime. Each perished in his turn, Danton by Sanson's guillotine, Marat under Charlotte Corday's knife, Robespierre in one of the tumbrils of Thermidor.

But the Terror was not confined to them. Its records have enshrined only the names of its illustrious victims, together

1793 with an impressive catalogue of "historic last words": the Du Barry: *"Encore un moment, monsieur le bourreau"*; Manon Roland: *"Liberté, que de crimes on commet en ton nom!"*; Camille Desmoulins: *"J'ai trente-trois ans, l'âge du sans-culotte Jésus"*; Bailly: *"Je tremble, mais c'est du froid"*;

1794 no less a person than Danton: *"Tu montreras ma tête au peuple, elle en vaut bien la peine."* The reply to Lavoisier of one of his judges is also worth recording: "The Republic has no need of chemists." Literature has kept a lively memory of the last line that Chénier wrote: "Weep, Virtue, if I die." But no one has troubled to remember the tens of thousands of anonymous citizens who faced death without any fine phrases.

The suspects who escaped the guillotine but did not succeed in getting out of the country came to a bad end. Con-

1793 dorcet took poison: Roland stabbed himself; Pétion was eaten by wolves; the boy Louis XVII was slowly dying in the Temple prison. At Lyon the condemned were blown from the mouths of cannon; at Nantes they were drowned; at Angers they were shot to music.

Did the new France need these hecatombs? It would be a mistake to think that the Terror was the work only of bloodthirsty fanatics. Those responsible for it held the opinion that "purges" were necessary for the health of a true republic. A still stronger reason was that they killed in order to avoid being killed. Having purged, they went in terror of being purged in their turn. They feared too the reprisals of a possible reaction no less than the violence of the enthusiasts. Robespierre, even at the height of his power, had to take measures to protect himself from Right and Left alike. On the Right he was threatened by the followers of Danton, on the Left by those of Hébert. But he did not **1794** escape his fate. Barras, Tallien, and Fouché profited from a moment of national weakness to replace the rule of doctrinaires by one of shady speculators.

The Revolution had now reached another stage. The prison gates were thrown open, and through them emerged 400,000 men and women who had been detained. Among them, miraculously saved from the guillotine, were Hoche, Florian, Du Pont de Nemours, Thomas Paine, Joséphine de Beauharnais, Rouget de l'Isle—composer of the *Marseillaise* —and even Dr. Guillotin, inventor of the mechanical head-chopper. It was the turn now of the assassins of yesterday to be assassinated in their turn or deported.

The theorists tried their hands at putting together yet another Constitution, on a basis of five Directors and two Chambers. It was no great advance on its predecessors. The **1795** clubs were still busy organizing "days," and the Royalists tried to do the same. Rome, however, had ceased to be an inspiration, and become a sideshow. France was sick of violence and sacrifices and general rottenness.

The Great Reforms

Sterile though it was in the field of political experiment, the Revolution has a fine record of successful reforms. The monarchy had tried in vain to introduce some of them. It had needed a revolutionary earthquake to clear the ground of old habits, ancient traditions, and "vested interests."

A general leveling began on the night of August 4, 1789—

that amazing night when, in the space of a few hours, the achievements of a thousand years were turned upside down. In an access of enthusiasm and panic all privileges were abolished, those of cities as well as of nobles, provincial rights as well as feudal. Gone forever were personal immunities, titles of nobility, the rights of primogeniture, ecclesiastical tithes. But with them went common-land pasturage and collective franchises. When, however, the time came to pass on from generalities to details, discussion continued for a whole year in an atmosphere of bitterness. It seemed almost as though those taking part in it were already regretting the tidal wave of the 4th of August. But what had been done could not be undone. The classes, the provinces, the cities had lost their dusty liberties. In return they had acquired equality. All Frenchmen now addressed one another in the second person singular, and used the title "citizen," in a sacred frenzy of fraternity. Henceforward Brittany and Franche-Comté (which now was neither *Franche* nor *Comté*) would have precisely the same rights as Orléans or Berry. The people of Alsace and Flanders were compelled to speak French. France, "one and indivisible," had taken the place of the old partitioned, decentralized France of the monarchy. Paris had become the sole head of a single body.

Nor did economic reforms lag behind. In spite of the *cahiers*—which had reflected the old sectional interests—all internal tolls and customs dues were abolished. Freedom of movement was given to local products, to the trade in and transport of grain. More than once did popular feeling, reacting to the fear of famine, rebel against the law, and this same fear compelled the Revolution to act in opposition to its own liberal theories in the matter of foreign trade. It hesitated to allow the export of wheat and, with the object of protecting the nation's industries, levied a tax of from five to fifteen per cent on the importation of manufactured

1789

1790

1791

goods, sometimes going so far as to prohibit them altogether. The Convention closed the frontiers more completely than Colbert had ever dared to do.

Industrial organization was reformed from top to bottom.
The Constituent Assembly proclaimed the right to work,
which meant no less than the suppression of the guilds and
their out-of-date regulations. But the associations of jour-   **1791**
neymen, which had been left untouched, increased the
number of strikes. Forced to choose between individual liberty and the liberty of the unions, the middle-class Revolution decided for the former. The journeymen's associations
were suppressed and wage-earners forbidden to combine.
"Citizens belonging to certain trades shall henceforward be
forbidden to band themselves together in protection of
their common interests. Only the interests of individuals
and of the nation will be recognized." Any workman who
attempted to disobey this ruling was liable to the death
penalty. Equality is no joking matter.

This unyielding attitude was the expression of a doctrine.
In its building of a new society the Revolution had made a
clean sweep of the past and chosen to start again from zero.
With a similar merciless logic, repudiating the old administrative frontiers and the old units of measure, it had carved
out a brand-new nation, offering it, as one part of its achievement, a brand-new decimal system for the reckoning of
weights, measures, and the calendar.

The provinces had been the product of time, geography,
and history. The Constituent Assembly would have liked to
accept the proposal made by Sieyès to divide France into
equal squares. In fact they had to adopt the compromise   **1790**
measure—which was better than nothing—of creating
eighty-three Departments, and giving them names derived
from purely physical features—rivers or mountains (with
one accidental exception, Calvados, which, through the intervention of a small and unspectacular rock, received the

name of a Spanish ship that had run aground). There was
much competition between towns for the privilege of acting
as local capital. More than once the color of their politics
was the deciding factor. To the parishes, now stripped of all
religious significance, was given the fine name of communes
—in compensation for those communal liberties which they
had seen so recently vanish forever.

Reform in the system of measurement was even more
drastic, and nature was called in to assist in establishing the
standard unit. The meter is the millionth part of one
quarter of the earth's meridian (approximately). From this
meter were derived all the divisions of surface measurement,
of volume, of capacity, and of weight. *Toises, onces, pintes,*
and *perches* were now to be things of the past. Their place
1793 was to be taken—much to the relief of future schoolboys—
by the kilometer, the cubic meter, the liter, and the hectare,
with multiples and submultiples reckoned in tens, hundreds,
and thousands. But a long time was to elapse before resistance to this novelty was overcome. For many generations
Frenchmen continued, in spite of the decrees of the Convention, to reckon as their ancestors had done, in *lieues* and
arpents. Certain crafts too remained loyal to the duodecimal
system (jewelers still use carats, and printers "points" for the
different sizes of type).

There was another domain in which nature responded
but ill to the decimal system. Even after '89 the number of
days taken by the earth to circle the sun could not be expressed by a complete multiple of ten. The moon, too,
moved around the earth twelve times in every year. In a
fine access of ambition it was decided that the year of the
Republic's birth should be known as "Year I" (with a
Roman numeral!), the actual date coinciding admirably
with the autumn equinox. The annual period was still to
consist of twelve months, but these were to be renamed.
1793 The first suggestion was to give them such ridiculous titles

as Tennis Court, Bastille, Redcap, and Pike. Fabre d'Églan-
tine, the poet and author of *Il pleut, bergère*, set himself—
between two bouts of speculating in India Company stock—
to find more charming substitutes. The ones he put forward had a fine pagan flavor, and ended in *ôse, al, aire*, and
idor. Each month was divided into three periods, each of
ten days (*décades*), to which, at the end of every year, were
added five or six feast-days called "*sans-culottides*." The
Convention even went so far as to decree that each day
should contain ten hours, and each hour ten minutes. The
100,000th part of the day was to be the equivalent of
the pulse-beat of a man of average stature. But sundials and
the human pulse refused to recognize the decision, and the
public showed a spirit of non-co-operation.

The changes made by the Revolution in the fields of law
and education, on the other hand, were both practical and
lasting. Local customary law was abolished in favor of a
single code. The old Parlements were swept away, and with
them went the manorial and royal courts. A judicial system
of three degrees was organized, with juries in all criminal
cases. Schools, too, were set up in three degrees, open to all
children. The École Normale was founded, and, with it,
the École Polytechnique, the Conservatoire, the Museum,
and the Archives. It is only fair to point out that these titles
sometimes gave no more than a new label to existing institutions. But in many instances the Revolution cleared the
ground entirely for the building of a young society proud
of its youth. Whether it broke with the past or merely re-
adjusted it, it built with its eye on the future.

The Religious Battle

In some respects, however, the Revolution was led to con-
tradict its own principles. Was it, for instance, concerned to
institute a regime of liberty, equality, and fraternity in reli-

gious matters? Not a few of its leading spirits were Protestant. At Montpellier and at Nîmes the Revolution began with clashes between Catholics and the adherents to the Reformed church. In Paris many of the key positions were held by Protestants. Necker and, at a later date, Cambon were in charge of finance. Barnave urged the Constituent Assembly to nationalize Church property. Marat, a Swiss and the child of a Calvinist family, waxed lyrical over the massacre of priests. Jean Bon Saint-André, a former pastor, was a member of the Committee of Public Safety. In a sense the Revolution and the Reformation were blood-sisters, because each derived from a passion for individual liberty.

The *philosophes* had made the Catholic religion a target for their mockery. The people had grumbled against Church tithes. It was inevitable, therefore, that the Revolution should turn against the Church, which was an intermediate body between the individual and the State. Having laid hands on Church property, having first suspended and then forbidden monastic vows, having secularized civil status, it went farther and attempted to transform bishops and curés

1790 into civil servants. It insisted on their taking an oath to the Constitution on pain of dismissal, and subsequently of imprisonment. Nearly all the bishops and more than half the parish priests refused. They were replaced, and it was Talleyrand who consecrated the new occupants of episcopal sees. But the faithful abandoned the churches presided over by the "jurors," and secretly frequented the refractory priests in barns and cellars.

In the west the people of La Vendée and Brittany rose in revolt as champions of their King and their faith. It was war

1793 to the knife, war without quarter either given or received. Whites and Blues vied with one another in both heroism and ferocity. The rebels swept forward to Nantes, to Laval, and even as far as Le Mans. But, in spite of Charette's leadership, they could do nothing against the artillery of the Republic.

This insurrection led to a greater intensification of persecution. The zealots of the Convention ordered the destruction of crosses on the public roads and issued instructions that priests were to marry. In Paris the new Church of Sainte-Geneviève was renamed the Panthéon, in accordance with the fashionable passion for all things Roman. Within its precincts Mirabeau, Voltaire, Marat, and Rousseau were buried. All over the country cathedrals and churches were secularized or transformed into clubs and barracks, prisons, storehouses, and brothels. The browbeaten Archbishop of Paris laid his pectoral cross and his episcopal ring on the table of the Convention.

Over the new calendar, which excluded all Church festivals, the strife waxed bitter. Sundays had been replaced by the "*décadi.*" No mercy was shown to the peasant who refused to work on Sunday, to the tradesman who kept his shop open on one of the "*décadi.*" The observance of Christmas and Easter was forbidden. The celebration of the anniversary of the King's execution and of the taking of the Bastille was made compulsory. There was a law against the selling of fish on Christian fast-days. The names of the saints were removed from the calendar, their places being taken by names borrowed from nature—dandelion, cow, or dung. Pumpkin was substituted for Saint Francis, pig for Saint Catherine. Many sans-culottes adopted these vocables instead of their baptismal names.

Even place-names were secularized. Saint-Denis became Franciade; Dunkerque, Dune Libre; Saint-Lô, Rocher de la Liberté; Saint-Antoine, the faubourg de Gloire. This process of "renewal" was applied also to names with a royalist connotation. Bourg-la-Reine was rechristened Bourg-Égalité; Île Bourbon, Réunion; Place Louis XV, Place de la Révolution, and later Place de la Concorde. Lyon, which was in disgrace, was renamed Commune Affranchie. There was a solemn ceremony at which a crucifix and a copy of the Gospels were publicly burned, and a mitred donkey was made to drink the contents of a chalice.

But it was not enough to replace ancient names with new ones. For the condemned faith younger faiths must be substituted. Four alternative religions emerged in turn from the fertile imaginations of the reformers. The first of them was an apotheosis of the Goddess of Reason, organized by **1793** Chaumette, with a chorus girl from the Opéra posing at Notre-Dame at the foot of a cardboard mountain. At Besançon the Jacobins appointed twelve apostles to preach this same doctrine of Reason. But Robespierre, who was a deist, would have nothing to do with such pagan atheism. He preferred another form of paganism, with a real divinity, which should enable the government to found a true republican code of morality. He sent Chaumette to the scaffold, and requested the Convention to decree a metaphysic em- **1794** bodying two specific dogmas: the existence of a Supreme Being, and the immortality of the soul—Lucretius revised by Rousseau. On this occasion a statue of Atheism was solemnly burned at the Tuileries. The deputies attended carrying bouquets of flowers. There were also young girls garlanded with roses, and old men with myrtle and vine-shoots. David designed the setting, superintended the making of the wreaths, and organized the procession. There were choirs, hymns, speeches, and an invocation to the Eternal—a modern version of the former good God. Streamers announced that "the Revolution is the daughter of heaven." In the provinces the state religion was celebrated with equal splendor, and there was not a country town where, to an accompaniment of much drinking, tripods burning incense were not set up beside the tree of liberty.

The Supreme Being lasted for an even shorter time than the Goddess of Reason. He fell with Robespierre. But religious freedom was restored only in theory. Actually Catholics were persecuted for a long time to come, and dancehalls continued to flourish in monastic houses and churches. The Directory invented two new faiths: theophilanthropy,   **1796** to which it made over the principal churches of Paris, and which it subsidized from its secret funds; and the *"culte*   **1799** *décadaire,"* which ordained that secular services should be held three times each month in honor of agriculture, marriage, youth, and the sovereignty of the people. But the people remained obstinately faithful to their "superstitions."

Of this prolonged attack on liberty of conscience little remained but ruins, which were never again restored. The Revolution itself undertook the task of expelling Mirabeau and Marat from its Panthéon, but it did nothing to replace the bells it had melted down, nor did it restore the looted treasures or the mutilated statues. Notre-Dame de Paris never recovered the ninety figures of her gallery of kings (true, they were only Jewish kings), nor the Church of Saint-Denis the statues of its façade or the bodies of the   **1793** kings buried within its precincts, which had been dug up and thrown into a common ditch. "In the space of three days," said Chateaubriand, "men destroyed the achievements of twelve centuries." The embalmed hearts of Louis XIII and Louis XIV, taken from the Church of Saint-Paul, were pounded into dust and used as an ingredient in his pigments by a painter who happened not to be squeamish in such matters. At Chartres the cathedral escaped being torn down only by a miracle. An architect intervened to point out that the debris would block the streets. The disappointed iconoclasts had to rest content with burning the statue of Notre-Dame de Sous-Terre. At Strasbourg the spire of the cathedral was saved from destruction by the ingenuity of a citizen who crowned it with an immense Phrygian cap of red tin. Nor was it only the churches that

suffered, but the great country houses as well, and everything that served to recall the ancient despotism. The wreck-
ers painted over or scraped away the fleurs-de-lys, parceled
out the estates, scattered the furniture. Versailles and Vincennes were all but razed to the ground, but luckily escaped
with the removal of their contents. Saint-Germain was put
up at auction. Marly was knocked down to a spinner who
sold off the stones of which it was built. Gaillon, the residence of the archbishops of Rouen, was demolished by its
new owners, and even Jeanne d'Arc's house at Domremy did
not escape damage.

All this was very different from the spoliation and destruction that France had suffered in the civil wars of past centuries. It was not the work of fanaticism and hot blood. It
was carried out by order of the public authorities and paid
for at fixed rates—so much for defacing armorial bearings,
so much for reducing crosses to the likeness of tree-trunks,
for chipping away angels' wings, for tearing down paneling.
The demolitions at Saint-Eustache were invoiced at 31.745
livres. The cleaning up was methodical and estimated on a
commercial basis. It was the true expression of a revolution
that had been systematically planned and executed.

The Social Struggle

It may have destroyed the privileges of birth, but it strengthened those of wealth. So completely had it been organized
by and for the rich that its first Constitution gave the fran-
chise only to those who had property. It had set out to establish universal equality. Logically, therefore, it ought to have
leveled social conditions. The true end of liberty is anarchy;
of equality, communism. More than one revolutionary realized this, and some found the prospect distinctly alluring.
The State had already laid hands on the property alike of
Church and *émigrés*. It had seized hoarded wealth. Why

then did it not take the further step of abolishing private ownership?

That, certainly, was what the extremists would have approved. In spite of the example of the Gracchi and their agrarian laws, what they demanded was not so much the dividing up of the great estates as their confiscation. "All real property," said Barère, "belongs to the State." "It is the rich man who is the thief," wrote Brissot in a monograph on the rights of property. The men of the Mountain were left far behind by the Enragés, and, compared with such leaders as young Varlet and the Abbé Jacques Roux, Marat seems an angel of light. "How can we speak of equality," asked Jacques Roux of the Commune, "when the rich man, by reason of his monopoly, can exercise the power of life and death over his fellows?" There were petitions, there were calls for insurrection against the merchants and against their protectors in the Convention—"those vile hirelings of tyranny." Hébert threw in his lot with the Enragés so as not to diminish the circulation of his *Père Duchesne*:

Country? Hell!—what do businessmen know of country? So long as they thought that the Revolution was useful to them they backed it up, but what they really wanted was to put themselves where the aristocrats had been. . . . The swine are no better than a pack of turncoats.

And again:

Public opinion is controlled by a lot of rotters who put on a great act of serving the interests of the people. With one hand they caress them, and with the other give them a punch in the nose. . . . The damned monkeys pose and posture as Revolutionary leaders, making believe it's liberty they're defending, when all the time it's their own gold!

But the Enragés went just too far. Jacques Roux was arrested and stabbed himself. Hébert switched to an attack **1793**

on the "famine-mongers"—businessmen and farmers—until
1794   a day came when Robespierre, deciding that he was an embarrassment, sent him to the guillotine.

State control, however, had gained ground. There was a
tax on the rich, there were forced loans from the rich, and
large incomes were confiscated. The Stock Exchange was
closed, joint-stock companies dissolved, manpower requisitioned. Foreign trade became a state monopoly. In every
field equality was encroaching on liberty, collectivism on the
individual.

The property of all enemies of the Republic was confiscated. Now, in order to be an enemy of the Republic it was
necessary only to spread false news or to cause anxiety about
the means of subsistence; and since all such confiscated
property was distributed to "indigent patriots," there was a
sudden big increase in the number of beggars.

Is it true to say that the Republic did genuinely declare
war on the rich? On the old rich, yes, but not on the new.
Army contractors were busy making hay while the sun
shone. Highly placed politicians were in a position to order
the arrest of large property-owners and to buy their land at
cheap rates. After Thermidor and under the Directory it was
the gorged who ruled the roost.

Jacques Roux had a successor, a man who waxed indignant over poverty and corruption and longed for the coming
of true equality. For Gracchus Babeuf the Revolution was
nowhere near being over. It still had to organize the communal ownership of wealth. His followers were a strange
mixture, ranging from Prince Charles of Hesse to Drouet,
the postmaster who had stopped Louis XVI at Varennes.
But the "Manifesto of Equals" did not catch on with the
crowd. The communist plot was broken up by the police
1796   of the Directory, and Babeuf, like Jacques Roux before him,
committed suicide.

There could be no doubt about it: the egalitarian revolution had miscarried. For the feudal privileges, around which the original argument had raged, it had substituted the privileges of wealth, and from now on opposition within the revolutionary fold dared not show its head.

The Struggle of Finance

The real drama of the Revolution was financial. No Frenchman could avoid it. Each day the producer worked, the tradesman sold, the housewife bought. Each day the problems of getting bread and making money had to be faced. Each day the treasury was only too well aware of the yawning gap between increased expenses and uncertain receipts.

The monarchy had been embarrassed by the need to cover the public deficit. The Republic was even more so. The taxpayers had been recalcitrant in the old days, and they obstinately refused to change their spots. Had not their first step been to destroy the fiscal system? The new Assemblies strove to construct a different one that should be less **1790** unjust and easier to work. There was to be a land tax, a tax on investments, and a license system for traders. The general result was far from satisfactory. Though the word *tax* was avoided, the good will of those liable for contributions was woefully lacking. Appeals made for voluntary gifts fell on deaf ears.

In the absence of tax revenue, loans were the only alternative. But those who want to borrow cannot always do so. Even the Frenchmen who were wholeheartedly behind the Revolution entertained doubts of its solvency and were unwilling to loosen their purse-strings to help it. In vain did the treasury implore the citizens to save. The sums forthcoming from that source were laughable. In order to inspire confidence, and to keep in step with the passion for unifica- **1793** tion, Cambon transferred all state bonds into one single type bearing a dividend of five per cent. But his loans suc-

ceeded no better than their predecessors. Expedient followed expedient. The Directory set the coping-stone on this
1797   policy with a resounding bankruptcy, as a result of which,
out of a total of three billions of debt, two billions were annulled.

Life, however, had to go on. To the costs of the centralized State were added the obligations no longer assumed
by the provinces and the clergy—maintenance of hospitals,
unemployment relief, education, the mass purchase of
grain. The nationalized estates had only earth and stone to
1789   offer, whereas what the treasury needed was money. How
were these two or three billions tucked away in landed property to be turned into liquid capital? Pétion launched the
idea of issuing paper. The scheme would provide the State
with resources, and the purchasers of national property with
the means of paying for what they had bought. The new
notes were called *assignats*. Their circulation was controlled
only by the supply of paper and the speed with which the
printing-presses could work. The first issue amounted to
400 million, a figure that had increased by the end of the
Constituent Assembly to 1,300 million, by the beginning of
the Convention to two billion, by its end to nineteen billion, and under the Directory to thirty-nine billion. In all,
the Revolution turned out forty-five billions of assignats.
1796   When at last it was decided to destroy the plates, it was only
to have recourse to others less discredited. The *mandat* succeeded the assignat. The Directory issued paper to the value
of 2,400 million livres, the equivalent of sixty-two billions
of assignats. In the final stage it represented some 107 billions of notes, or thirty-six times the issue made by Law, and
forty-eight times the volume of legal tender circulating at
the end of the monarchy.

To this state paper inflation must be added all the
credit bills issued by the Departments, by the communes,
and by individuals. Anyone was free, in the name of liberty,

to make these issues. There was what amounted to a monetary deluge. The Chouans of La Vendée were not slow to take a hand, and manufactured their own I O U's repayable "on the return of peace."

But the public was far from being convinced that this flood of money had a solid backing. There was a wide preference for gold or silver. At first the Revolutionary paper had been a matter for joking ("a crown is a crown, but assignats are so much toilet paper"). In the long run, however, it became an object of detestation. The peasants were unwilling to sell their crops except in exchange for hard currency. The rate of exchange of the Louis d'or, both official and black-market, moved from 24 livres to 70 at the time of Robespierre's fall, to 2,600 when the Convention was in its death-throes, and to 18,000 when assignats were being pitched into the gutter. Prices soared correspondingly, until a pound of bread cost 150 francs, a pound of sugar or coffee 1,600, and a pair of shoes 20,000 livres.

The Revolution did everything it could to put a stop to this disastrous process of depreciation. To the security provided by the national property of Church and Crown it added the goods of the *émigrés*, and latterly those of condemned prisoners. The guillotine became an instrument of treasury manipulation.

What could not be obtained by credit the Terror extorted by the threat of force. There was a general freezing of prices and wages, as under Diocletian; a war against hoarding; domiciliary visits and searchings, as in the time of the gabelle; rationing of foodstuffs; bread-cards, sugar-cards, meat-cards. There was no shortage of these commodities; not all the harvests were bad. But the owners of land, producers, and merchants alike would not sell for paper. The executioner had to be employed to bring pressure to bear on them.

It seemed on the surface that the policy of maximum

1793

prices really was slowing down the devaluation of the assignats. What in fact was happening was that stagnation in the official rates of exchange was merely acting as camouflage for rises on the black market. There were queues at the shops, a certain amount of looting, attacks on food convoys. The Republic made a great pother about despising gold ("dung" it was called officially), but that did not stop its officers from buying as much as they could from those who were hoarding it. Gold, which was not a Republican product, fled or went underground.

1794   It was to cries of "Down with the maximum!" that Robespierre fell. Speculation was rampant, poverty extreme. The peasants had given up sowing (in addition to their other troubles, all fit men and horses were being requisitioned); bread was being made of bran and maize, bean and chestnut flour. There was famine. Suicides and uprisings were frequent. Police reports bristled with harrowing accounts. But inflation had its profiteers as well as its victims. Ministers and representatives trafficked shamelessly in shortages. Gamblers, contractors, and money-lenders made fortunes. Eighteen hundred dance-halls were doing a roaring trade in Paris.

Many Frenchmen, despite the general distress, were prospering. They bought national property on credit and paid for it in depreciated paper. For a few handfuls of worthless notes they acquired immense estates. For the price of a lump of butter they could have a field; for that of a cow, a country house. The purchasers of national property—numbering 1,200,000—felt themselves henceforward bound hand and foot to the Revolution, which had enriched them. The assignats had a way of turning men into Republicans.

1797   And so it came about that the financial disaster of the Revolution spelt victory for its politics. It mattered little that paper went down before real standards, that salaries were paid in grain, that barter replaced commerce, that bank-notes were devalued officially to one three-thousandth part of their original worth, that the old currency, dribbling from secret hide-outs, recovered its role of genuine money and reduced paper to nothing. Assignats and *mandats*, far more effectively than dogmas and speeches, were the foundation on which the Republic was built.

At War

There was another ordeal lying in wait for the Republic, and from this one, the ordeal of war, it emerged triumphantly. The new France had begun by flying the banner of fra-   1789
ternity and declaring a state of perpetual peace with the whole human race. The Constituent Assembly had, indeed, issued a decree in which war, as an instrument of policy, was solemnly renounced. Foreign powers welcomed this pacific attitude, because it left their hands free. Far from complaining of the Revolution, they helped it forward with discreet subsidies. England, intent on being mistress of the seas, and Prussia, no less intent on being master of the Continent, gave help to the Jacobins, to say nothing of Mirabeau and Danton. In the eyes of these two nations—one the mother of parliaments, the other with a weakness for philosophers—every allowance could be made for Revolutionary France.

What brought about the sudden change from goggling pacifism to wild aggressiveness? In the first place, opportu-   1791
nity makes the thief. Since the papal enclave of Avignon was clamoring to be annexed, it was clearly necessary that the free union of the two neighbors should be brought about. The door was now open to every sort of abuse. The *émigrés* in the Rhineland, headed by Louis XVI's brothers, were blustering and threatening. Although they were enemies of the Queen, and some of them of the King as well, they made a great show of hastening to their assistance,

perhaps in the hope of compromising them still more completely. If only they could involve Austria in the quarrel!
The mere name Austria made the French see red. They forgot that their former enemy was now an ally, and felt the
age-old hatred stir within them. The Girondin deputies, under the leadership of Brissot, thought this opportunity of
stirring the Revolutionary fires too good to be missed. The
Simon Pures could now be measured by the yardstick of
their attitude to Austria. The King was actually negotiating
with her. (In point of fact, he had just become godfather
to a little Habsburg princess who was given the name of
Marie-Louise.) Farewell now to dreams of fraternity! Eu-

1792 rope must be set on fire that France might have air to
breathe. War was voted amid scenes of enthusiasm, war
against Austria—in other words, against kings. The Revolution was on the march to free the oppressed peoples and
cast down the tyrants from their seats.

So began the great adventure that was to last for twenty-
three years. France, in turn conquering and threatened, was
soon to find herself facing a coalition of all Europe—Austri-

1793 ans and Prussians, Russians and Spaniards. From the very
moment that Belgium was invaded, England was up in
arms. Never had she permitted, nor ever could permit, a
hostile power to hold the coastline of the Low Countries.
Tirelessly, to the very end, she poured out money and blood
without counting the cost in order to keep France from the
mouths of the Scheldt; and in the end she had her way.

But in the early stages all went well for the Republic. She
had ready to her hand the strongest army in the world—
strong by reason of its permanent cadres, all trained in the
military schools of the monarchy, strong by reason of its
armament, which was incomparably superior to that of any
possible enemy (Valmy was a gunners' victory; Fleurus saw
the first use of a balloon in battle); strong in numbers supplied by the country with the largest population in Europe;

strong with an enthusiasm which the prospect of booty, and
the great crusading hope of establishing liberty among the
peoples, kept at fever pitch; strong, finally, because of the
indifference of the foreign kings, who did not really feel
that their own thrones were in danger and who were not
particularly eager to reinstate the Bourbons. They were far
more interested in Poland, which they now set to work to
partition at their leisure.

With the rhythm of the seasons, defeat alternated with
success, and France was several times invaded. The army,
which responded badly to discipline, and had no great liking
for being paid in assignats, was more than once on the
verge of mutiny. Desertions were frequent. The military
contractors made fortunes, and the generals, more or less
suspect, had sometimes to choose between emigration
(Dumouriez) and the scaffold (Custine and Beauharnais,
the husband of Joséphine). But in the most tragic moments
the Republic could find in herself the resiliency that alone
could save her from disaster. Its basis was twofold: mobilization on a scale never before envisaged—1,200,000 men—and
the appearance of an organizer of genius, Carnot, the disciple of Vauban.

In the heat of battle the Revolution became warlike. Her
new passion found expression in her new songs. *"Formez vos
bataillons!"* was the exhortation of the hymn of the men
from Marseille. *"Le France invoque le Dieu des combats,"*
said the *Chant du départ.* *"Vive le son du canon!"* sang the
Carmagnole. A single theme inspired all of them. The
troops were called upon to "lay low the flag of tyranny," to
swear "eternal war on all the kings of the earth," those
kings, "drunk with blood and pride," who were invited to
"go down into the tomb." In France there was no longer
any question of being loyal to a king. The idea of "country" commanded something quite different. The nation in
arms had given birth to nationalism. Clootz and Paine were

arrested for the reason that they were foreigners. Humanity as a whole went for nothing now that the *sovereign people was on the march*.

Those, however, to whom it brought deliverance were less enthusiastic. The inhabitants of Belgium and the Rhineland at first acclaimed the victorious French. It was not long, however, before they realized that the price of liberty was high—requisitions, pillage, forced loans, the seizure of Church property. The French armies lived on the countries they conquered. Far from being a burden on the treasury, they were expected to add to its resources. Belgians and

1795 Rhinelanders grew indignant and revolted. But it was too late! The whole of the left flank of the Rhine was annexed and divided up into twelve Departments, which it was hoped would be productive of public revenue.

After a brief interval the war started again—not that, strictly speaking, it had ever stopped. At sea England was blockading the coasts of France. On land Austria had still

1796 to be overcome. In the young Bonaparte the Directory found a general who was competent beyond their wildest

1798 hopes. By way of Italy the Corsican marched on Vienna. At Malta and in Egypt he flung down the gauntlet to London. Two brilliant campaigns turned an undersized political soldier into the idol of the mob. Arcole, Rivoli, the Pyramids—names that went to the head like wine; Mulhouse and Geneva restored to France; Rome and Luxor occupied; Holland and Switzerland, Genoa and Cisalpine Gaul transformed into satellite republics. What an achievement! Not Richelieu, not Louis XIV, had ever planned on such a scale. At a single blow the Revolution, which had become bogged down in its religious, social, and financial experiments, with its guillotine, its Supreme Being, and its paper money, had renewed its youth on the battlefields of Europe.

The Dictator

Men can find consolation in glory, but they cannot live off it. The Directory had shown itself incapable of lifting the national economy out of its condition of slump, of balancing the national finances, of rescuing France from poverty. Everywhere throughout the country there was unemployment, and that at a time when England was renewing her industrial equipment and making great technical strides. The treasury could no longer depend on paper to get it out of its difficulties. Customs dues were re-established; an attempt was made to levy a tax on capital, which was redistributed on political grounds by corrupt tribunals. On the last day of the regime only 167,000 francs remained, the **1799** balance of a last-minute loan made by the banks to a government that had been reduced to begging for help. The five-per-cent state bonds fell to seven francs. Recruits refused to obey an order for general mobilization. Organized gangs held up travelers and peasants. Rouen welcomed the Chouans. Toulouse was beleaguered by Royalists. Paris was ready to surrender to the first-comer as the only hope of avoiding chaos.

A return of the Bourbons, however, was impossible. The former regicides and those who had acquired national property had uneasy consciences. They feared reprisals and confiscation. Furthermore, the *émigrés* had all the appearance of traitors. Nobody wanted Louis XVIII, but who could be made king in his place? There were some among the Directors who hoped for a soldier to prolong the life of the Republic. Barras, the most corrupt of them all, and Sieyès, the most crafty, joined together to carry through a *coup d'état*. But who was to be the chosen general? Hoche was dead, Joubert was dying, Moreau declined to be a candidate. Salvation lay in Bonaparte alone.

He had given pledges to the Revolution. This under-

sized Corsican scion of a family of minor landed gentry had
been trained in the military schools of the monarchy and
had been a militant Jacobin. What he had achieved against
the Whites, at Toulon, and in the streets of Paris, was matter of common knowledge. The peace that he had imposed
on Austria, though it had not lasted, redounded as much to
his credit as did any of his victories. He was a man of peace
rather than of war. After his return from Cairo, through
the English blockading squadrons, he kept about him in
the public eye a vague splendor of Oriental mystery. The
country as a whole approved of the way in which he had disobeyed the Directory by signing a treaty with Austria and
by abandoning the army of Egypt. It was in love with his
youth and his bluntness, with the dry style in which his
proclamations were worded. The Napoleon of these early
days was already a legendary figure. Ambitious he may have
been, but Joséphine, his lovely Creole, the woman he had re-
1799 cently married, was even more so. She had useful connec-
tions—Barras, to begin with. In two days of Brumaire the
coup was completed: France had found a master.

Like his contemporaries, Bonaparte unconsciously continued the Greco-Roman parody in which the Revolution
had taken such delight. With his education he could
scarcely have done otherwise. He had been bred on Livy,
Plutarch, and those *Institutes* of Justinian which at one
period of his life were his chosen bedside book. What,
really, had he been seeking in Egypt? His presence there
was not a serious threat to the lines of communication with
India: he had been more an embarrassment to the Turks
than to the English. Without, perhaps, realizing it, he had
been led to follow the road of Alexander, Cæsar, and Augustus.

David, the scenic designer of the Republic, had turned
his back on Robespierre. This former President of the Convention was more than ready to give his services to the dic-

tatorship. He would act as "producer." Was he not himself a dictator of the arts? Girodet, Gérard, Gros, all of them his respectful disciples, commemorated on canvas the exploits of the Corsican hero. Napoleon may not have many poets to his credit, but at least he had his painters. David it was, too, who, feeling the way the wind was blowing, expressed in his picture of the Sabines the reconciliation of all Frenchmen which had been brought about by the Consulate. He celebrated the coronation in paint, and ten years later, with his *Leonidas at Thermopylæ*, gave form and imagery to the period of the great defeats.

1799

Bonaparte was no whit behind David in playing the Roman. Whence, if not from Rome, did he derive the title of Consul? In order to obtain ratification of his successive upward moves in the hierarchy, he multiplied the holding of plebiscites (which produced genuine majorities). For the purposes of his new legislative machine he revived the Senate and devised a Tribunate. He appointed prefects in the Departments. Repudiating Robespierre's wig, he wore his hair like Titus, like all the Roman emperors (and his soldiers called him "little crop-head"). His fashion in hairdressing was a preliminary step to the assumption of the crown.

Joséphine had a wish to be "Empress of the Gauls"—and why not? The Republic, treading the long road of Roman history, had taken the place of the monarchy, and now it was the turn of the Empire to succeed the Republic. France was true to the Roman model. Napoleon's thoughts were fixed on Cæsar rather than on Charlemagne. He did better than Charlemagne, for he brought the Pope to Paris, and received from him, in Notre-Dame, the anointing and the sanctified oil. But he set the crown on his head with his own hands. He donned for the occasion a version of the robes worn by the Roman imperators.

1804

Emperor and builder, he was possessed by a passion for

antiquity. He topped his standards with the Roman eagle. He filled Fontainebleau and Compiègne with sober furnishings, with objects veneered in mahogany and adorned with sphinxes and griffins and caryatids of gilded bronze. Of such things was the Empire style composed. His new palaces were reminiscent of temples—the Stock Exchange, the Palais Bourbon, and that Shrine of Fame which was to be known later as the Madeleine. He set his heart on having a Triumphal Arch, and, until the one at the Étoile should be ready, made do with the Arc du Carrousel, which was a copy of the gateway set up by Septimius Severus. He set his heart on having a column to commemorate the deeds of the Grande Armée. It was copied from Trajan's, and was afterward called the Colonne Vendôme.

This version of Roman history differed from its original by being spanned at breakneck speed. The French Republic, including the Consulate, lasted for twelve years; Cato's for a period forty times longer. The French Empire lasted for ten years, a period fifty times less than that of Augustus. Invasion put an end to both.

The Conciliator

What precisely did Napoleon represent? The Revolution booted and spurred? The monarchy restored? Historians, according to their fancy, have painted him as heir of the Jacobins and of the Bourbons. He would have liked to be both. "I am part and parcel," he said, "of all that has happened from the days of Clovis to those of the Committee of Public Safety." The coins that he had struck after his coronation bore the double legend "*République Française*" and "*Napoléon Empereur.*" He was compelled to conciliate the two tendencies and to reassure the world, because he had need of the world. He authorized the return of 52,000 *émigrés*, but filled the Senate with former members of the Conven-

tion. He restored the Gregorian calendar, and concluded
with the Holy See a concordat which recognized the Catho-   1802
lic religion as that of the majority of Frenchmen. But he
confirmed the purchasers of national property in their holdings. He chose as his residence the Tuileries, but not Versailles. He restored a nobility consisting of 9 princes, 32
dukes, 388 counts, and 1,090 barons, but he handed out
these titles to his generals and to former agitators. Talleyrand became Prince of Benevento, Fouché Duke of Otranto,
Cambacérès Duke of Parma. Danton's widow was created a
baronne.

Between the liberties of the Capetian monarchy and the
equality of the Revolution he chose not to choose, but to
reject both alike. He gladly sacrificed equality, which ill
suited the temperament of the French, with their passion
for decorations (the Legion of Honor was founded under
the Consulate) and hierarchy (the Empire revived the title
of Marshal). He sacrificed all the liberties that got in his
way. The Legislative Assemblies voted laws when instructed
to, and without debate. The press was muzzled. In the
course of a single year the number of newspapers circulating
in Paris fell from seventy-three to nine. Trade-unions continued to be forbidden, and no worker could be taken on unless his labor-card was in order. France had become a police
state. Education was reorganized under public control. In
the *lycées* (it is worth noting the fine Greek note struck by
the name!) and in the Imperial University the young were
to learn, in periods marked by the roll of a drum at start and
finish, the histories of Sparta and of Rome. Instead of allowing the Departments to be controlled by elected councils
and elected officials, Napoleon installed prefects on whose
loyalty he could rely. It was only Paris now that counted,
and in Paris there was only one master who counted. Triumph of centralization.

He was far, however, from dictating events. Instead, he

submitted to them. Dominant though his character was, it was constantly being dominated. His wish was to appease, but circumstances compelled him to deal harshly. Because the Simon Pures of the Revolution could not forgive him for Brumaire, he banished them. Because the Simon Pures of the monarchy insisted on regarding him as a usurper, he had them shot. To bombs and plots he replied with the firing party: Enghien, Cadoudal.

All his reforms were hybrids, children born of a mixed parentage—Capetian tradition on the one side, modern principles on the other. In this double origin lay sometimes their strength, sometimes their weakness; which it was depended wholly on whether the compromise in question happened to be judicious or clumsy. How was it possible to come to terms, at one and the same time, with the old and the new, with the State and the individual? Napoleon the great leader was hesitant when he found the road blocked by an obstacle. When necessity forced him into the position of arbitrator, he was timid.

The first thing to be done was to get some sort of order into the nation's finances. The Consulate in its early stages lived from day to day, borrowing from the banks and from big business. The Empire built up a working-fund by demanding caution-money from its officials (which was an indirect way of re-establishing the system of office by purchase). In order to rescue the treasury from its condition of embarrassment some sort of fiscal system was restored. Direct taxes were of Revolutionary origin. The full weight of them fell on goods rather than persons—agricultural land (the value of which was established by survey), trades, rents, 1804 doors, and windows. But certain indirect levies, inherited from the monarchy, were also reinstated, and these struck at such commodities as drink, salt, and tobacco. The whole conception was the first case of a marriage between equity and yield.

Monetary reform was governed by the same spirit of compromise. The old livre of Tours, with its duodecimal divisions, was repudiated. The Convention had wished to institute a new, so-called Republican unit, and then later had proposed the franc, containing ten tenths and one hundred centimes. This coin was, within a small margin of error, the equivalent of the now defunct livre. It had a bimetallic definition—an agreed weight of silver (4.50 grams), and an   1803
agreed weight of gold (290 milligrams). Why was not a single standard decided on? The answer to that question is—indecision.

To make up for lack of currency it was necessary to have recourse to paper. But the memory of the assignats stood in the way of any large-scale activity. A few private banks made a cautious issue of notes. Napoleon wanted to have his own ·
bank and his own paper currency. He founded the Bank of   1800
France, and granted it the privilege of issuing notes in Paris (an old privilege resurrected!). It was neither a public nor a private bank, but a hybrid. Its notes, convertible into metal on sight, were not even legal tender. It was open to anyone to refuse to accept them in payment. Another case of hesitant and overcautious action.

Was the Consul Emperor any more adventurous in the field of law? He set on foot, and carried through, a great work, the effect of which was to give France a complete legislative system: a penal code, a commercial code, a criminal code, a code of procedure, but, above all, a civil code. It fused into a single whole ancient customary law, Roman   1804
law, royal ordinances, and Revolutionary right. In so far as it confirmed property rights (donations, bonds, agreements), and subordinated married women to their husbands, it was traditional. Its innovations were confined to making all citizens equal in the eyes of the law, to abolishing the right of primogeniture, and to establishing divorce. In short, it bolstered up property and weakened the family.

Imperfect though they may have been, these Napoleonic achievements were, all the same, astonishing. *Lycées*, prefects, taxes, money, legal code—through them the structure of French life was reshaped with a flick of the fingers, and the results were destined to last for a very long time. Napoleon took a personal interest in everything, even to drawing up a statute for French actors. His vitality was prodigious. He never rested. He neither wanted to nor could. There can be little doubt that he would have liked to go down to history as the peaceful architect of the new France. But war was on the doorstep and demanded his presence. He was condemned to play his part as the warrior architect of Europe.

The Conqueror

The Revolution had confided to Napoleon the duty of safeguarding its conquests. Where that was concerned there could be no compromise. But he had no wish to increase the territorial size of France. She was quite large enough already. His sole ambition was peace, and peace fled from him. It was the unattainable phantom that he chased through every war and every annexation. Napoleon was a conqueror only from necessity.

Had his enemies been merely the great powers of the Continent there would have been no difficulty about achieving his ambition. With his old veterans and his conscripts, with his guns and his cavalry, he was strong enough to take them all on, and to beat them too, as he proved. He held the secret of lightning marches and outflanking movements. But of what use was that? Marengo settled nothing; Austerlitz settled nothing, nor Jena, nor Friedland, nor Wagram, because after every battle he had to fight another battle, after every peace treaty impose another treaty, and because it needed but one single defeat to undo all the work he had already done.

The reason for this was that behind Austria, Prussia, Russia, behind the alliance of those three countries, which was forever being renewed, stood England, and England never laid down her arms. The most she ever did was to allow the Consulate a twelve-month breathing-space. She could not **1803** consent to leave the French in occupation of the Belgian coast. When war flared up again, it was obvious that one or other of the two main adversaries must be beaten to her knees.

Napoleon, mindful of Cæsar, made preparations to invade the island. If once he could cross the Channel with the **1805** 130,000 men whom he had concentrated at Calais, it would be all up with England. But the Emperor lacked the fleet that Louis XVI had had—and he lacked a Nelson. Contrary winds delayed the covering squadron, and off the Spanish coast, at Cape Trafalgar, it was sent to the bottom, carrying with it all hopes of an invasion. The end now was inevitable. No matter what the Emperor might do, in spite of his 100,000 "stalwarts," in spite of his marshals, in spite of his "star," disaster on land was bound to follow defeat on the high seas.

For ten years the illusion continued. For ten years, to the roll of drums, useless victories enslaved the countries of Europe. Napoleon galloped from capital to capital—to Vienna, to Rome, to Madrid, to Moscow. But it was another capital that he aimed at and never reached—London.

Unable to conquer the English by force of arms, he tried to break their will by setting up a blockade—this time using a financial weapon. He closed the Continent to British ex- **1806** ports, hoping thereby to undermine her trade balance and so ruin her. The idea was a good one. Strategy so conducted *could* have strained a "nation of shopkeepers" to the breaking-point. But it needed only a small leakage to bring the scheme to nothing. Napoleon was like a property-owner whose land lies on the banks of a river in flood. He builds a

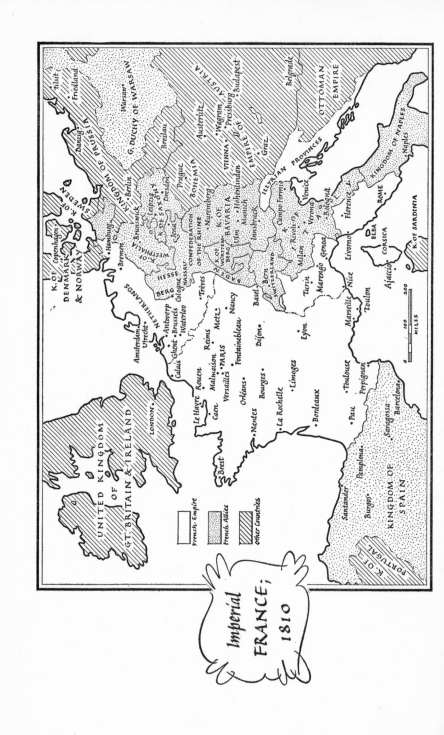

Imperial FRANCE; 1810

French Empire
French Allies
Other Countries

UNITED KINGDOM OF GT. BRITAIN & IRELAND

LONDON

K. OF DENMARK & NORWAY

K. OF SWEDEN

KINGDOM OF PRUSSIA

G. DUCHY OF WARSAW

AUSTRIA

OTTOMAN EMPIRE

Tilsit
Friedland
Danzig
Warsaw
Breslau
Belgrade

Copenhagen

Hamburg
Bremen
Berlin
Leipzig
Dresden
Prague
BOHEMIA
Austerlitz
Wagram
Pressburg
Budapest

NETHERLANDS
Amsterdam
Utrecht

K. OF BRUNSWICK
K. OF WESTPHALIA
K. OF SAXONY
Jena
Nuremberg

VIENNA
Hohenlinden
Graz

ILLYRIAN PROVINCES

HESSE
BERG
NASSAU
CONFEDERATION OF THE RHINE
K. OF WÜRTEM-BERG
K. OF BAVARIA
Munich
Innsbruck

Antwerp
Brussels
Waterloo
Cologne
Trèves
BADEN
Basel
SWITZERLAND
Bern

EMPIRE OF

Campoformio
Venice
Verona

Calais
Ghent
Reims
Metz
Nancy

Le Havre
Rouen
Malmaison
PARIS
Versailles
Fontainebleau
Dijon
Besançon

Turin
Milan
Marengo
Genoa
Bologna
Florence
ROME
Livorno
ELBA

Brest
Caen
Orléans
Bourges
Limoges
Lyon

Marseille
Nice
Toulon

KINGDOM OF NAPLES
Naples

CORSICA
Ajaccio

K. OF SARDINIA

Nantes
La Rochelle
Bordeaux
Toulouse
Pau
Perpignan

Santander
Pamplona
Burgos
Saragossa
Barcelona

KINGDOM OF SPAIN

K. OF PORTUGAL

0   100   200
MILES

dike to hold back the rising waters and then has to spend all his time rushing hither and thither to stop the holes.

Closing France to English merchandise meant closing Europe as a whole. But to shut Europe off entailed an extension of the blockade by either persuasion or force. Smuggling was active. How could it be kept from the Dutch and German coasts, from the Russian and Italian harbors? Napoleon installed his brother Louis in the Low Countries, his brother Jérôme in Westphalia, his brother-in-law Murat in 1807 Naples. At Tilsit he signed a treaty with the Tsar, Alexander, who undertook to buy nothing from England. Then, to make doubly sure, he annexed such parts of the coastline as were suspect. He made Rome the administrative center of a French Department, and held the Pope as a hostage at 1810 Fontainebleau. Genoa, too, and Leghorn became French prefectures, as did Bruges and Antwerp, Amsterdam, Bremen, and Hamburg. But it was only too obvious that this monstrous Empire of 130 Departments, with its tentacles feeling their way to the coast, was not a sound political unit. It was merely a wartime makeshift, serving to build a wall against which English trade should dash its head.

History has been too ready to accept things at their face value, and to take seriously Napoleon's declaration that he was "by the grace of God and the Constitution Emperor of the French, King of Italy, Protector of the Confederation of the Rhine." It has disseminated the belief that he was dreaming of universal dictatorship just because he laid hands on Venice and Illyria, Portugal and Spain. It is even possible that Napoleon, in his moments of blindness, deceived himself. But the demands of the war against England recalled him quickly enough to the realities of the situation. If he extended the boundaries of his Empire beyond all measure, if he multiplied the number of his satellites, if he showered thrones on the members of his family and on his marshals, it was with the sole object of keeping his own crown on his head. The conqueror had a panic fear forever at his throat, the fear of defeat, of that single defeat which would bring the whole edifice tumbling about his ears. He was fighting in a mood of desperation. At moments of crisis, haunted by the figure of his destiny, he would, even when completely alone, recite in a loud voice lines from Racine's tragedy *Mithridate* or from Voltaire's *Mort de César*.

How could he seriously pretend that he had brought liberty to the world when all he had given it was his own tyranny? If Europe had been French in the days of the Bourbons, that had been because of France's cultural supremacy. Napoleon made her French by force of arms, and Europe refused to accept the yoke. The former subjects of the Papal

1808 States failed to appreciate the closing of convents and the dissolution of religious orders. The Spaniards, who wanted to have nothing to do with Joseph Bonaparte, but remained faithful to their own Bourbon King, rose against the occupying power. The Germans discovered that they were a nation. The Poles were sacrificed to the Russians, and the Russians wanted to be free to buy what they needed from the English. Which way should he turn? Whither send his troops? There could be no question now of crossing the Channel. It was the turn of the English to do that, and land

1812 men in Portugal and Holland. Resolutely the Russians resumed the struggle. They must be forced back into the system. Smolensk, Moscow. The Russians retreated, leaving an emptiness behind them. The Kremlin burned. The Grande Armée was in danger of being cut off from its bases. Retreat —in the teeth of bitter cold, with the Cossacks attacking all

1813 the time. Collapse. Prussia rose in arms. Saxony turned traitor. Leipzig—300,000 allied troops against 100,000 French. The conscripts were too young. France was at her

1814 last gasp. Invasion: English in the south, Germans, Austrians, Russians in the east. The final jerks and spasms. Paris occupied, for the first time since the days of Henri IV.

Mock monarch of the isle of Elba, Napoleon tried one
last gamble. He landed in the Gulf of Juan, hurried to Paris,   1815
made an offer of peace to the world. It was refused. A hundred days of reprieve. On the Belgian plain, which had been
the stake of so many wars, Wellington and Waterloo put
an end to the adventure. One last echo of antiquity: "I return, like Themistocles"—but it was the fate of Bajazet that
awaited the fallen Emperor. An uncrowned king upon the
rock of St. Helena, his only future now was to wear the
crown of martyrdom and to create a legend.

A Colossus with Feet of Clay

In France itself, as in the outer world, the Empire had been
proved a fragile thing. Napoleon realized its weakness and
knew the cause. Like the first of the Capetians, he had had
to impose himself on all those who, seeing him Emperor,
had thought: "Why not I?" More than once he deplored
the fact that he did not come of a line of kings. "If only I
had been born upon the throne!" he said with bitterness.
The whole of his policy had been framed to the end of overcoming that initial, that irreparable inferiority.

A self-made general, he mistrusted soldiers even more
than civilians. His first concern was to show himself different from those other generals who in the old days had been
his seniors or his companions. He fettered them with honors
when he did not dismiss them in disgrace. Deliberately he
painted a picture of his own sobriety against the background
of their plumes and brocades and gold lace. In his little hat
and his riding-coat, with his hand stuck between two but-
tons, he posed for the albums of posterity. He pinched the
ears of his veterans, he was the friend and idol of his men.
"Soldiers, I am satisfied with you!" Thus did he arm himself against the military hierarchy. In the Legion of Honor
(a Roman word, that *Legion*) he systematically mingled sol-

diers and civilians in such a way as not to create a Prætorian élite. He was at pains to posture for the great public. Roche-sur-Yon he renamed Napoléon-Vendée; Pontivy, Napoléon-ville; Réunion, Île Bonaparte. The great Paris street that later became the rue de la Paix he christened rue Napoléon. The civil code has come down to us as the Code Napoléon. But names are even more precarious than deeds.

Every dictator is at the mercy of a dagger or a plot. Against the "Corsican ogre" the Royalists conspired, the peasants of the west rose again and again. Against the despot the Republicans murmured. Against the oppressor foreign peoples were ever ready to revolt. At Schönbrunn a German student tried to kill the tyrant. How keep the danger at arm's length? How force the hand of destiny? Napoleon knew that the individual man is mortal, but that a family endures. He wanted to found a dynasty. By giving kingdoms to his brothers and sisters he sought to protect himself. "One of these 1809 days I shall have seven or eight sovereigns on my hands," said Madame Mère with philosophic resignation. The Em-1810 peror repudiated Joséphine, who had failed to give him a child. He tried to marry the Tsar's sister, and finally let his choice fall on the daughter of the Austrian Emperor, on that Marie-Louise who was the grand-niece and god-daughter of Marie-Antoinette. Thus did Bonaparte be-1811 come a relation of the Habsburgs and the grand-nephew of Louis XVI. Better still, a son was born to him. A crown must be found quickly for the child. He was made King of Rome, since Rome was all the fashion and ranked as the second city of the Empire. Napoleon would find his shield and buckler in heredity. After the Capetians would come the Bonapartes.

But on the day of the child's christening there were cat-calls in the Paris streets. A bad sign. When Napoleon was lost in the snows of Russia, a former aristocratic Republican, 1812 General de Malet, spread a rumor that the Emperor was dead, and for a brief moment he seized supreme power. Nobody on that day thought of the King of Rome. Never would the Bonapartes reign—that was quite certain. Ten years of glory are no substitute for ten centuries of continuity.

Napoleon had more than once already had proof of the mistrust that he inspired. Even at the height of his fame lenders had been hard to find. Neither the solid conduct of his finances nor the brilliance of his victories served to convince those with money tucked away. Holders of Bank of France notes took fright on the very eve of Austerlitz, and stood in queues at the pay-desks to change their paper into specie. Paying out had to be checked, and notes lost ten per cent in terms of real money. The sun of Austerlitz saved the franc, but the panic had proved how nervous the great public was.

On whom could the Emperor rely? Public opinion was sullen. His own family sponged on him. The most intimate of his collaborators were prepared at any moment to betray him—Fouché, Talleyrand. The best of his marshals were ready to abandon him, Bernadotte and Murat in order to keep their own thrones, others from sheer apathy. Each time that he was exploited or deceived, he burst out in terrible fits of anger. He threatened, but his words were rarely followed by acts. For all his violence, was he not really just an erratic creature of impulse? He knew what he wanted, but knew its vanity as well. He sought to drug himself with constant business, drowning anxiety in work.

At the moment of his fall the Senate, which he had filled with his creatures, gave him not a single thought. The question of the succession was not even raised. Automatically the throne reverted to the man who could claim it by virtue of the old fundamental law of the realm, to the brother of Louis XVI, who for twenty-three years had lived in exile and, since the death of the Dauphin, had assumed the title of Louis XVIII. He had lived on foreign subsidies; he suf-

1814

fered from the gout. There was nothing attractive or glorious about him. He had only one outstanding quality: he was
a Bourbon, a Capetian. It was enough that he should reassure the holders of national property and accept the support
of the regicides. Because he could boast of ancestors, and
the Corsican hero could not, he was, beyond all doubt or
discussion, the true heir.

The Balance-sheet of a Quarter of a Century

Only twenty-six years had elapsed since the summoning of
the States-General, and now the way was open for brother
to succeed brother. But how much had happened in those
twenty-six years! They counted for more than many centuries. To evoke the feel and sense of them we have had, not
to stride across the generations in seven-league boots, but to
bend down and watch men and women, like teeming insects, living their daily lives. While the Revolutionary storm
was still raging we were compelled to register each crash of
thunder, but now, with the violence stilled, it is time to
reckon up the damage.

The roaring wind had swept away much rubbish. It had
cleansed the land of France of a deal of outworn lumber.
But it had been responsible as well for many victims. More
than a million men had perished in the wars, but the old national vigor was not abated, and the population had actually
increased. From twenty-seven million it had risen to twenty-
nine. Paris now housed 650,000 souls. But though these figures show an absolute growth, relatively they mark a diminu-
tion. France had formerly accounted for one quarter of the
population of Europe; now it contained only a fifth.

The French standard of living had been lowered. As a result of the Revolution the number of landed proprietors
had swollen, but recurrent conscription had mobilized all
men who were physically fit, and constant requisitioning

had taken a sad toll of horses. It was only with great difficulty that the peasants could now farm their land. Cultivation had fallen in twenty-five years from thirty-three to
twenty-five million hectares—in other words, from two
thirds of the national territory to less than one half. Shortage of grain was frequent. But potatoes and tomatoes became articles of common consumption, and great strides
were made in the breeding of livestock.

The most serious problem was that of sugar. The black
men of Santo Domingo, disfranchised by a decree of the
Constituent Assembly, had risen in rebellion. The island
was lost, and with it went all the cane crop of the Antilles,
which had been the mainstay of French trade. The Jacobins, in a fine uprush of abnegation, had taken an oath to
abstain from sugar. The Empire, with a clearer eye for the
practical, had experimented in extracting sugar from beets.
But the beet industry, which later was to be so prosperous,
was only just beginning.

Industry as a whole suffered during the Revolution from
consumer poverty. Textile production diminished by two
thirds. As a result of the blockade, manufacturers were deprived of raw materials. So severe was the crisis that Napoleon modified his decrees to the extent of permitting certain   1810
importations under license. His action amounted to a le-
galization of smuggling, and this struck at the very roots of
his Continental blockade. It did, however, enable France
to receive the cotton necessary for her looms. Their number
increased, and they became more and more frequently mechanized. Steam began to be used as a motive power in the factories, though as yet to a not very large extent. Gas-jets made
their appearance in Paris. Jacquard developed a mechanical
shuttle for use in the weaving of silk. Philippe de Girard invented a machine for spinning flax. De Wendel introduced
English methods of smelting. Chevreul discovered the formula for the stearic candle. But all these novelties were still

in the experimental stage. Not yet could they produce any fundamental change in industrial methods. The State encouraged them, but was not greatly concerned in the production of weapons.

The men of science worked on in apparent indifference to political storms. Chappe devised an aerial telegraph which, by means of visual signals, could accelerate the sending of messages. Blanchard invented the parachute. Fulton launched his first steamboat on the Seine. French chemists, trained by Lavoisier, made a number of fruitful discoveries—chromium, iodine, chlorine for use in laundry-work, and a method for producing caustic soda. Gay-Lussac established the law of the dilation of gas, Berthollet the law of affinities.

Napoleon, who took an interest in everything, was far from being indifferent to scientific progress. As he had backed David in the latter's attempt to lay down the law to art, so did he make Laplace his dictator in the Institute, and Cuvier at the Museum. Laplace had developed a theory of astral movements which satisfied the master's sense of discipline. The idea of a celestial police system was wholly to his taste, as was the descriptive geometry of Monge, and Lagrange's exposition of analytic mechanics. On the other hand, he had no fancy for Lamarck and his doctrine of evolution, preferring Cuvier, who had classified the animal kingdom with a fine Imperial rigor.

Napoleon could not, however, bring the literary men to heel. They were obstinate in valuing liberty above dictatorship. Chénier had declared war on Marat. Chateaubriand declared war on the Emperor—but, then, on whom did Chateaubriand not declare war? The haughty Viscount was incapable of admitting that anyone or anything could be his superior. It was the Emperor's failing that he surrounded himself with poetasters, though he longed to have, like Louis XIV, his Molières and his Racines. It was only later

that the poets began to sing his praises and to magnify his
achievements—when they were no longer compelled to do
so and could play a minority part. The best man of letters
in the Empire was still the Emperor.

He was also the great patron of the art galleries of France.
Masterpieces poured into the country from Cairo, Rome,
and Florence. As the result of numerous treaties the Louvre
—called the Musée Napoléon—received the artistic riches
of Europe: Rembrandt's *Night Watch*, Rubens's *Descent
from the Cross*, Titian's *Assumption*, the Medici *Venus*, the
Laocoön, the *Apollo Belvedere*—and, at its doors, perched
on the Arc du Carrousel, pranced the four horses brought
from the Basilica of St. Mark at Venice. But all these trophies, when the Empire fell, went back to the cities from
which they had come.

As the Louvre lost its acquisitions, so did France. By the
terms of the Treaties of Vienna she was compelled to withdraw behind her ancient frontiers, and even farther. She   1815
still held Avignon, but lost many cities of the Sarre and the
Ardennes. Although she recovered some of the colonies that
the English had occupied during the war (Guadeloupe,
Martinique, Saint-Pierre and Miquelon, Senegal, Réunion—
all of them trading-centers for the Indies), she failed to
make good her claims to Santo Domingo and Île-de-France
(Mauritius). Louisiana was sold by an impoverished treasury to the United States for eighty million francs (about
fifteen million dollars).

Peace was an expensive business: an indemnity of seven
hundred million francs to the victorious Allies; occupation
costs amounting to twelve hundred million, to say nothing
of the poverty caused by invasion. The English were encamped in the north, the Prussians between Paris and the
Loire, the Russians in the east, the Austrians all the way
from Burgundy to the Dauphiné. Twelve hundred thousand
foreign soldiers were spread throughout the length and

breadth of France, and one hundred and fifty thousand remained there for more than three years.

Such was the final reckoning of the great adventure.
What remained to set against cost in human lives, in loss of
territory, in loss of money? Philosophically, a body of ideas
that were to ripen and ferment throughout the coming century; politically, an irresistible tendency to centralization.
The same passion for unity had animated Revolutionaries
and Emperor alike. The old pattern of the monarchy had
been shattered. France had been made one and indivisible.
But those who had brought about this result had paved the
way for unity in Germany, for unity in Italy. On the Rhine,
Richelieu's achievement was tottering. By exalting nationalism the Republic had given a stimulus to Germanism. By
making a confederation of what had been a kaleidoscope
Napoleon had prepared the federation of the German states
under the ægis of Prussia. Similarly, by reviving the name of
Italy, by breaking down local systems and local loyalties, he
had worked for the reawakening of the Italian people. It was
for the nineteenth century to lay the coping-stone upon his
labors, at the expense of French supremacy and French
security.

For the moment Germany and Italy were but vague fore-
bodings. But Russia, for the first time in her history, had appeared in the West. For England, mistress of the seas, and
firmly ensconced at all the crossroads of the world, the way
was clear. Her industrial and commercial power had the
firm backing of money. The supreme victor in the struggle
was London.

To sum up. If in the kingdom of the immaterial the
twenty-six years just past had brought to France prestige and
glory, in that of the real they had laid the foundations of
foreign mastery.

CHAPTER VII

SUNSET

(after 1815)

The Last of the Kings

HE DESCENDANTS of the Ca-
petians returned, but not to the throne of their fathers. The
storm had passed. France had roughed out a restoration, but
what rose from the grave was not the ancient monarchy.
Kingship by divine right was dead. The two brothers of
Louis XVI who wore, in turn, the crown and restored the
white lilies of the Bourbons inherited willy-nilly some part
of the Revolutionary legacy—the codes, the departments,
the prefects, and even the two legislative Chambers.

From now on, the French were sworn followers of the
representative system. The Assemblies had bred a taste for
parliamentary speech-making. But the men of the new dis-
pensation, torn between a desire for ordered government
and a longing for adventure, were destined to move from
monarchy to anarchy, from the domination of one man to
the domination of all. The older France had never been concerned to find a political formula, but had left the centuries
to do their work. The new France was in search of herself.
From Constitution to Constitution, from republic to dictatorship, from *coup d'état* to revolution she moved, fated
to tread the road of recurrent experiment. Wearied by authority, she groped her way to liberty. Pestered by liberty,
she longed for authority. In just such a way do children act
when weary of their toys, or old men grown sick of dieting.

The Bourbons who returned to Paris had formerly behaved as feudal nobles. Power, which works a great change
in men, made conscientious kings of them. Louis XVIII
was by no means lacking in subtlety, nor Charles X in courage. But it was their turn now to deal with aristocrats. In
the southern provinces bands of extremists established a
"White Terror." Many of the homing *émigrés* were filled
with rancor. The Chambers were composed of "ultras," of
men like Chateaubriand, who, reviving the opposition tactics of the former Parlement, sought to extend their own prerogatives at the expense of the King's.

This "feudal" clique (I need hardly point out that I use
the word as meaning the descendants of the ancient feudal
nobility) was a fact. It would be straining the language un-
duly to suggest that there existed, also, some sort of "popular" opposition. To use that term of public opinion would
be to do the latter too much honor. Ordinary, decent
Frenchmen were fully conscious that the foreign troops had
been got rid of earlier than had, at one time, seemed likely;
that France had resumed her position as a free agent among
the other powers of Europe; that the financial muddles had
been straightened out, and that it was now possible for men
to work in peace. But these benefits did not send them into
ecstasies. Faced by disaster, human beings are apt to feel
astonishment, whereas they regard good fortune as a normal
state.

But if, for the moment, there were no public disturbances,
conspirators were hard at work to find how best trouble
might be fomented. Lafayette began once more to play a
prominent part. Several secret societies, modeled on the Italian Carbonari, dreamed of imitating the Revolutionary
clubs. The Revolution had become a legend, and men's
minds were obsessed by it. This was especially true of the
King, who had no intention of letting himself be held a pris-

oner in Paris, like Louis XVI. A single "incident," a few barricades were sufficient to send Charles X on his travels again.

Should a republic be proclaimed? Memory of the guillotine and the assignats was still too vivid. The lure of the
house of Capet remained too strong. But the Bourbons had
shown themselves to be clumsy. It might be better to take
a chance with the Orléans branch. After all, had not the
right of primogeniture been suppressed? For centuries the
Orléans branch had schemed and plotted. Now at last their
moment had come. The attempts made by Gaston d'Orléans under Louis XIII, and by Philippe-Égalité under
Louis XVI, had miscarried. Where they had failed, Louis-
Philippe, the son of the regicide, succeeded, without particularly meaning to. Lafayette summoned him to the throne.
The Chamber made him King of the French.

It needed a considerable amount of optimism to believe
that this middle-class, liberal monarchy, which reinstated
the tricolor but refused universal suffrage, had much hope
of lasting. Born of rioting, it was at the mercy of rioting. It
satisfied neither the legitimists nor the Republicans. There
was, indeed, little to be expected from such a king. Intelligent he might be, but nobody could call him glamorous. He
was an easygoing husband and a good father. His umbrella
became a national joke, his pacific nature a lasting reproach.
When Belgium rose against the Dutch and wished to place
itself under the wing of a French prince, Louis-Philippe refused to accept the proposal for fear of offending the English. On two, on three occasions he chose retreat rather than
defiance. He was obstinately wedded to peace. His subjects
began to get bored. Of their great and glorious twenty years
they remembered only the triumphs and forgot the miseries. It was the will of destiny that this same Louis-Philippe
should be the man to raise in the Place de la Concorde the
obelisk of Luxor, which reminded all who saw it of the cam-

paign of Egypt; that by him should be completed that Arc de Triomphe at the Étoile which commemorated the achievements of the Grande Armée. Béranger made songs about the vanished hero: "He wore a little hat. . . . Tell us about him, Grandma, tell us." The young Hugo wrote an *Ode à la Colonne*. It was one of Louis-Philippe's sons who **1840** brought the Emperor's body from St. Helena to the Invalides. But monuments and songs and ceremonies are bad substitutes for deeds. The French were avid for greatness.

They were avid too for change. Romanticism in painting and in letters was the expression of a wish to break with the past. The classical tradition in the arts now merely provoked a snigger. The rage was for the younger writers, for the men who had freed themselves from the older conventions of prosody and drama, who were breaking the cadence of the Alexandrine line and thumbing the nose at the three unities. The "battle" of *Hernani* preceded by some months the fall of Charles X. Théophile Gautier's red waistcoat was in a sense the forerunner of the red flag. Chateaubriand had attacked the monarchy from the Right; Lamartine, the champion of the Girondins, attacked it from the Left. All the intellectuals were busy taking sides.

It is true that the great peasant mass of the French people remained unmoved. The sound and fury of the romantics meant nothing to it. But nobody thought of consulting it. Universal suffrage would have saved the monarchy. A limited suffrage, which gave the vote to a disgruntled middle class bred on Voltaire, brought about its overthrow. The secret societies were rich. In the Chambers, in the streets, a mounting tide of rebellion rose against the younger branch of the royal house. There were riots at Lyon, at Grenoble, in Paris. At Strasbourg and Boulogne a nephew of the great Napoleon tried to seize power. A legitimist tide swept across La Vendée. To a grumbling mutter of plots and insurrections the reign of Louis-Philippe drew to a close.

Louis-Philippe was no less mindful than Charles X of what had happened to Louis XVI. When his throne began to totter he put up no sort of a fight, but hurriedly departed—in a cab. Like Charles X, he was to die in exile. **1848**
France had rejected the last scions of the house of Capet. She had had her fill of them, had had her fill of kings who could do no more than give her prosperity and a quiet life. What she wanted was to live dangerously.

The Republican Road to Cæsarism

But revolutions do not come by chance. They arise from deep-seated causes of which even their leaders have no conception. Thus it came about that each of the three revolutions—1830, 1848, as well as 1789—was heralded by a staggering rise in the price of grain. Dear bread is a necessary preliminary to political earthquakes. During the same winter in which Louis-Philippe vanished into thin air, the unemployment figures rose to 780,000. The disease, in both its causes and its effect, was international, a strange disease that started in Belgium with potato blight and then flamed across Europe, bringing ruin to farmers, closing the outlets of industry, and creating an economic crisis with all its accompaniment of forced sales, bankruptcy, and misery. The temperature of discontent rose in Poland and in Italy and was to rise very soon in Spain, in Germany, and in Austria. Thrones were set trembling, and the way was blazed for the glowing movement of socialism. Paris played its part in the general turmoil by sacrificing a dynasty.

This time, there being no substitute king available, a republic was set up, a republic of workmen and poets, a republic born of panic and exaltation, exaltation in men's minds, panic on the Bourse. The fashion now was to ape the pro- **1848**
letariat. Intellectuals sported caps and untidy clothing. Beards sprouted in triumph on innumerable chins. In a

double sense they were the sign and symbol of liberation—
because under the restored Bourbons they had been the prerogative of the fire brigade, and because the classicists, like
the Romans, had been clean-shaven. Only when bearded
could men seriously frighten the middle classes.

But, very naturally, the middle classes did not like being
frightened, and the peasants shared their feelings. Both were
alarmed by the working-class disturbances. The state of the
taxes (an additional forty centimes, and the possibility of a
capital levy) most certainly did not appeal to them. Conse-
1849   quently, no sooner did universal suffrage become vocal than
its non-revolutionary complexion was at once evident. So
far as the mass of the French people was concerned, the
sooner the supporters of Bourbons and Orléanists came to
some sort of an agreement, and the monarchy was again established, the better.

Who, then, was to save the Revolution? The Man of Destiny, as fifty years earlier, was to be a Bonaparte. The Emperor's son, the boy who should have been Napoleon II, had
died in Vienna as a colonel in the Austrian Army. But a
nephew was available. Had not Cæsar been the nephew of
Marius, Augustus the nephew of Cæsar? Louis manipulated
to his own advantage the legend of the eagles. In order to
run no risk of becoming Louis XIX, he at first went under
the name of Louis-Napoleon, as a halfway house to Napoleon pure and simple. He presented himself to the people
as the man who could carry on the tradition of the soldier
of liberty, the man who was heir to the martyr of St. Helena.
He gave a new twist to the Napoleonic idea more in accordance with the taste of the times, making it into something social, industrial, and humanitarian. Louis-Napoleon
was the friend of the poor, the enemy of bad employers. He
had as allies the Carbonari, the Freemasons, and the socialists. He promised prosperity, a lightening of taxation, and
free trade. When the French were called upon to elect the

first president of Republic No. 2, they rallied enthusiasti- **1848**
cally round the person of this popular prince. Five million
votes were cast for Bonaparte as compared with two million
for his rivals. In the ears of the mob his name had the sound
of glory. The conservatives felt that he stood for ordered
government. The Revolutionaries regarded him as an instrument of revenge on an Assembly of monarchists.

But the Constitution so arranged matters that a Royalist
Assembly and a prince posing as the disciple of Rousseau
were brought face to face. A clash was inevitable. The
Chamber was niggardly in the matter of credits to the President. The President countered with a *coup d'état* on the an- **1851**
niversary of Austerlitz. The Chamber was dissolved. The recalcitrants of Right and Left were arrested. Victor Hugo,
who had been a legitimist under the Bourbons and a peer of
France under the Orléanses, had just recently become a sup-
porter of the Republic. He failed to convert himself in time
and withdrew into a flamboyant exile.

Two successive plebiscites, showing an increased majority, ratified the operation. As President for ten years (which
was the stipulated period of the Consulate), then hereditary Emperor, the nephew set himself to follow in his uncle's **1852**
footsteps. Napoléon le Petit, the sulking Hugo called him.
Like his forerunner, Napoleon III attempted to mediate between the supporters of authority and the enthusiasts for
social reform. He silenced parliamentary opposition, but
granted to the workers the right to combine into unions.
Like the Revolutionaries, he wore a beard, but it was neither shaggy nor unkempt.

Like the First Empire, the Second was insecurely based.
It was difficult to believe in length of life for a dynasty that
had emerged from a *coup d'état*. In the intervals between
plots and bombs the beneficiaries of the regime dulled their
anxieties in a round of pleasures. The Empress made Biar-
ritz fashionable. Morny started a vogue for Deauville. It was

the period of Mabille, of Hortense Schneider, and of Offen-
bach's operettas. Paris grew, sprawled, and swelled. But the
Prefect Haussmann pierced it with great strategic avenues
so as to make the erection of barricades more difficult.

The nephew resembled the uncle in being a warmaker.
The uncle had received war as part of the material legacy of
the First Republic. The nephew sought a basis for his own
wars in the spiritual heritage of the Second. It was his duty
1854   to attack tyrants and to bring aid to oppressed peoples. As
the ally of England—a liberal nation—he fought against the
Tsar of Russia in the Crimea. In Lombardy he freed the
1859   Italians from the yoke of the Austrian Empire. Wars of prestige: nonsense wars. To celebrate Sebastopol and Magenta
it was felt necessary to construct the boulevards of Paris.
Napoleon had no gifts as a soldier, and still less as a poli-
1860   tician. The Italian campaign brought him Nice and Savoy,
but it resulted in Italian unity. By weakening Austria he
paved the way for the unification of Germany in the interests of Prussia. In pursuit of a pointless Mexican adventure,
1870   France wasted her energy. When Prussia leaped upon her,
the Empire collapsed. Defeated and made prisoner, Napoleon III died, like his uncle, in exile, but without the aureole
of St. Helena. For the second time France had learned to
her cost that dictatorship, born of a Republic in dissolution,
could lead only to disaster.

Marianne

In little more than sixty years nine separate regimes had followed hard on one another's heels. Would the French ever
find a safe anchorage? On the morrow of defeat they could
still show a majority for the monarchy, and universal suffrage once again elected an Assembly predominantly faithful to the throne. But it was the kings now who hung back.
In vain were the two branches of the royal house reconciled.

Henri, Comte de Chambord, had no desire to wear a paste-board crown and wield restricted power. He would be king or nothing. For Henri IV Paris had been worth a Mass. For Henri V it was not worth an abjuration.

And so it came about that France got to be republican, and she became so to an accompaniment of savagery. How? The communist revolution served Republic No. 3 in good stead. Though it was confined to Paris, the news of it spread terror in the provinces.

The Commune was proclaimed under the mocking eyes of the Prussian troops who had occupied the forts of the Paris region. The capital, exacerbated by a long siege, fell a victim to Jacobin emotion. Obsessed by the memories of 1871 '93, the insurgents restored the Republican calendar, re-vived the Terror, massacred their hostages, and pulled down the Vendôme Column. Certain institutions, however, for some strange reason made them feel shy. They thought nothing of burning the Tuileries and the Hôtel de Ville, and they were prepared to destroy the Louvre and the Sainte-Chapelle, but they respected the Banque de France and the gold in its vaults. Being both honest men and simpletons, they hesitated to lay hands on private property, which their doctrine condemned, but their integrity protected. Imbued, at one and the same time, with feelings of chauvinism and a passion for brotherhood, they longed for revenge no less than for the reign of the International. They were dreaming innocents eager to follow in the footsteps of Marat and Robespierre.

Far from serving the cause of socialism, they were uncon-sciously instrumental in laying the foundations of a reac-tionary republic. They provided the insignificant Thiers—who became head of the provisional government—with an excuse for taking violent measures of repression. Once Paris was reconquered, executions and deportations fol-lowed by tens of thousands. Middle-class and country opinion thought that the Republic was capable of restoring order. It did so, in a bath of blood.

As a result its weaknesses were forgiven. Men averted their eyes from its origins, which were reminiscent of those "foreign baggage-wagons" which for so long had been a reproach to Louis XVIII. The French, with their passion for horses and uniforms, grew used to a simple and unspectacular regime, which raised to power—or to the lack of it—a succession of elderly gentlemen in frock-coats and striped trousers. As though to disguise this triumph of the old, they gave to their Republic, in marble and in plaster, the face of a young woman wearing a Phrygian cap. This ageless and, as her enemies said, brainless female was christened Marianne —a name she inherited from a secret society.

Marianne was an honest enough lass, not particularly strait-laced, perhaps even a shade too free-handed, but anxious only to please everybody. Her failings were those that noticeably appeal to the French. She was very ready to sacrifice the public interest to private profit. The elector was the soverign master. He might at times be capricious or unjust, but, by definition, his caprices and injustices were such as satisfied the majority. The law, in the eyes of which all are equal, did at least see to it that all were educated and that all received state assistance. It guaranteed respect for the public liberties—freedom of thought, freedom of worship, and freedom of the press. There was no oppression in these matters—except by accident.

Very quickly, as electoral promises succeeded and outdid electoral promises, the Royalists lost their majority. The parties of the Left always offered more than those of the Right, and sometimes they were actually as good as their word. As the result of a slow downward slide, and as the peasant voters gradually lost their preponderance, France moved in the direction of a secular regime with a vaguely socialist complexion. But the socialism was respectable and well-mannered, and, on the surface at least, it respected public order.

The Constitution of the Third Republic was laconic and remarkably elastic, qualities that ensured its continuance. Conceived by monarchists to allow of the presence of a puppet king, it easily adapted itself to the requirements of parliamentary democracy. The Presidents, letting their constitutional rights fall into abeyance, became no more than figureheads to be trotted out at inaugural ceremonies and state banquets. The Presidents of the Council, whose functions were never clearly defined, came to play the most prominent part in the political life of the nation, though party warfare rarely left them time to become genuine leaders. In the forty-four years of the Republic which elapsed between the two Franco-German wars forty-five ministries passed across the stage at the double. Their average length of life was rather less than three hundred days. The permanent staffs of the administrative offices, however, outlived governments, and the civil service came to be the only guarantee of continuity.

In the absence of graver troubles, public opinion turned for its thrills to a number of abortive attempts to seize power, all of them of a more or less Ruritanian nature (Boulanger, who was a general; Déroulède, who was a poet); to several scandals, which were quickly covered up—a trade in decorations in which a President's son-in-law was concerned, an affair of parliamentary corruption in connection with Panama Canal stock; a case of alleged espionage (was Captain Dreyfus innocent?); the struggle between secularists and Catholics (the persecution of the congregations, the break with the Vatican, the separation of church and state). There were a few assassinations and one or two cases of rioting, but nothing that need seriously disturb the nation's peace.

1888

1892

1897

France was too much occupied with her internal troubles —on which the party system throve—to spare much attention for anything beyond her own frontiers, except, however, that she did round out her colonial possessions. Content to feel that she was growing, she did not notice that other powers were growing too, and very much more quickly. She paid but small attention to the development of the German Empire, which had been revived under the ægis of Prussia. Taught by defeat, the French had come to be peace-minded. Made flabby by progressive advances in material well-being, they were now a home-loving people. Warlike escapades no longer tempted them. Besides, were wars really possible between the nations of the modern world? Such things belonged to an age long past. The German Socialists gave their sworn word to the French Socialists that they would never countenance a resort to arms. France dozed on in a mood of comfortable optimism. A majority of the electors voted against the three-year period of military service, which the imminence of catastrophe had made it necessary to revive.

Then came the summer of 1914. Born of invasion, it was at the threat of invasion that the Republic woke at last.

Technical Developments

All through the century separating 1814 from 1914, kingdoms and republics alike had benefited from technical developments and from the Industrial Revolution. It has been customary to credit the political regimes of the period with the birth of a thousand marvels, whereas in fact they merely watched them happening.

All over the world, first steam, then electricity, had completely revolutionized the economic life of the nations. What the eighteenth century had discovered the nineteenth century applied. In the sending of messages the telegraph and the telephone did away with the obstacle of distance. In the transporting of human beings and of freight the railway, the steamship, and later the internal-combustion engine and the airplane changed the whole appearance of the planet. The organization of labor and the coming of mass production increased the number of commodities available and brought comfort within the reach of the many. Towns took on a new look. All were proud of their railroad stations and of the avenues leading to them. The center of social gravity moved away from the church. As time went on, garages and gas stations sprang up alongside the roads, ousting the old blacksmith's shop.

France played her part in most of these changes. Two Frenchmen, Niepce and Daguerre, developed a method of fixing and retaining pictures made by light. The brothers Lumière found out how to register and to reproduce the visual records of movement. With Serpollet, France became one of the pioneer countries in the building of automobiles, and with Clément Ader was an early practitioner of a new form of aviation which could challenge the achievements of the dirigible balloon. Blériot was the first man to fly the Channel in a machine that was heavier than air. Charles Cros invented the phonograph simultaneously with Edison. Branly was one of the first scientists to make radio possible. All these things were technical contributions of the first importance.

French economy, too, had its share in a movement that was making itself felt everywhere. In the course of a single century the production of coal shot up from one million tons to forty million. The whole of French industry turned over to steam as a motive power, and, later on, to electricity. The countryside was covered by a spreading network of more than 30,000 miles of railroad tracks, and close to 125,-000 of telegraph wires.

But in these activities France was no longer the leader. What was it she lacked? The security, perhaps, and the po-

1816

1895

1890

1877

litical continuity which encourage inventiveness, or, maybe, the steady perseverance that all must have who seek to turn to practical account the discoveries of the research scientist. But even more than moral energy she needed the material sources of industrial power—coal first and foremost, without which the nineteenth century would have been stranded; coal, which was mined far from Paris, Marseille, Lyon, and Rouen, and from nearly all the French manufacturing centers.

England forged ahead of France because she had much richer coal deposits. Her population had at first been smaller than that of France, with the result that, since English labor was scarcer and dearer, she had been driven to develop and extend machinery in order to make up for her shortage of manpower. France could never catch up with her rival across the Channel in the industrial race. She had to rest content with following at a considerable distance when it came to increasing the number of her blast furnaces, equipping her textile-mills with English machinery, or replacing her wooden sailing ships with steamboats of iron. Again, she could do no more than imitate the Germans in the field of industrial chemistry and in the substitution of synthetic for vegetable dyes. Every time some technical invention took a forward leap, France jogged quietly along. She had none of the vigor of the younger nations and seemed almost to regret her ancient ways. It was only with considerable hesitation, and at the end of the century, that her peasantry adopted the threshing-machines, the harvesters, and the reapers which their fathers had known so well how to do without. Her workers more than once gave expression to their fear of the competition represented by the devilish machines, which seemed determined to drive them into unemployment. Her poets bewailed the vanished days of three-masted ships, packets, and coaches—all of them things conducive to dreamy reveries. Her men of affairs were profoundly suspicious of the railways. Such newfangled ideas, they seemed convinced, would plunge them all into bankruptcy.

Her farmers, thinking it impossible to compete with the low prices obtaining in England, sought the protection of a tariff wall. High duties struck a heavy blow at imported grain, foreign sugar, cashmeres, cotton goods, and metallurgical products. Silks, shawls, and Indian textiles were forbidden. When the younger branch of the monarchy took the dangerous step of reducing the customs dues on iron and fabrics, it prudently raised those on linen thread and hemp and on oil-seeds. The measure was to the advantage of the producers, but not of the consumers.

It was only under the Second Empire that France ventured to experiment in liberalism. Her economists urged it; the example of England was tempting. Napoleon III, who had lived in England for many years, dreamed of free trade, and sought to gain with the consumers the popularity he so badly needed. He signed a trade agreement with the English, reduced import duties to less than twenty-five per cent of their former figure, and opened the frontiers. But he put up the backs of employers and peasants alike, who were demanding protection. In the economic field Bonaparte stood forth as the champion of liberty, while the opposition seemed to be playing the role of its convinced adversary.

Thus it came about that the first step taken by the Republic was to re-establish the tariff barrier, and this it raised doggedly in the interests (especially) of crops, sugar, and livestock. When it came to voting, the consumers had no way of asserting themselves, whereas the producers, particularly in the rural districts, knew how to make themselves heard.

Poverty, the Mother of Socialism

In spite of this defensive strategy, prices fell in the course of the century. Commodities in the world at large, and not in France alone, increased more rapidly than the means of payment, except in the years immediately following the discovery of gold in California and Australia and in the twenty years after its first appearance in South Africa. Apart from these two periods (when there was a general upward movement) prices showed a tendency to fall. From 1820 to 1896 the average drop was in the neighborhood of one half. Making all allowance for later recoveries, the prices of 1914 were still twenty-five per cent lower than those of 1814—a victory for improved technical methods.

But wages, in the meantime, had at first weakened. In the hope of competing in the commercial field, employers had demanded more work from their men, and had paid it badly. In the spinning and weaving industries they had imposed a thirteen-hour day, and had roped in women and children at a low rate. In mines and factories slavery reappeared in a new form. This policy of low wages led to the mass production of a proletarian class. The effect of industrial capitalism was to produce great fortunes and abject poverty. It treated labor as a mere object of merchandise. Gone were the easy days of family workshops and the masterpieces of craftsmanship. The workman now left his slum only to spend his day in a prison.

What could he do to improve his position? The penal code forbade the assembly of more than twenty persons except by special permission. The Revolution had deprived 1848 the wage-earners of the right of banding together. The Second Republic did not restore it. The most it did was to enroll the unemployed at two francs a day. Not until the coming of the Second Empire was there recognition of the 1864 workman's right of association. The Third Republic re-

stored the right of corporate action. From then on, the   1884
unions set about reviving the old journeyman system.

These slow conquests were the fruit of much agitation.
Only in the teeth of the law could workers gather together
at a spot close to the Hôtel de Ville, on La Grève, or the   1833
banks of the Seine, and there *faire grève*, or organize a strike.
Step by step the theorists of the labor movement built up a
new doctrine that opposed the necessity of joint action to
the revolutionary glorification of the individual. The idea
of association sprang from a nostalgic longing for the old
guilds. The word *socialism* was born, the true child of
poverty.

It was the child too, in its way, of feudalism. The great
nobles of past centuries had dreamed of creating states
within the State. The workers' leaders of the new century
dreamed of building labor fiefs within the structure of society. It is significant that the earliest Socialists were by
birth aristocrats.

Among them were to be numbered the Baron de Sis-
mondi, and Louis Blanc, who was the son of *émigrés* and
had started life as a legitimist; Filippo Michele Buonarroti
too, the owner of a great Tuscan name and a disciple of
Babeuf; as well as Prince Bakunin, who moved in the noblest Russian circles in Paris and opposed his anarchism to
the communism of Marx in the war against capitalism.
"Neither God nor master!" was his cry.

Aristocrat of aristocrats, Saint-Simon was the supreme
apostle of the movement. He had in the bosom of his own
family an example to follow in that same Saint-Simon who,
during the Revolution, had speculated in national property.
He claimed descent from Charlemagne. The society of the
future which he wished to build would be without either
marriage or inheritance, but it would be constructed on a
rigid hierarchical pattern. As the messiah of industrial bless-   1829
edness, he preached the religion of science. Men might

smile at his two popes and his forty disciples; they might imprison the maddest of his successors, but, for all that, he founded a school, and the greatest financial geniuses of the century were drawn from the ranks of his adepts—Lesseps, piercer of isthmuses, and the Péreire brothers, of railroad fame. Napoleon III had been his pupil, and might to some extent be described as a Saint-Simon in power.

There were other Socialists, however, who preached different variants of Socialism. Fourier sketched a system of phalansteries. Cabet, following in the footsteps of Sir Thomas More, shifted Utopia to Icaria—and inspired a handful of unfortunates to give, in Texas, a practical expression to his dreams. Proudhon denounced all property as theft, and hoped to find in a system of mutual exchange the key to every social problem. Thus did French Socialism stammer in a babble of high-minded fantasies.

But it surrendered to that German Socialism the Bible of which was written by Karl Marx. His aim was the elimination of capital—in other words, of free enterprise and private property. The means to this end was to be the class war, which implied the abolition of frontiers: "Workers of the world, unite!" The Workers' International was established, which adopted a common hymn (a French one) and a yearly day for voicing its claims—the 1st of May (a date of American origin).

Socialism in France never succeeded in shaking the fabric of capitalist society. How could it triumph in a nation of peasant proprietors? At most, the threat of the "dark night of capitalism" set a few bourgeois trembling in their shoes. It did, however, infiltrate into the laws and into daily life. Trade-union action enforced a number of social reforms—for instance, the first of the employers' liability, and workers' pensions, schemes. The working-day was limited to ten hours, and a weekly day of rest was made compulsory. There was an increase in nominal wages, though after the discov-

1840

1867

1900

ery of gold in South Africa the rise in prices again outdistanced the purchasing power of the average workingman,
which improved only at a very much more cautious rate.

Between 1850 and 1900 the weekly wage of a miner (in
other words, of the best paid of all workers) rose from 2.14
francs to 5.40—that is to say, it more than doubled itself.
But during the same period coal, per ton, increased from
less than ten francs to over twenty. Expressed in terms of
wheat, the workman's annual income (rather less than 1,000
francs) amounted at the close of the half-century to thirty-
nine quintals, or less than twice what a day-laborer in the
days of Saint Louis, 650 years earlier, had received for a task
that had taken fewer hours to perform and had been a great
deal less exhausting. It was very little in excess of what the
same type of workers had earned in the reign of Louis XI.

Poverty remained abject in the industrial slums. Society
had come to be organized on a pattern of mutually exclusive castes. The lower classes cursed and envied the upper,
who, in their turn, were puffed up with pride of money and
social eminence. For the century which had brought about
equality in law had witnessed an increasing inequality in
fortune, with the result that the rich middle class, the bankers and millowners, the army officers and ironmasters, were
now more arrogant than the aristocrats had ever been.

The consequent social antagonisms would have constituted a grave menace had it not been that the great mass of
Frenchmen, standing midway between the privileged trade-
unionists and the privileged capitalists, served to keep the
nation on an even keel. The real strength of France was in
her sturdy race of parsimonious countryfolk. So long as
nothing occurred to undermine their prosperity, so long as
they could tuck away their dividends and the profit from
their crops, French stability would never be seriously threatened.

The Rise of State Control

The final stage of social organization as envisaged by Marxian Socialism is, logically, the complete suppression of private property, and the vesting of all wealth and all control in society as a whole—which can mean only the State—at the expense of individual freedom and individual enterprise. The supreme object of Socialism is the redistribution of wealth. How to create it is a problem that the Left-wing theorists have not faced with the same enthusiasm.

Stealthily but steadily in France state control began to encroach upon private enterprise. This it did in several ways. By increasing taxation the State began to nibble away at the great fortunes and at the same time to build up its own resources. Slowly but surely it assumed the direction of more and more of the nation's economic activities. It developed public expenditure on an enormous scale and thereby swelled the total of its own bounty. Nor was this increasing power of the State a phenomenon peculiar to France. It was something that was happening, to a greater or less extent, all over the world.

More and more the State's main function was becoming one of fiscal organization. The system of taxation inherited from the monarchy and the Revolution, and settled on a firmer foundation by the Empire, was on the whole not a bad one. But those responsible for finding the money remained disgruntled. They complained, as they always had done, but at least they paid more punctually, because an expanding economy and the greater availability of liquid assets made doing so less painful. Though they had to hand over nearly one sixth of their incomes, they found some consolation for being subjected to the extortions of the treasury in the knowledge that, at least, they were no longer "subjects."

The fiscal privileges of an earlier age had now been super-

seded by privileges of a different type, and these met with
the approval of the majority. The rural population was deliberately favored. Those, for instance, who distilled spirits
for their own consumption were exempted from having to
pay duty. Immunities and rebates of many different kinds
flourished—a state of affairs much to the taste of the French,
who have always loved inequalities.

At the taxpayer's death, however, the State came into its
own. The inheritance tax amounted to a death-tax. The revenue authorities made sure of getting their share, at first a
moderate one, but later increasing. The scale of duty rose
in proportion to the size of the property to be taxed. A new
inequality was introduced into legislation. In vain did the
liberal economists raise a cry of "Thief! Thief!" The State
remained deaf.

Tax-gatherer and legatee, it aimed at performing numerous other functions as well. The Revolution had entrusted
to it the triple duty of being judge, soldier, and schoolmas-
ter. All these fields of activity it strove to enlarge, by making
justice free, military service obligatory, and education the
concern of the administration. Law for all, barracks for all,
schools for all. The total number of government employees
was trebled in sixty years.

To these legitimate employments it added others which
could only very doubtfully be so described. For many years
it had assumed control of forests and stud-farms. Why
should it not, like the Pharaohs of old and Imperial Rome,
take over the functions of producer and merchant? The
mails, to which the telegraph and the telephone had given
new life, were a standing temptation. It turned them into a
state monopoly. The manufacture and sale of tobacco, and
later of matches, seemed to be eminently taxable. It absorbed them into its patronage. It allowed the bankers and
the industrial magnates to embark on great schemes of rail-   1909
way construction, but only as a temporary measure which it

felt free to take over at the first opportunity. It tried the experiment first with the western network.

And so the State became manufacturer, transport agent, and employer on a non-profit-making basis. It cared little about the consequences. The more it swallowed, the greater did its appetite become. It sought to compensate for its impotence at the top by an extension of its powers at the bottom.

The increase in its budgets was in line with its ambitions. The annual total of State expenditure had been one billion francs under Louis XVIII. By the time of the Second Empire this had risen to two billion, by the end of the century to close on four billion, and at the outbreak of the First World War to five. These figures are eloquent of the increased expenditure on the army and the social services.

How many of these hundred budgets showed a surplus? Less than half—to be precise, forty-two. Only under the Restoration did surpluses exceed deficits (nine to seven). Under Louis-Philippe balanced budgets decreased (six to eleven). The Second Republic had none at all to its credit (zero to four). The Second Empire was more fortunate (five to fourteen). The Third Republic came out equal (twenty-two to twenty-two).

In order to stop the holes and enable the State to undertake various activities that fell outside the budget estimates, the successive regimes borrowed wherever they could. In a single century the capital value of the national debt increased from 1.3 billion francs to 33—or twenty-five-fold. The service of the debt, which, in the long run, absorbed a quarter of the budget, was a source of grave anxiety to those responsible for government finance. How was it possible to get rid of this dead weight? It was part of the price to be paid for state control.

Diminuendo

So absorbed were the French in their task of seeking a political equilibrium and a sound social organization that they
failed to notice the downward movement of France from
her position as a great power. Conscious of her past glories,
they could not imagine that their own future would be less
brilliant. Where, if it came to that, was there any indica-
tion of decadence? Statistics showed nothing but progress.
To see that France was falling behind in the race, it was necessary to compare her achievement with that of the nations
that were moving forward at a still quicker rate—old nations, like England, now rapidly expanding; new nations,
like the United States, putting forth new buds; nations that
France herself had mothered, like Germany and Italy. Only
when such a comparison was made could it be seen that the
importance of France was diminishing. The progress shown
by absolute figures merely disguised the fact of a relative
decline.

To begin with, France had ceased to be the most densely
populated country of Europe. That the number of her people should have risen from twenty-nine to forty million was
not enough. In the course of the same century Great Britain
had leaped from eighteen to forty-five. France had fallen
from the first place to the fourth among the Western powers. The proportion was no longer one Frenchman to every
five from the rest of Europe, but one to every ten.

Thanks, no doubt, to improved methods of sanitation,
the expectation of life increased and mortality diminished.
The total of deaths in 1816 was 724,000 (or 245 per 10,000
of the population); in 1913, 702,000 (or 177). The birth-
rate, on the other hand, was falling. In the same period it
diminished from 969,000 to 746,000, which showed a decline, per 10,000, to 188 annual births as compared with
329. The first year in which deaths exceeded births was at

the beginning of the Second Empire. Whole provinces became underpopulated—not only the mountainous regions of Gascony, Franche-Comté, and Burgundy, but even fertile Normandy. The evil increased with the coming of the Third Republic. Between 1871 and 1914 there was a deficit in seven separate years.

What were the causes of this demographic crisis? It was due in part to a defective legal system (a code which laid it down that all estates should be shared equally among the heirs), in part to psychological reasons (a growing taste for comfort), and to a weakening of spiritual life (a contraction of the Christian idea). But it was not only quantity that suffered, but quality as well, and this was due to the increasing ravages of alcoholism. The number of retail drink establishments—the pillars of an elective regime—swelled from 280,-000 in 1830, to 483,000 in 1913. The consumption of wines and spirits per head was quadrupled. At the same time the population of the country districts diminished. The rural workers could no longer compete with the output of the factories. The children of peasant families fell victims to the lure of the cities, with their pleasures, their wages, and their smoke. Paris, like a great leech, was sucking the blood of the French people. Every railway led to the capital, with the result that its population rose to three million, and this figure, moreover, did not include the teeming multitudes inhabiting the suburban slums.

But enough of these profound speculations! In certain districts economic decline was very real, and only crude, imperfectly digested statistics could disguise the fact. Agriculture was no less hard hit by the exodus to the towns than it had been by the causes which had produced that exodus. Though the figures for production and yield in cereals of all descriptions and in potatoes and beets increased, though the acreage of grassland expanded, the general area of land under cultivation showed a slight decrease, and certain crops diminished or disappeared altogether. Plants from which dyes were derived (madder, woad, and saffron) could no longer find a market, and the oil-producing growths (such as the colza bean and the poppy) had to be abandoned as a result of competition from the olive and from different species of exotic fruits. Some of the minor cereals, too, were badly affected, as well as a number of industrial plants (flax and hemp). The vines suffered cruelly from the attacks of fungi and of insects. Other parasites preyed on the silkworm. The bee industry and the production of honey were badly mauled by the sugar offensive. The breeding of horses, pigs, and horned cattle did, it is true, increase, but that of sheep declined owing to the growing quantities of imported mutton from Australia and the Argentine. In spite of a protectionist policy and bonuses on production, in spite of improved cattle-feed, of better methods of breeding, and more efficient agricultural equipment, the French peasants as a whole showed no eagerness to modernize their farming technique. Because their soil was naturally fertile they left it to the younger nations to reap the benefit of innovations. They were not even anxious to improve their housing conditions. All they cared about was buying a few extra acres and so increasing the size of their holdings.

Industry, to be sure, did show itself receptive to modern methods, but it adopted them more slowly and with less success than did England or Germany. France had to import not only coal, but machine-tools. Against a forward movement in iron-smelting and cotton-spinning, and a development of such younger enterprises as automobile engineering and electricity, must be set a diminishing activity in the production of woolen and linen goods. In 1913 France could claim first place in world production only of silk and bauxite (which took its name from a village in Provence, once prosperous, but now abandoned). In aluminum and automobiles she came second; in the extraction of iron ore third; in coal-mining and smelting fourth; in cotton fifth; and in the marketing of salt and sugar sixth. She was nowhere at all in the fields of copper, lead, zinc, tin, gold, silver, or crude oil. For all that her foreign trade was twenty-four times larger in terms of money than it had been a hundred years earlier, it ranked only as fourth in importance, lagging far behind that of Great Britain, Germany, and the United States.

Her economy was shaken by a succession of crises inherent in a liberal system which inevitably produced a recurring rhythm of overproduction, bankruptcy, and underproduction. No country managed to break the vicious circle. But neither these crises nor the relative decline of their country seriously alarmed the French. They found consolation in the obvious fact of their increasing wealth.

The Financial Boom

The secret of that wealth lay in monetary stability. The franc of the Consulate, heir of the livre of Tours, held firm throughout the century. Neither invasions nor revolutions really endangered it. Indeed, the contrary was true, and hard times merely had the effect of consolidating it. The law of compulsory tender, which the Second Republic had to proclaim, enabled the Bank of France to eliminate the issue-houses in the Departments, and so to acquire a monopoly of note-issue. This law of compulsory tender, introduced after the war of 1870, lasted for seven years. It put paper into circulation the value of which was maintained at the legal rate. It had taken three quarters of a century for the paper franc to eliminate the memory of the assignats and to become a genuine currency. From now on, it had a secure basis of credit. French currency actually set an example. Just as many countries adopted the metric and decimal system, so did a number of currencies align themselves on the franc—Belgium, Switzerland, Italy, Romania, Greece, Spain, Serbia, Finland, Bulgaria, Colombia, Haiti, Argentina, and Venezuela in turn adopted it as a standard. Men began to dream of a universal currency, and came within an ace of seeing their dream realized.

But when the overproduction of silver reduced the value of that metal, the franc was forced to choose between it and gold. There was a general feeling that a gold standard was preferable. But this choice did not affect the stability of the national currency. In the world at large the Bank of France played the part of a great lady. She was in the happy position of being able progressively to build up her reserves and to increase the total of her issues, thereby giving to the national economy the monetary facilities it needed. In 1914, to the seven billions of specie in circulation were added six billions of notes, which were covered by four billions of gold. These thirteen billions were further increased, as means of payment, by the use of checks and clearing-house settlements. These the French adopted rather more cautiously than did the Anglo-Saxons, but they were made necessary by the accelerated movement of business dealings.

There is nothing to surprise us in this development or in the stability of French money in a century of instability. The development was the natural result of increased economic activity. The stability was, first and foremost, an expression of an antagonism inspired by the nightmare of revolutionary inflation. It became a dogma that money should be no less sacrosanct than the meter or grammar, and this dogma was supported no less by an organized State with strong fiscal resources, and in a position to borrow widely, than by those miracles of credit which satisfied all monetary needs.

Stock exchanges and banks are the temples of money. The Paris Bourse became a great international market. By an odd quirk of destiny the circulation of stocks and shares

found itself bound up with the system of universal suffrage.
So long as the right to vote had been limited to the owners
of landed property, the French people had concentrated on
the buying of land. When the vote ceased to be based upon
a property qualification, stock investment began to achieve
an immense popularity with those who were middling well
off as well as with the rich. There was scarcely anyone who
had not a savings-bank book, a government stock certificate,
a railway bond, or an industrial share tucked away in his
wallet. There was a universal tendency to put money, in
however small a way, into one of the grandiose industrial
enterprises or one of the new multiple stores. Everyone was
willing to take up the loans floated in Paris by foreign powers in search of money. France became the banker of Europe and of the world. Forty-five billions of her people's savings were invested abroad—in Russia, Spain, the Balkans,
Africa, and South America. The French, who are born mi-
sers, cut down their standard of living for the pleasure of pil-
ing up stock certificates. They were learning to behave like
ants just about the time when the State was beginning to
behave like a grasshopper.

The vast network of banks served to canalize savings and
stimulate business expansion. Credit houses made their appearance side by side with savings-banks. Most of them were
Jewish or Protestant, because Calvin, like Israel, had justified the lending of money at interest—Rothschild, Fould,
Péreire, Lazard, Vernes, Mallet, Mirabaud. These were the
names of the new nobility; these were the men who had
seats on the board of the Bank of France. Some of them
were sure to be found among the directors of thousands of
different companies, dabbling in railways, coal mines, and
blast furnaces. They were active, powerful, and ambitious.

Rubbing shoulders with these money-kings were the lawyers—the ministers of the middle class. Their politics were
firmly based on two great principles: the worship of prop-

erty and the respect for contracts. It was they who drew up leases, administered estates, opened wills. The generations passed, but they remained.

If the French were growing rich—capital and income were multiplied by eight in the century and a quarter between 1789 and 1914—the reason was that they were spending less than they were making. What was true of the individual was no less true of the nation as a whole. Up to the end of the Second Empire France was selling abroad more than she bought. It was only under the Third Republic that she began to show an adverse trade-balance (thirty billions of deficit in forty-four years), and this was due to the general increase in easy living. But the falling off in trade balances was more than offset by the profits of the tourist trade, by freight charges, transit dues, and the interest from foreign investments. It was the credit balance which she acquired in this way that made it possible for her to increase her gold reserves each year and to grant loans to other countries.

So overjoyed were her people by all this new-found opulence that they failed to realize the considerable risks to which their capital was exposed. If anything at all worried them, it was the fall in the bank-rate, which, owing to the amount of money available, had declined by the end of the century to 2.5 per cent. They deplored the low yield of their investments, but felt confident that the principal was safe. After all, the political revolutions had left property intact, and wars had not much affected money. They thought that the fine weather would last forever.

Colonial Expansion

Delighted by the knowledge that they could stuff their safes and their stockings with accumulated savings, they found a further satisfaction in the rebuilding of their colonial empire. The attitude they adopted toward it was that of the

city-dweller who discovers that he can afford a little place
in the country. Had not their ancestors set them an example, first with the kingdoms of the Levant—those products
of the Crusades, which they had had to abandon to the
Turks—and later with the American and Asiatic Indies—
which they had been compelled to hand over to the English? Of the former nothing remained—nothing, that is, except a solid legacy of prestige in the Mediterranean area. Of
the second there still remained a few islands in the Antilles,
Réunion, and five trading-stations in the East. The new Empire to which their thoughts were turning was to be predominantly African. Saint Louis had shown the way by electing
to die at Carthage. Louis XIV had forged the first commercial links with Morocco. For centuries past, the French had
had "factories" in Senegal and Madagascar. It was only natural that they should be attracted by this *terra ignota* from
which they were separated only by a sea of which nobody
now need be afraid. The Dark Continent appeared to them
in the guise of a natural extension of the mother country.

Neither the administration, however, nor public opinion could work up much excitement over distant discoveries and exotic conquests. The sons of the men who had
made themselves the masters of Europe refused to think
of Africa as anything more than a second-best. When the
State undertook some colonial enterprise, the man in the
street turned his back. When a few pioneers took a chance,
the State, in its turn, withheld official support. There was no
planned overseas expansion. Such activities as there were
were piecemeal—but they happened to be successful.

All alone, disguised as an Arab peddler, René Caillé es-
1829   tablished communication between Morocco and the Niger
by way of the mysterious Timbuktu. Charles X took an interest in the Barbary lands, and, in the face of British oppo-
1830   sition, made a foray by the Bey of Algiers an excuse to attack the town. He had a good fleet and a fine army. After a

siege of twenty days Algiers was taken, and the pirates were
driven from the Mediterranean. He had done something
that Charles V had failed to do. But the event aroused no
enthusiasm among the French. Three weeks later the authority of Charles X was overturned.

Louis-Philippe continued his predecessor's work and
brought about the pacification of Algeria. Wonderful lands   1848
were opened up for colonization. Eight weeks after the surrender of Abd-el-Kader he received the same sort of thanks.

Napoleon III's Mexican adventure miscarried, but he
did, at least, establish France in Cochin China and Cam-
bodia, and permanently occupied some of the southern Al-
gerian oases. He also enlarged his base in Senegal, and set
up another at Obock, on the shores of the Red Sea, which
was destined, after the piercing of the Isthmus of Suez, to
become one of the vital arteries of world trade.

It was a French diplomat, a relation of the Empress, who
first broached the idea of a canal and collected the necessary
capital. Once again the English veto had to be challenged.
Half a billion francs, most of which was drawn from French
savings, and ten years of work finally resulted in the splitting
of the desert. It was a titanic labor, worthy of the land of
the Pharaohs, and it completely changed the pattern of the   1869
world's trade routes. But for the Emperor's support Lesseps
could never have undertaken, still less completed, the task.
The Suez Canal is Napoleon III's chief claim to fame.
Scarcely ten months after the solemn opening ceremony he
was driven from the throne.

Did better luck attend the Republics? The Second, re-
peating a gesture made by the First, proclaimed the abolition of slavery—which, as a matter of fact, was abolishing
itself by stages. This sudden decision had the effect of letting loose 500,000 freed natives and plunging the Antilles
into a serious crisis. The Third Republic, which was set up
at the very moment when the countries of Europe were

busy sharing out the new territories among themselves, discovered that it had a colonial vocation. In order to establish
Algeria on a firm foundation, and to protect it against attack, it imposed a protectorate on Tunisia in the teeth of
Italian opposition, and then on Morocco, in spite of a no
less determined opposition from Germany. With the object
of building the trading-stations of Darkest Africa into a
solid whole, it took possession of the Sahara. From Senegal,
Joffre marched to the Niger. From the Gabon, Brazza advanced into the Congo. From the Ubangi, Marchand
reached the Nile. From north, west, and south three columns converged on Tchad. The conquest of Madagascar
completed the Empire of Africa, of Tonkin that of Indochina. "Greater France" now extended over four and one
half million square miles, or nearly one tenth of the newly
discovered territories, and embraced a hundred million people, or more than a twentieth part of the population of the
globe.

This successful achievement had been a laborious affair,
and it remained very insecure. More than once the State, or
the political parties, thwarted colonial initiative. The Minister who wished to embark on the Tunisian campaign was
forced to resign, and the same Minister was bitterly opposed
and publicly mocked for casting envious eyes on Tonkin.
1892   The extreme Republicans, with Clemenceau at their head,
1898   demanded that Egypt should be surrendered to English ambitions, and censured Major Marchand for daring to press
forward to Fashoda. In order to appease the English the Republic surrendered such rights as it still had in Newfound-
1911   land. To appease the Germans it handed over a portion of
the Congo. In these ways was the colonial adventure sullied
by political maneuvers and diplomatic withdrawals. The
State backed the pioneers with completely inadequate
means. The new lands were regarded merely as sources of

raw materials to be exploited in the interests of the mother
country, and scarcely at all as overseas markets.

Great though the task was, there was nothing grandiose
about it. Such magnificence as it displayed was due to the
men who did the work—Bugeaud, Galliéni, Lyautey. Its beginnings were often mean and petty, and it was never carried out in conditions that could assure its durability—there
was no powerful fleet, which alone makes it possible to defend an overseas empire, nor was there that excess population at home which is the sole guarantee of its effective settlement and successful exploitation.

Cultural Expansion

Was the national sun setting? It could still bathe the world
of the spirit in radiance. Because of her scholars, her men
of science, her writers, and her painters, France seemed
scarcely to have moved from her zenith, though at times
the light was dimmed by passing clouds.

In the fields of pure and applied science she made great
contributions to the technical advances of the century. Le-
verrier, merely by employing the magic powers of computa-
tion, revealed the existence of the planet Neptune. Henri
Poincaré was the high priest of mathematical research.
Berthelot achieved the synthesis of organic bodies. Laënnec
showed how auscultation could open up vast new prospects
to medicine. Claude Bernard laid down a method for physi-
ology. Pasteur formulated the theory of microbes. Pierre
and Marie Curie discovered radium. Ampère, Arago, and
Becquerel took their place among the wonder-workers of
electricity.

To be sure, most of these masters were fully conscious of
the limits of their knowledge. But the mob, intoxicated by
the triumphs of mind over matter, lost all sense of the rela-

tive. It was only too ready to believe that science was, or
soon would be, capable of every kind of miracle, and the
apostles of the new religion could be sure of finding in every French village a Café de Progrès, where, between drinks,
they could expound the articles of their faith. One odd result of the new materialism was that it played into the hands
of superstitions new and old. The nineteenth century witnessed the heyday of table-turning and spiritualism.

French literature split into two streams. Down one channel rolled the waters of classicism, with Balzac, Stendhal,
Musset, each in his fashion intent on painting a picture of
the human comedy. Diverging from it was the swifter current of the innovators—of all those who, turning their backs
on the lessons of the classic age, and delighting in breaking
all its rules, were eager to dumbfound their contemporaries.
That the men of every generation despise their immediate
predecessors is a matter of course. The men who came after
the French Revolution were more than usually anxious to
deny the past, and to advertise the fact. In their eagerness
to achieve liberation, the more daring authors found themselves, more often than not, laughed out of court, though
they did on occasion touch the sublime. The playwrights
shook themselves free of all constricting bonds and produced—melodramas. The poets broke with the old verse
forms, and some of their successors abandoned both feet
and rhyme. The novelists turned out serials for the newspapers—and not all of them had the genius of the elder
Dumas.

The arts no longer drew inspiration from Greek, Roman,
or even French sources. The romantics made a great show of
adoring northern mists, and suicides à la Werther, and Lord
Byron. Then they discovered the Orient and peopled it
with stage Moors and fancy Turks. In spite of Hugo, that
great hammerer of words, they soon went out of fashion.
The writers who came after them could startle their readers

only by dint of dealing in the bizarre, the squalid, or the ma-
cabre. Baudelaire revived a classic form of diction with
which to give expression to morbid perversities. Others, following in his footsteps, set themselves to explore strange regions from which, on occasion, they returned with a load of
treasure. But more than one poet slipped into gibberish or
mystification; more than one prose-writer took refuge in the
gutter, and since everything, even bombast, even vice, grows
wearisome, the masters showed their wisdom by bringing
nobility both of manner and of matter back into fashion—
Mistral, for instance, by his restoration of the *langue d'oc*,
and Péguy when he sang his litanies in the *langue d'oïl*.

In painting, a similar ferment led to similar extremes, not
a few of them emotionally powerful. While the classic
school continued through Ingres and Carpeaux, and then
began to decline into the flabby academic, romantic pic-
ture-making, in the work of Delacroix, carried all before
it (as did music with Berlioz). Delacroix, too, turned his
back on antiquity and drenched his canvases in the brilliant
light of the East. He was reputed to be the son of Talleyrand, and there can be no doubt that he enjoyed a mysterious patronage which brought him many wealthy clients,
though that did not prevent him from—like Berlioz—erecting the freedom of the artist into an article of faith.

Free was what the artists were becoming to an ever increasing extent. They were haunted on the one hand by the
fear of being taken for mere hacks, and on the other by the
necessity of marking the essential difference between their
work and the products of an unexpected rival—the cam-
era. Turning away more and more from representational
painting, they created a subjective art, and concerned themselves with producing personal "impressions." When these
happened to be beautiful, the impressionists triumphed.
Corot, Manet, Degas, Renoir, and, in sculpture, Rodin enjoyed a world-wide reputation. And, since there is a cor-

respondence between colors and sounds—as Baudelaire showed in his theory of poetry—the musicians began to produce effects similar to those of the painters. Debussy, for instance, echoed Claude Monet. But liberty leads to anarchy, indifference to the object painted to abstraction. In order to explore the formula to the full, it was necessary to become either a Fauvist or a cubist. Very soon individualism was built into a school, and thereby ceased to be individual. The advance guard took refuge in the older methods, and were soon indistinguishable from the rear guard.

Abstraction was not possible for the architects, who remained the slaves of utilitarian ends. Not that opportunities for building were lacking. Napoleon III tore the guts out of Paris. The Louvre was completed. A gaudy new opera house was run up. The designers, not knowing how to achieve newness, relapsed into imitation. Viollet-le-Duc played at Gothic. He adorned Notre-Dame with a spire, and "restored" both Carcassonne and Pierrefonds. The neo-Byzantine made its appearance in the Trocadéro and on the summit of Montmartre. There was a rich crop of Renaissance railroad stations and town halls. Every style in turn was laid under contribution, and sham Louis XIII rubbed shoulders with bogus Moroccan. Architecture, in grave danger of finding itself strangled in the shoddy, was saved by the timely arrival of new materials. Eiffel built his tower of iron, and with the coming of cement every kind of adventurous experiment was possible.

1889

Furniture showed a sad falling-off. Gone were the pure lines of the Louis XVI style. Heaviness crept in with Louis-Philippe. Under the Second Empire there was an unholy alliance of black fabrics and gold fringes. The results, if they were inspired by anything at all, seemed to reflect the ideals of the undertaker's parlor. The mass deportations that followed the Commune had the effect of emptying the faubourg Saint-Antoine—the cabinetmakers' quarter—and France quickly lost her pride of place in the sphere of industrial art. Having formerly set their hearts on imitation Gothic chests and imitation Louis XV beds, the members of the middle class turned their attention to sideboards in the style of Henri II châteaux. The century went out in a horrid riot of stylized irises and water-lilies.

For a hundred years London had been the fountainhead of fashion, and Anglomania had struck deep roots. Dandies, and periodic expositions, watering-places and seaside resorts, English parks and English squares, cigarettes and sport—all these things came from across the Channel. But Paris was still the dictator of women's modes. Men might remain content with trousers if they liked, but ladies must follow the taste of Paris and adopt the crinoline, the parasol, the chignon. No one could say that the French had been stripped of their former greatness so long as they could still lay down the law to half the human race.

The German Invasions

Proud of her intellectual achievements, her colonial successes, and her wealth, France would have been happy in spite of her revolutions (and perhaps because of them) if only she could have lived in peace. Since the fall in her birthrate she no longer entertained ambitions of foreign expansion, but was perfectly contented to take her place among the satisfied and conservative nations. Now that she had ceased to be actively interested in Belgium and no longer clung tooth and nail to her overseas possessions, Great Britain, her old, traditional enemy, was prepared to be a friendly neighbor. But there was another enemy, a Continental enemy, stirring in its sleep beyond the Rhine.

The Germans, descended from the tribes described by

350 An Outline of French History

Tacitus, were only too ready to make of war their national industry. For two whole centuries the policies of Richelieu and the Treaties of Westphalia had kept them partitioned and powerless. But now Prussia meant to rebuild the Germany of Barbarossa. Already, at Waterloo, she had displayed her resources. Prussians had encamped as conquerors in France, gazing with wondering eyes upon her fertile plains, enjoying her mild and restful climate. They longed to return to this land of ease and prosperity, and return they did. Three times in three quarters of a century the Germans invaded France. Each generation was set on making the trip, arms in hand. Three times they found a convenient excuse—which had nothing to do with their real intentions—a dispute about the Spanish throne, an Austro-Serbian quarrel after the murder of an archduke, an ultimatum to Poland on the subject of Danzig. But on each occasion their real objective was Paris. Three times the assailant came, always bet-

1870   ter equipped, always stronger. First it was the Prussia of Bismarck, which after a victorious campaign lasting seven months seized Alsace and part of Lorraine, and at Versailles declared the Federation of the German States. Next it was

1914   the Germany of William II. In alliance with Austria, it stood firm for four years against France and a world coalition. It was eventually conquered, but not crushed. Although it was compelled to give back the two stolen provinces, it succeeded in consolidating its own internal unity—

1918   at the expense of the smaller princely houses—while the fall of the Habsburgs made of a mutilated Austria the inevitable prey of an acquisitive Germanism. Last scene of all, when the Germany of Adolf Hitler, mistress of all central Europe, firmly installed in Vienna, Prague, and Warsaw, allied with

1945   Mussolini's Italy and later with Japan, threatened and defied the rest of the world. She was defeated, but only after six years of war.

On each occasion France was found unprepared. In 1870

Napoleon began the war with empty arsenals, and blissfully
ignorant of the existence of the breech-loading rifle. In 1914
the Third Republic sent its infantry into battle still dressed
in their red trousers, and was short of both heavy artillery
and munitions. In 1940 she was without the tanks, the airplanes, the leaders, the effectives, and the morale without
which there can be no successful conduct of hostilities.

Except on the first occasion, under the Second Empire,
when she had fallen blindly into the net stretched by the
hunter, France had wanted to avoid war. In 1914 she had
implored Serbia to yield to the Austrian demands, and had
withdrawn her own covering troops six miles behind the
frontier. From 1925 to 1939 she gave up one vantage-point
after another, abandoning Mayence, allowing Germany to
rearm, tolerating the annexation of Austria and the rape of
Czechoslovakia, rather than break with the aggressor.

In each of the wars her frontier had cracked—at Sedan, at
Charleroi, and again at Sedan. In each of the wars she saw
the Germans firmly established in her own countryside—in
the first as far as the Cher, with forty Departments occupied; in the second as far as the Marne, with ten Departments invaded; in 1940 as far as the Atlantic and the Pyrenees, with one half of France under enemy control; in 1942
as far as the Mediterranean, with the whole of the country
in enemy hands. Paris, besieged and bombarded, surrendered in 1871; Paris was saved by Joffre in 1914; Paris fell
without striking a blow in 1940. On each occasion the
French government took to its heels and streamed along the
roads leading to Bordeaux.

In defeat as well as in victory there was no lack of glorious
set pieces, and the French dwelt on them in an endeavor to
persuade themselves that they had lost none of their martial
virtues. The cuirassiers of Reichshoffen, the poilus of Verdun, the troops of General Leclerc, do indeed bear witness
to the fact that not all Frenchmen faced collapse with ac-

quiescence. For every Bazaine, for every Gamelin, there has been a Foch and a de Gaulle.

But the last two wars were no mere Franco-German du-**1914** els, as the first had been. They set fire to Europe and the world, and if France saved the world on the Marne, the **1944** world saved France thirty years later, when English and American armies, under Eisenhower's command, landed in **1945** Normandy, drove out the German occupying troops, and never loosened their hold until they reached the Elbe and made contact with the armies of Soviet Russia. The liberation of France was no more than one episode in a universal rough-and-tumble.

France suffered terribly in her triple ordeal. Grandparents had learned in the siege of Paris how to put up with restrictions and eat rats. Parents had been introduced to ration-cards for bread and coal. Children saw rationing carried to its highest point of efficiency as the result of four years of blockade and enemy occupation. They experienced war taxation, and were initiated into the activities of the black market. They lived in a time of legalized famine.

With peace came the reckoning of the dead, the checking up of the ruins: 150,000 killed on the first occasion, then 1,500,000, then 600,000—a total for the three wars of 2,250,-000, to say nothing of the maimed and the gassed. Those lost were the finest elements of the population. Of material damage it is impossible to establish a full reckoning, of the houses reduced to rubble, of the factories burned, the bridges cut, the stations destroyed, the harbors ruined. An indemnity of five billion francs was paid to Bismarck. Losses in terms of money amounted, in the first war of the twentieth century to 150 billion gold francs, in the second to 200—a total of 350 billion, or the equivalent of 100,000 tons of fine gold, twice the amount of the gold reserves of the whole world, or the yield of five full years of the French national revenue. Certain types of damage too were irreparable and beyond computing—those, for instance, which involved the country's artistic patrimony: the Cathedral of Reims smashed; then that of Rouen. Others too were indirect in their incidence—among them the ravages caused by the Colorado beetle, which was brought to France in the baggage of the American armies and continued for years to prey on the potato crop.

1922

From these exhausting trials France emerged exhausted. No longer was war waged in lace ruffles. It had ceased to be an occupation for gentlemen and mercenaries. The whole fit manhood of the nation must now be mobilized, and civilians were no less deeply involved in the drama than soldiers. The French wars were no longer wars of expansion, fought on enemy territory, as in the days before the Revolution. France had had to endure seven invasions since the death of Louis XVI.

Then, too, after the wars, between the wars, peace was forever tottering on the edge of destruction, forever having to be defended, with no one knowing whether threats or concessions would be most likely to keep it intact. The Peace of Frankfurt, the two armistices of Rethondes, the Peace of Versailles, the armistice of Reims. There were Frenchmen who were stimulated by defeat, others who were cast down. Peace sent them to sleep. They confided their future to international insurance companies (League of Nations, United Nations), where there was much talk, while the aggressors put a new edge on their weapons. Compelled to beg for American aid in order to restore her economy and defend her territory, France has now fallen to the level of a country assisted and protected—she who for so long was the shield and buckler of others.

In Search of a Regime

Political systems rarely survive military disasters. Napoleon I was wiped out by Waterloo, Napoleon III swept away by Sedan. Republic No. 3 did not long outlast Hitler's invasion. Foch's victory had given it a respite. But it had
1920 not known how to turn that respite to account, nor how to set its house in order. Terrified by the thought that it might have found a master, it began by showing its gratitude to the "Tiger" Clemenceau—who throughout the whole war had held the defeatists in check—in a way that has become habitual with French governments. It carried on in a condition of prolonged instability—forty-three ministries in twenty years (an average lifetime for each of 170 days). Parliament succeeded parliament, each contradicting its predecessors. There were periodical outbreaks of scandal, and there were always evil tongues to implicate some eminent men of affairs. There would have been a deep gulf fixed between the legal country and the real had it not been for the fact that a majority of Frenchmen remained loyal to the regime, from reasons either of self-interest or of sentiment.

One novelty there was which had the effect of modifying
1920 to some considerable extent the structure of domestic politics. The Socialist Party split into two sections, one of which joined the Communist International. This body was entirely under Russian control, which meant that from now on, all one-hundred-per-cent Marxists would take their orders from Moscow—somewhat as the members of the Catholic League of the sixteenth century had obeyed the injunctions of Madrid. Confronted by this party inspired from abroad, and strictly disciplined, the other political groups in the country crumbled away into a condition of fragmentation and impotence.

As a result of these divisions, even more than of the misdeeds of the Communist opposition, the parliamentary machine began to function so badly that more than once it broke down altogether. The Chambers consented to their own dissolution and delegated their powers to the Executive. Decrees took the place of laws, and democracy, almost without realizing what was happening, found its feet set on the slippery slope to dictatorship. This evolution was in the ordinary run of things. There is a certain type of Frenchman who grows weary of the excesses engendered by liberty, and longs, in a muddle-headed way, for authority. Both the First and the Second Republic had ended in the rule of a Cæsar, **1940** and it was only logical that the Third should find one too. The moment it began to fall apart under the pressure of invasion, it passed into the control of a soldier.

Who was he? Philippe Pétain had once been the savior of Verdun, but now he was no more than an aged, peace-loving Marshal, ready for every sacrifice and every humiliation. Like the Cæsars, he had been raised to the throne by the political Left. A Popular-front Chamber, by an enormous majority, entrusted him with the supreme power. From Vichy, his precarious capital, he carried through a policy that had a markedly socialist complexion. Those members of the community who had put money aside had their bearer-bonds taken from them. The liberal economy was declared bankrupt. Production and prices were controlled. Factory committees were instituted, and the 1st of May—traditionally associated with Marxist claims—was given an official blessing as the festival of labor, which was as good as to say, abstention from labor. But the conservative-minded were reassured by increasing police activity.

Thus, on one side of the picture stood Pétain, the grandfatherly despot of an occupied France, and, on the other, **1940** de Gaulle, calling upon his countrymen to fight the Germans. General versus Marshal; London versus Vichy. Pétain had signed the armistice, de Gaulle had repudiated it. Where did the true France lie? It was no new problem. History had faced it more than once before—when, for instance, Frenchmen had had to choose between Charles V and the English Henry VI, between Mayenne and Henri IV of Navarre, between Louis XVIII and Bonaparte. Who should be acclaimed as loyal, who branded as traitor? Most Frenchmen followed Pétain so long as German strength remained unshaken. They rallied to de Gaulle only when the conviction grew daily more certain that the moment of revenge would come. And so it was that France hedged, staking her all, turn and turn about, on Pétain the shield and de Gaulle the sword. But in the long run the shield became a colander, while the sword showed itself to be well and truly tempered.

When the hour of deliverance sounded, de Gaulle was ac-

1944 claimed by the crowd, but disowned by the political parties.
1946 He managed to get the Constitution of the Third Republic repudiated by a referendum, but it was without his help, and against his wishes, that Republic No. 4 was set up. He suffered the same ostracism as that which had been visited on Clemenceau and like him was made a victim of ingratitude.

The Fourth Republic is, to all intents and purposes, not very different from the Third. It may have four Chambers, but two of them, at least, perform no function. It may have given the vote to women, but the electoral map of the country has not, as a result, been greatly modified. Young Marianne, like her elder sister, is having her fill of weak governments and old scandals.

But behind the chaos of institutions the old ordered life of France continues. The labels too of the more revolutionary parties show signs of an increasing mildness. The Communists, though Red as Red can be, now sing the *Marseillaise* and wave the tricolor. The Socialists are forgetting Karl Marx, the radicals are turning conservative, and the former republicans of the Left are now the liberals of the

Right. A disenchanted public opinion gives but scant attention to the quarrels of politicians. France still lives.

The Monetary Collapse

France still lives, but the franc is on crutches. It has emerged
in a pitiable condition from the strains and stresses of two
great wars. The wars themselves, however, were no more
than the starting-point of financial catastrophe. The post-
war periods, even more than the actual fighting, were what
proved fatal to the franc. The proof of this may be seen in
the fact that Belgium, which has suffered just as much as
France from invasion, if not more, possesses a healthier currency. Responsibility, in the case of France, lies first and
foremost with governments. On the very morrow of victorious wars Parliament succeeded in losing the ensuing peace.

After a full century of stability the franc abandoned the
gold standard. It became an unconvertible currency, and diminished in value in proportion as the State issued greater
and greater quantities of paper. A day came when the flight   1926
from the franc became a headlong stampede. Men began to
wonder whether French economy was once again to become
the victim of a galloping inflation, as in the days of the assignats. Just in the nick of time Raymond Poincaré turned   1928
up to restore confidence and to peg the franc. He achieved
stability at 58.95 milligrams of fine gold—or one fifth of its
former value.

The respite was not of long duration. The treasury was
soon in difficulties and had recourse to an increased note-   1936
issue. In order to stop a run on gold a compulsory rate was
re-established. Inflation followed, depreciation, the reign of   1939
paper. Exchange-control, which was revived on the outbreak
of the Second World War, disguised and retarded the new
debasement. Inflation pursued its evil way. By mid-century

the note circulation had passed the 1,500-billion point, and had reached a figure 250 times the total of 1914. On the free market for gold the franc represented 1.8 milligrams of metal, or 160 times less than before the two conflagrations. In other words, it had fallen in the space of thirty years to a level five times lower than that reached by the livre of Tours in five centuries.

Together with the value of gold and the rates of exchange, prices rose prodigiously. Ten years after the Treaty of Versailles they were six times what they had been. Five years after the end of Hitler the index figure stood at 150. Consols, true to the rule, had not moved, with the result that holders of government bonds were ruined, as were all those who lived on fixed incomes and had been already badly hit by the failure of the Russian and Balkan debtors. Landlords, finding their rents frozen by extraordinary legislation, were, in many instances, condemned to poverty. Wages rose very slowly in comparison with prices. Producers, who could charge what they liked and could live off the black market, made fortunes. Many farmers renewed their equipment, mechanized their estates, paid off their debts, and bought additional land. The whole face of society was changed to the advantage of the new rich and at the expense of the new poor. Scarcely any gold was left in the vaults of the Bank, but a considerable quantity was locked away in private safes.

The government, which was primarily responsible for what had happened, might have derived considerable benefit from the turn of events, because devaluation meant an easing-up in the service of the national debt. But, owing to the fact that Germany had shirked her obligations and wriggled out of the reparations agreements, it was compelled to spend a great deal of money on rebuilding and pensions. Moreover, it had vastly enlarged the field of its activities. The national budget, which had taken a whole century to move from one to five billion, increased ten times in fifteen years, and by the 1950's had reached a figure in excess of 2,000 billion. Except during the years immediately following Poincaré's stabilization, it showed a deficit.

Was it that collectivism was quietly gaining ground, or was it simply that electoral competition was pushing the State into playing the part of universal provider? Whatever the cause, the sphere of private enterprise is being increasingly invaded by government activities. Officialdom has taken over the railroads, civil aviation, coal-mining, electricity, gas, the big banks, the insurance companies. The State has adventured into the world of the cinema, has laid its hand on radio, controls credit, prints newspapers, manufactures airplanes and automobiles, engages in the extraction of potash and in the bulk buying of wheat. It has become the biggest banker, the biggest industrial organization, the biggest traffic concern, the biggest employer of labor, in France. It has under its orders three million civil servants, who strike whenever the fancy takes them. 1946

The growth of state control has been accompanied by a steep rise in taxation, which now accounts for one third of the national revenue. Standards are now so different from those of the nineteenth century that comparisons are impossible. Taxes, instead of being levied on goods, are levied on persons. An income tax, with an occasional capital levy, has taken the place of the old tax on expenditure. The rate constantly rises. Returns are compulsory. The system varies with the electoral category of the taxpayer. Inequality flourishes. The French get their own back by cheating. This perpetual failure to pay taxes is undoubtedly one of the key themes of their history.

As a result of the monetary collapse, old articles of faith are vanishing—intangibility of the unit of payment, respect for property and contracts, respect for the State, respect for the public service, love of saving. The virtues that formerly made France great may not be dead, but they are sleeping.

Progress and Decline

From trial to trial France, like the rest of Europe, has been gradually moving down the slope of a relative decline. But her disappearance from the stage of history has never been absolute, nor is she beyond all hope of recovery.

She has, in the first place, suffered from a demographic crisis. In the five years immediately preceding Hitler's invasion her birth-rate fell to the lowest point ever known, and the effect on her population was already apparent. In the same period the number of retail drink-shops passed the half-million mark, beating all records. In order to find the necessary manpower she had to import foreign labor. The irrigated districts around Nice were resettled with Piedmontese, the valleys of the Garonne and the Gers with Italians, the Ardennes and the countryside of Caux with Belgians, the Department of the Yonne with Dutch, of the Lot with Spaniards, of the Nord with Poles. But, as in the distant periods of her history she managed to absorb long-heads, short-heads, Celts and Romans, Franks and Norsemen, so now only a few generations will pass before she has assimilated the greater part of her newest immigrants. Late in the day though it is, France, liberated and once again becoming prolific, is offsetting the collapse that haunts an old and empty land, and can already show an increase of cradles over coffins.

The law of numbers is, throughout the world, taking toll of the French language. In all countries things have gone badly for royal courts and the intellectual élite, and it was they who consistently spoke French. English now is supreme in business. In diplomatic documents and at international conferences it fights for leadership with the tongue of Voltaire, and sometimes wins. Its triumph marks the success of practical considerations over mere prestige, of present needs over historical values.

In the world of thought and scholarship, too, she has had to stand up to younger competitors. But her writers and her painters still enjoy the benefits that Paris can bestow as the cultural capital of the world. Paris still gives a cachet to ephemeral fashions and resounding achievements, still presides over new philosophies and new modes in hairdressing. Paris still sets the seal of her approval on reputations, giving her hall-mark to the painters of the Dutch, Spanish, or Japanese schools, to Swiss architects, Polish poets, Argentine composers, Russian dancers, or Negro singers. She still has her Quartier Latin, her Montparnasse, her Saint-Germain-des-Prés. France shows no sign yet of throwing up the sponge.

Her men of science are hard at work, though with a technical equipment which, to other more fortunate nations, sometimes seems to be laughably inadequate. Her engineers are fitting her out anew, and as best they can with the niggardly credits that come their way. Generally speaking, French science is quick off the mark where new ideas are concerned. Her industries rarely lag behind in finding practical use for the discoveries of the laboratory, but, the first fine gesture made, the earliest successes registered, they have a way of sleeping on their laurels and letting themselves be outdistanced. France might well have taken the lead in the motion picture, in automobile design and aviation—but along came Hollywood with its first unpretentious studios, along came Ford and Chevrolet to beat Citroën and Renault at their own game, along came Lindbergh to snatch the prize of the Atlantic flight from Costes. The modern age is American, not French.

Though poor in coal, France was among the first nations to realize the immense possibilities of hydraulic power. She has harnessed her torrents and her rivers, and is busy electrifying the whole of her railway system. Since the coming of the internal-combustion engine, gasoline has been the trump card in all economic affairs. France has scarcely any of her own, and has been driven to get a controlling interest in part of the Iraq production. At the dawn of the atomic age she finds herself without uranium or heavy metals. Except in the matter of iron, she enters the battle for raw materials ill equipped.

At the end of each of her wars she set herself bravely to rebuild her shattered industries, but there were some that could not be efficiently renewed, others that had already become out of date. In the world of textiles silk has had to stand up to the attack of artificial fibers. Lyon has had to make an adopted child of rayon. Troyes has come round to nylon. The methods of shipbuilding which produced such masterpieces as the liner *Normandie* are now too expensive. House-building is suffering from rent-control. The railroads are losing money and have ceased to work many of their lines. The old canals are silting up. In those spheres of industry where she can still hold her own and make money, she has had to beg America for the necessary machinery, to be paid for with American credits. France often pats herself on the back for being the country of the golden mean. If she is, that is because she is no longer in a position to be a country dedicated to greatness.

The farmers have used the profits that came to them as the result of war and inflation to modernize their machinery. The conditions of agriculture have been completely revolutionized. Fertilizers, reaper-thresher combinations, artificial insemination—all these things have brought about enormous changes. Crop yields are better, livestock breeding has improved, oil-producing plants are coming back into favor. But once the years of shortages are over, the problems of abundance will have to be faced. Where will it be possible to find a market for all the superfluous wheat, wine, and distilled spirits? The French peasant will never be satisfied for long.

Are the industrial workers satisfied with *their* lot? The great unions are now all-powerful. They have won their battle for the eight-hour day, the forty-hour week. They have forced the not seldom restive employers to grant holidays with pay, pensions, insurance against the risks of sickness, accident, and unemployment. Married men with families now draw extra allowances. The old maxim "To each according to his labor" has been changed, and we are within measurable distance of saying: "To each according to his wants." Individual initiative lacks stimulus. There is little encouragement to save, and production-costs are a heavy load on the back of industry. But at least the workers have won the right to a more self-respecting way of life.

With these many problems—which seven hundred years ago the guilds had already studied and sometimes even solved—the civilized nations of today are all at grips. France is merely sharing in something that is going on everywhere. Her effort to achieve a human way of life will be fruitful on condition that she does not take back with one hand what she has given with the other. For wars have a way of interfering with pension schemes and vacations with pay. Inflation inevitably forces down the standard of living. In short, there can be no social security so long as in the military and monetary fields the nation is unsafe.

The Twilight of the Ages

Political speakers like nothing so much as to laud the eternal values that made France great. It is a theme for the platform, not for the historian. No nation is eternal. All nations are born, and all nations die. So, too, do cities. Those nations alone endure that have the will to do so.

France has endured till now, and her future length of life depends upon herself. The orators who nurse her in illusions assure her that the world cannot do without her.

That sort of remark is comforting, but false. The world has
managed to do without Athens and without Rome. It is by
no means safe from a renewed assault by the barbarians.
France, which has outlived so many invasions, might well
fail to survive another mass movement of peoples.

Already her Empire shows signs of breaking up. The ap-
1945 peal for human equality has put colonists and colonies out
of fashion. The word *empire* has given place to *union*, but
1947 even *union* is showing signs of strain. Syria and Lebanon,
after twenty years of solidarity with the French bloc, have
won their freedom. Indochina is stirring. The old trading-
stations of the Indies are yielding to appeals for nationalism. The Arab peoples are muttering. The Negroes are voicing their claims. All over the world men are beginning to
realize the weakness of the "whites." Everywhere the cry
goes up for national autonomy. Nationalist aspirations are
beginning to ferment at the very moment when the statesmen of the world make a great show of calling for international collaboration.

The French respond somewhat apathetically to this general threat of dislocation. The major political problems no
longer work on their emotions, unless they have an immediate effect upon their individual interests. They want wheat
to be dear and bread cheap. Their one ambition is to drink
and eat well (even if it means being badly housed), to own
a cottage and cultivate a small garden. The ideal way of life
for many is to retire at the earliest possible moment on a
state pension. They can no longer work up any very great
excitement over electoral contests that do not center at the
parish pump. Only habit keeps them loyal to the slogans of
democracy. They are much more interested in the next
game of *boules* or the next Tour-de-France bicycle-race.

But this self-regarding, slippered Frenchman conceals another of a different kind: a Frenchman who is at all times
ready to take the initiative, who will gladly face death on

the barricades if he so much as suspects that liberty is being filched from him, who will rediscover his love of country when faced by an invader whom he has failed to stop on the frontier, who will work without ceasing in the hope of surprising his neighbor or beating a record, who will discover wonders if only to prove that he is still capable of achieving prodigies. That is the Frenchman who climbs impossible mountains and risks his life in the depths of prehistoric caves. That is the Frenchman who is ambitious to fly ever farther and ever faster. That is the Frenchman who, at any moment, may produce a masterpiece.

Taking all these contradictions in her stride, France has remained herself, true to the constant elements of her history. A temperamental weakness for the negative has led her people under each regime to disown what went before, and then, in double-quick time, to behave in exactly the same way. From this it follows that her story may seem at times to be an almost wanton alternation of ordered government and anarchy.

In the twentieth century, as in all the twenty centuries of her history, her people are still in a state of permanent rebellion against the central power—at least, in two clearly defined spheres of social life. First, that of the taxpayer, who wants a state pension for himself, yet will not lift a finger to provide the State with the means to provide it. It is for somebody else to do that. The old love of inequality is far from being dead. The French have always been concerned to build a body of privileges, each man for himself, and only incidentally to abolish the privileges of others. Second, what may perhaps be best described as "feudal grouping." Within the State other states have grown up, all striving to usurp the powers that belong to government. The weaker the state machine, the more outrageous does their arrogance become. Feudatories, whether lay or ecclesiastical, guilds or trade-unions, one and all have been animated by the same ambition—the Gallic tribes refusing to unite, the dukes of Burgundy in arms against the king, Philippe d'Orléans sapping the monarchy, or, in later days, the great banks and business houses, the employers' federations, the trade-union council, and the nationalized industries. Under whatever colors the revolt has marched, the object has always been the same—to weaken or damage the State.

It is possible to draw comfort from this long continuity in rebellion. After all, two thousand years have passed and France is not yet dead. Can any man say with certainty that after the sun in his glory, after the great storm, she is now moving through the twilight to an engulfing night? She is still capable of producing dazzling flashes, and has already proved that a nation may both be and have been. Twice at least—once in the course of the Christian centuries, and again, later, in her classic age—she led the world. Ten times, no doubt, she has been within measurable distance of vanishing altogether under the threat of foreign pressure—English, Austro-Spanish, German—or because she was being undermined from within. We cannot read the secrets that history may have in store. It may well be that France will again surprise the world, not by the violence of her death-throes, but by the glory of her resurrection.

SOME COMPARATIVE DATES

In the History of France		In the History of Other Countries

CHAPTER I

B.C.

Bronze Age	2500	2500	The Pyramids
Iron Age	900	900	Homer
Founding of Marseille	600	600	Solon in Athens
The Celts in Gaul	500	500	Confucius
The Belgæ in Gaul	300	321	Break-up of the Empire of Alexander
The Romans in Provence	121		
Marius at Aix	102		
Cæsar in Gaul	59		
Alesia	52		

A.D.

Roman citizenship granted to the Gauls	212		
Ausonius	330	330	Constantine in Byzantium
Death of St. Martin	395	395	Division of the Roman Empire

CHAPTER II

Attila in Gaul	451	476	The last Emperor of the West
CLOVIS	482		
DAGOBERT	628	630	The Arabs at Mecca
Charles Martel halts the Arabs	732		
PEPIN anointed King	754		
CHARLEMAGNE	771		
Oath of Strasbourg	841		
Treaty of Verdun	843	860	The Norsemen in Iceland
Eudes halts the Norsemen	885	895	The Hungarians on the Danube
The Norsemen in Normandy	911		
HUGUES ascends the throne	987	960	The Sung dynasty in China

In the History of France		In Other Countries	
JEAN II (the Good)	1350		
Battle of Poitiers; capture of the King	1356	1356	The Turks pass the Dardanelles
Treaty of Brétigny	1360		
CHARLES V (the Wise)	1364		
CHARLES VI	1380		
Battle of Agincourt	1415	1415	The burning of John Huss
Treaty of Tours	1420		
Siege of Orléans	1428		
CHARLES VII crowned at Reims	1430		
First standing army	1445	1445	The Portuguese at Cape Verde
Formigny	1450		
Castillon	1453	1450	Gutenberg, the first Bible
LOUIS XI; Villon	1461	1453	The Turks at Constantinople
Charles the Bold killed	1477		
CHARLES VIII	1483	1483	Birth of Luther
Conquest of Naples	1494	1492	Fall of Granada; Columbus in America
LOUIS XII	1498		
Ravenna	1512	1498	Vasco da Gama
FRANÇOIS I; Melegnano	1515	1502	Leonardo da Vinci: *Mona Lisa*
Battle of Pavia	1525		
Rabelais: *Gargantua*	1532	1515	Machiavelli: *The Prince*
Jacques Cartier in Canada	1534	1520	Luther excommunicated
HENRI II	1547	1540	The Society of Jesus founded
Recapture of Calais	1558		
FRANÇOIS II	1559	1556	Philip II of Spain
CHARLES IX	1560	1558	Elizabeth of England
Massacre of Saint-Barthélémy	1572	1572	Camoëns
Assassination of the Duc de Guise; Montaigne's *Essays*	1588	1588	Defeat of the Armada
HENRI IV	1589		
Peace of Vervins	1598	1598	Death of Philip II

CHAPTER V

HENRI IV assassinated;		1602	Shakespeare: *Hamlet*
LOUIS XIII	1610	1609	Independence of Holland
Richelieu, Minister	1624	1618	Thirty Years' War begins
Corneille: the *Cid*	1636	1632	Rembrandt: *Anatomy Lesson*
LOUIS XIV, Battle of Rocroi	1643		

In the History of France		*In Other Countries*	
Treaty of Westphalia; Pascal			
proves atmospheric pressure	1648	1648	Civil War in England
The Fronde	1649		
Treaty of the Pyrenees	1659		
Death of Mazarin	1661	1660	Restoration of the Stuarts
Molière: *The Misanthrope;*			
Perrault, the Colonnade of			
the Louvre	1666		
Racine: *Andromaque*	1667		
Treaty of Aix-la-Chapelle	1668		
Peace of Nijmegen	1678		
Mansard, Versailles	1682	1682	Peter the Great
Revocation of the Edict of		1687	Newton, the law of
Nantes	1685		gravitation
Treaty of Rijswijk	1697	1697	Charles XII, King of
Fénelon: *Télémaque*	1699		Sweden
Treaty of Utrecht	1713	1714	The Hanoverians on the
Louis XV; Philippe, Regent	1715		English throne
Watteau: *Embarkation for*			
Cythera	1717		
Law's inflation	1720		
Dupleix, Governor of the		1740	Frederick II, King of
Indies	1742		Prussia
Battle of Fontenoy	1745		
Voltaire: *Candide*	1759	1752	Franklin's lightning
Rousseau: the *Social*			conductor
Contract	1762	1760	Catherine II
Treaty of Paris	1763		
Lorraine becomes French	1766		
Corsica becomes French	1768		
Cugnot, first steam carriage	1770		
Dismissal of the Parlements	1771	1772	First partition of Poland
Louis XVI; Gabriel, the			
Trianon	1774	1774	Goethe: *Werther*
Treaty of Versailles;		1781	Battle of Yorktown; Kant:
Montgolfier's balloon	1783		*Critique of Pure Reason*
David: *Oath of the Horatii*	1785	1785	Mozart: *Marriage of Figaro*
Assembly of the Notables	1787	1788	First Congress of the
The States-General	1789		United States

| In the History of France | In Other Countries |

CHAPTER VI

Constituent Assembly; taking of the Bastille	1789	
Legislative Assembly	1791	
The Convention; First Republic; Valmy	1792	
The Reign of Terror	1793	1793 Second partition of Poland
Treaty of Basel; the Directory	1795	1795 End of Poland
Treaty of Campo Formio	1797	
Bonaparte in Egypt	1798	
The Consulate	1799	1799 Schiller: *Wallenstein*;
Napoleon declares himself		Volta's battery
Emperor; the Civil Code	1804	
Trafalgar; Austerlitz	1805	
Jena; Gay-Lussac; the dilation of gases	1806	
Russian campaign	1812	1812 Byron: *Childe Harold*
Leipzig	1813	1813 Davy, electric light
Waterloo; LOUIS XVIII	1815	1815 Congress of Vienna

CHAPTER VII

Ampère, electromagnetism	1820	
CHARLES X; Delacroix: *The Massacre of Chios*	1824	
Hernani; capture of Algiers; LOUIS-PHILIPPE	1830	1830 Independence of Belgium
Opening of the Paris and Saint-Germain railway	1835	
Surrender of Abd-el-Kader	1847	1845 Wagner: *Tannhäuser*
SECOND REPUBLIC	1848	1848 Marx: *Communist Manifesto*
Napoleon III, Emperor	1852	
Hugo: *Les Misérables*	1862	1859 Darwin: *Origin of Species*
Sedan; THIRD REPUBLIC	1870	1861 American Civil War; formation of the Kingdom of Italy
Pasteur, inoculation against rabies	1885	
The Eiffel Tower	1889	1866 Sadowa
The Curies, radium	1898	1888 William II, Emperor of Germany
France in Morocco	1911	
Battle of the Marne	1914	1912 The Balkan War

372

Some Comparative Dates

In the History of France

In Other Countries

In the History of France		In Other Countries	
Battle of Verdun	1916	1917	Russian Revolution
Foch triumphant	1918		
Treaty of Versailles	1919		
Devaluation of the franc	1928		
France invaded; Pétain	1940	1933	Hitler, Chancellor
France liberated; de Gaulle	1944	1941	Pearl Harbor
FOURTH REPUBLIC	1946	1945	Potsdam conference

INDEX

THE READER *is warned that this index is selective. To have given a reference to every mention of place or person would ludicrously have overweighted a short book every page of which is a pincushion of names. Only such entries, therefore, have been listed as bear to some extent upon the main argument or usefully stress the narrative.*

A NOTE ON THE TYPE

This book was set on the Linotype in ELECTRA, *designed by W. A. Dwiggins. The Electra face is a simple and readable type suitable for printing books by present-day processes. It is not based on any historical model, and hence does not echo any particular time or fashion. It is without eccentricities to catch the eye and interfere with reading— in general, its aim is to perform the function of a good book printing-type: to be read, and not seen.*

The typographic and binding designs are by W. A. Dwiggins.

The book was composed, printed, and bound by The Plimpton Press, Norwood, Massachusetts.

WAD